THE CAMBRIDGE COMPANION TO
JAMES BALDWIN

This *Companion* offers fresh insight into the art and politics of James Baldwin, one of the most important writers and provocative cultural critics of the twentieth century. Black, gay, and gifted, he was hailed as a "spokesman for the race," although he, at times controversially, eschewed titles and classifications of all kinds. Thirteen original essays examine his classic novels and nonfiction as well as his work across lesser-examined domains: poetry, music, theatre, sermon, photo-text, children's literature, public media, comedy, and artistic collaboration. In doing so, *The Cambridge Companion to James Baldwin* captures the power and influence of his work during the civil rights era as well as his relevance in the "post-race" transnational twenty-first century, when his prescient questioning of the boundaries of race, sex, love, leadership, and country assumes new urgency.

Michele Elam is Professor of English, Olivier Nomellini Family University Bass Fellow in Undergraduate Education, and former Director of African and American Studies at Stanford University. She is the author of *Race, Work, and Desire in American Literature, 1860–1930* (2003) and *The Souls of Mixed Folk: Race, Politics, and Aesthetics in the New Millennium* (2011).

A complete list of books in the series is at the back of this book.

THE CAMBRIDGE
COMPANION TO

JAMES BALDWIN

THE CAMBRIDGE COMPANION TO
JAMES BALDWIN

EDITED BY

MICHELE ELAM
Stanford University

CAMBRIDGE
UNIVERSITY PRESS

CAMBRIDGE
UNIVERSITY PRESS

32 Avenue of the Americas, New York NY 10013-2473, USA

Cambridge University Press is part of the University of Cambridge.

It furthers the University's mission by disseminating knowledge in the pursuit of
education, learning and research at the highest international levels of excellence.

www.cambridge.org
Information on this title: www.cambridge.org/9781107618183

© Cambridge University Press 2015

First published 2015

A catalogue record for this publication is available from the British Library

Library of Congress Cataloguing in Publication data
Elam, Michele, author.
The Cambridge companion to James Baldwin / [edited by] Michele Elam,
Stanford University.
pages   cm. – (Cambridge companions to literature)
Includes bibliographical references and index.
ISBN 978-1-107-04303-9 (hardback) – ISBN 978-1-107-61818-3 (paperback)
1. Baldwin, James, 1924–1987 – Criticism and interpretation.   2. African
Americans in literature.   I. Title.   II. Series: Cambridge companions to literature.
PS 3552.A45Z 6526   2015
818'.5409–dc23   2014043430

ISBN 978-1-107-61818-3 Paperback

For
Harry Justin Elam, Jr.

CONTENTS

ix

CONTENTS

ILLUSTRATIONS

NOTES ON CONTRIBUTORS

ALIYYAH I. ABDUR-RAHMAN is Associate Professor of English, African and Afro-American Studies, and Women's, Gender, and Sexuality Studies at Brandeis University. She is the author of *Against the Closet: Black Political Longing and the Erotics of Race* (2012).

NICHOLAS BOGGS is Clinical Assistant Professor in the Department of English at New York University. He has published essays in *Callaloo* and *James Baldwin Now*. His book-in-progress about James Baldwin's collaboration with French artist Yoran Cazac has been supported by a fellowship from the MacDowell Colony and a grant from the Jerome Foundation.

RADICLANI CLYTUS is Assistant Professor of English and American Studies at Brown University, specializing in nineteenth-century (African) American cultural productions. His forthcoming book, *Graphic Slavery: American Abolitionism and the Primacy of the Visual*, examines the ocularcentric roots of American anti-slavery rhetoric.

SOYICA DIGGS COLBERT is Associate Professor at Georgetown University. She is the author of *The African American Theatrical Body: Reception, Performance, and the Stage* (2011) and has published in *Theatre Journal, Theatre Topics*, and elsewhere.

ERICA R. EDWARDS is Associate Professor of English at the University of California, Riverside. She is the author of *Charisma and the Fictions of Black Leadership* (2012) and has published in *American Quarterly, Callaloo*, and *American Literary History*.

MICHELE ELAM is Professor of English, Olivier Nomellini Family University Bass Fellow in Undergraduate Education, and former Director of African and American Studies at Stanford University. The author of *Race, Work, and Desire in American Literature, 1860–1930* (2003) and *The Souls of Mixed Folk: Race, Politics, and Aesthetics in the New Millennium* (2011), she has published in

American Literature, *African American Review*, *Theatre Journal*, and *Genre*, among others.

DOUGLAS FIELD is Lecturer in twentieth-century literature at the University of Manchester. He is the editor of *A Historical Guide to James Baldwin* (2009) and founding coeditor of the *James Baldwin Review*. He is author of *James Baldwin* (2011) and the forthcoming *All Those Strangers: The Lives and Art of James Baldwin* (2015).

CHRISTOPHER FREEBURG is Assistant Professor at the University of Illinois at Urbana-Champaign and author of *Melville and the Idea of Blackness: Race and Imperialism in Nineteenth-Century America* (2012). He is working on a monograph on Baldwin and everyday life. He has published widely on race and American literature, including the forthcoming "James Baldwin and the Unhistoric Life of Race."

JACQUELINE GOLDSBY is Professor at Yale University. She is the author of *A Spectacular Secret: Lynching in American Life and Literature* (2006), which won the Modern Language Association William S. Scarborough Prize (2007), and coeditor with Philip Brian Harper of *The Autobiography of an Ex-Colored Man* (2012).

DANIELLE C. HEARD is Assistant Professor at the University of California at Davis. The recipient of a Mellon Mays fellowship, she is the author of the forthcoming *Buggy Jiving: Comic Strategies of the Black Avant-Garde*.

E. PATRICK JOHNSON is Professor, Chair, and Director of Graduate Studies in the Department of Performance Studies and of African American Studies at Northwestern University. A scholar/artist, Johnson is the author of *Appropriating Blackness: Performance and the Politics of Authenticity* (2003) and coauthor (with Mae G. Henderson) of *Black Queer Studies: A Critical Anthology* (2005).

META DUEWA JONES is Associate Professor of English at Howard University. She is the author of *The Muse Is Music: Jazz Poetry from the Harlem Renaissance to the Spoken Word* (2011), which received an honorable mention for the Modern Language Association William Sanders Scarborough Prize. Her current book-length project examines contemporary black writers' visually expressive aesthetics and black visual artists' literary engagements with photography, painting, poetry, and other texts.

D. QUENTIN MILLER is Professor and Chair of English at Suffolk University. His publications include *Re-Viewing James Baldwin: Things Not Seen* (2000) and *"A Criminal Power": James Baldwin and the Law* (2012). He is currently completing

The Routledge Introduction to African American Literature; his next projects include books on John Edgar Wideman and American literature of the 1980s.

BRIAN NORMAN is Associate Professor of English at Loyola University Maryland, where he founded the program in African and African-American Studies. He is the author of *Dead Women Talking: Figures of Injustice in American Literature* (2012), *Neo-Segregation Narratives: Jim Crow in Post–Civil Rights American Literature* (2010), and *The American Protest Essay and National Belonging* (2007).

MAGDALENA J. ZABOROWSKA is Professor at the University of Michigan and author of *James Baldwin's Turkish Decade: Erotics of Exile* (2009), winner of the 2009 William Sanders Scarborough Prize; *How We Found America: Reading Gender through East-European Immigrant Narratives* (1995); and the forthcoming *James Baldwin in the Company of Women*.

ACKNOWLEDGMENTS

This edited collection came together in a truly collaborative spirit. The editor would like to thank those whose names appear in the table of contents. They enthusiastically formed a close community in dialogue about all things Baldwin. In honor of Baldwin, who loved good conversation over food and drink, the contributors met over meals to talk, confer, share insights, and trade resources during the writing of their respective essays whenever they found themselves together at a conference. One important member of this group, who we wish could have appeared in the table of contents, José Esteban Muñoz, passed away as he was completing his essay for this volume. We would like to honor him here with the recognition that his influence runs throughout this *Companion*. The editor would also like to acknowledge the following individuals whose efforts were essential to the completion of this book. Ray Ryan, the senior editor of English and American Literature at Cambridge University Press, always appreciated the necessity for a *Cambridge Companion* to this brilliant writer and thinker, and encouraged my vision for it. Jennifer DeVere Brody contributed substantially to an early version of the essay on Baldwin and children's literature and was an important advisor throughout. Nigel Hatton prepared both the Chronology and Further Reading sections. Alice E. M. Underwood, PhD student in comparative literature at Stanford University, with good-natured attention to both duty and detail, helped copyedit and proofread the essays and assisted at every stage with the preparation of the manuscript for press. Harry J. Elam, Jr., offered vitalizing intellectual and emotional support, which enabled his wife to spend a joyful sabbatical entirely devoted to Baldwin's works. He deserves special credit for encouraging her to spend a marvelous week in New York in the spring of 2014 with no other charge than to attend all the inaugural events of the city's "Year of James Baldwin." Finally, the editor wishes to acknowledge a debt to her daughter, Claire Elise. Currently an undergraduate, she and her peers are among the target audiences for this collection, and we hope it leads them to a James Baldwin who speaks as powerfully to their time as he has to the generations before them.

1924   James Arthur Jones, first child of Emma Berdis Jones and a father never revealed, is born on August 2 in Harlem Hospital, New York, New York.

1927   Emma Berdis Jones marries the Reverend David Baldwin and James is given his stepfather's surname. His parents have eight additional children: George, Barbara, Wilmer, David, Gloria, Ruth, Elizabeth, and Paula.

1929   Baldwin attends Public School 24.

1935   Baldwin attends Frederick Douglass Junior High School where his influences include the poet, teacher, and literary club advisor, Countee Cullen.

1938   Baldwin begins preaching at Fireside Pentecostal Assembly.

1942   Baldwin graduates from DeWitt Clinton High School, where his classmates include Sol Stein and Richard Avedon. He leaves the church.

1943   The Reverend David Baldwin dies. The funeral was held on James's nineteeth birthday, which was also both the day his stepfather's last child was born and the day of the Harlem Riot of 1943.

1946   Baldwin has his first book review, on Maxim Gorki, published in *The Nation*. With the help of Richard Wright, he wins a Eugene Saxton Memorial Trust Fellowship.

1948   Baldwin wins a Rosenwald Foundation fellowship and publishes his first short story, "Previous Condition." Fed up with racism in the United States, where he "was going to kill somebody or be killed," Baldwin moves to Paris.

1949   "Everybody's Protest Novel" published in *Partisan Review*.

1951   "Many Thousands Gone," a critique of Richard Wright, appears in *Partisan Review*. This leads to a rift between Baldwin and Wright.

1952   Meets Ralph Ellison. Begins writing *The Amen Corner*.

1953   Publishes *Go Tell It on the Mountain*, his first novel. Langston Hughes writes to Baldwin with congratulations. Baldwin's mentor and friend, the painter Beauford Delaney, moves to Paris.

1954   Awarded Guggenheim fellowship.

1955   Publishes essay collection, *Notes of a Native Son*; Baldwin's first play, *The Amen Corner*, staged at Howard University. Meets E. Franklin Frazier and Sterling Brown.

1956   Awarded National Institute of Arts and Letters *Partisan Review* fellowship. Publishes second novel, *Giovanni's Room*.

1957   Meets the Reverend Martin Luther King, Jr. Travels to the American South as correspondent for *Harper's Magazine*. The short story "Sonny's Blues" appears in *Partisan Review*.

1959   Awarded Ford Foundation grant.

1961   *Nobody Knows My Name*, Baldwin's second essay collection, is published by Dial. Baldwin finishes writing his third novel, *Another Country*, during his first trip to Istanbul.

1962   Baldwin visits Africa (Dakar, Senegal; Conakry, Guinea; and Freetown, Sierra Leone) for the first time. *Another Country* is published by Dial.

1963   "The Fire Next Time" is published in *The New Yorker* and subsequently in book form by Dial. Baldwin appears on the cover of *Time* magazine. He receives the George Polk Memorial Award.

1963   In May, Baldwin meets with Attorney General Robert Kennedy at his home in McLean, Virginia, bringing a group of civil rights activists and artists, including Lorraine Hansberry, Harry Belafonte, Jerome Smith, Kenneth Clark, and Clarence B. Jones.

1963   Leads a civil rights demonstration in Paris on August 19.

1964   Completes his second play, *Blues for Mister Charlie*, while in Istanbul. *Atheneum* publishes *Nothing Personal*, a photo-essay collaboration with Richard Avedon.

1965   *Going to Meet the Man*, Baldwin's first short-story collection, is published by Dial. Baldwin travels to Israel.

1966   Baldwin completes *Tell Me How Long the Train's Been Gone*, his fourth novel, in Rumeli, Hisari, Turkey.

1967   "War Crimes Tribunal" is published in *Freedomways*. Baldwin asserts that any official international tribunal should be held in Harlem.

1968   *Tell Me How Long the Train's Been Gone* published by Dial. Baldwin moves to Los Angeles to work on the script for "The Autobiography of Malcolm X." Raises funds for the Reverend Martin Luther King, Jr., and the Southern Christian Leadership

Conference. Deeply affected by the assassination of King on April 4, Baldwin quits the Malcolm X project and returns to Europe.

1969 "Negroes Are Anti-Semitic Because They're Anti-White" published in *Black Anti-Semitism and Jewish Racism* by Richard W. Baron.

1970 Baldwin falls ill with hepatitis. Sedat Pakay makes the twelve-minute film *James Baldwin: From Another Place*, released by Hudson Film Works; portions of this film were incorporated into the American Masters/PBS biography of the author.

1971 Baldwin's essay "An Open Letter to My Sister, Miss Angela Davis" appears in *New York Review of Books*. Baldwin purchases a home in St. Paul-de-Vence, France. Travels to London for appearance on television program *Soul* with poet Nikki Giovanni.

1972 Dial publishes both *One Day When I Was Lost: A Scenario Based on "The Autobiography of Malcolm X"* and *No Name in the Street*, Baldwin's third essay collection. Collaborates with Ray Charles at the Newport Jazz Festival.

1973 Professor Henry Louis Gates, Jr., interviews Baldwin, the dancer Josephine Baker, and novelist Cecil Brown in St. Paul-de-Vence.

1974 *If Beale Street Could Talk*, Baldwin's fifth novel, is published by Dial Press. Baldwin celebrates his fiftieth birthday in St. Paul-de-Vence.

1976 *The Devil Finds Work*, Baldwin's meditation on the film industry, is published by Dial. The children's book *Little Man Little Man: A Story of Childhood* (illustrations by Yoran Cazac) is also published by Dial.

1978 Begins first of three teaching stints at Bowling Green College. City College of New York awards Baldwin the Martin Luther King Memorial Medal.

1979 Baldwin teaches at the University of California at Berkeley. Dial publishes Baldwin's sixth novel, *Just above My Head*. Beauford Delaney dies. Baldwin travels to Russia for the first time.

1980 Participates in dialogue with Chinua Achebe on the "African aesthetic" as part of a meeting of the African Literature Association at the University of Florida. Makes a trip through the American South, which forms the basis of the television documentary *I Heard It through the Grapevine*.

1981 "The Evidence of Things Not Seen," Baldwin's essay on Atlanta child murders, is published in *Playboy*.

1983   *Jimmy's Blues: Selected Poems* is published by Michael Joseph. Begins teaching literature and African-American studies at the University of Massachusetts, Amherst, where he stays for several months with regular visits to his home in St. Paul-de-Vence.

1984   Baldwin is hospitalized for exhaustion.

1985   The made-for-television adaptation of *Go Tell It on the Mountain* appears. *The Price of the Ticket: Collected Non-Fiction, 1948–1985*, is published by St. Martin's Press. An expanded version of Baldwin's essay on the Atlanta child murders, titled *The Evidence of Things Not Seen*, is published by Holt, Rinehart and Winston.

1986   Baldwin is made an officer of the Legion of Honor in France during a ceremony presided over by president François Mitterand. Baldwin makes a trip to Russia with his brother David.

1987   Baldwin is diagnosed with cancer of the esophagus. He works on "The Welcome Table" and other writing projects while being cared for by his brother David. Dies at home on December 1. Viewings take place in St. Paul-de-Vence and Harlem and a funeral service is held at St. John the Divine. Thousands attend and hear Baldwin eulogized by famed writers such as Amiri Baraka, Toni Morrison, and Maya Angelou. Baldwin is buried on December 8 at Ferncliff Cemetery, Hartsdale, New York.

MICHELE ELAM

Introduction: Baldwin's Art

A People's Prophet

The cover of our *Companion* features Beauford Delaney's 1963 portrait of James Baldwin (1924–87), one of the most important writers and provocative cultural critics of the twentieth century. In Delaney's portrait, Baldwin's luminous, outsized eyes – "world absorbing"[1] orbs – seem to promise not just sight but insight. Haloed by the saturated yellow that the artist often favored in his paintings, Baldwin is solitary, almost sainted. The image is representative of the way Baldwin so often is portrayed in paintings and photographs, and indeed, how many have come to think of Baldwin: as a solitary genius whose eloquent literary jeremiads about race in America set him a bit above and apart from the world in which he wrote. This common characterization of Baldwin dovetails with the opinion that great artists must rise above their time and place, must achieve distance from the mundane and the temporal – that is, from the concerns of money, of politics, of family, of the specificities of race, class, gender. That view of "art for art's sake" often conjures images of a starving artist locked for months in a bare Parisian studio, forsaking not only food and friends but all the imperatives of the here and now in order to create something eternal and enduring.

And it is true that in many ways, Baldwin seems to fit that picture of a peerless man unmoored. Born in 1924 to a single mother in Harlem, alienated from a cruel stepfather, he was, as one interviewer put it, "black, impoverished, gifted and gay." When asked about coming into the world with so many challenges, Baldwin said wryly that he had thought he'd hit the "jackpot," the "trifecta."[2] Becoming a self-described nomad, he searched for a place to belong and for love that, according to his biographers, more often than not went unrequited.[3] As one of his characters puts it, "I saw myself, sharply, as a wanderer, an adventurer, rocking through the world, unanchored."[4] Disgusted with racism in the United States, he chose exile in 1948, and, in fact, much of his oeuvre was written outside the country of his birth,

1

Figure 1.1. Beauford Delaney (1901–1979), *James Arthur Baldwin (1924–1987), American Author*. 1963. Pastel on paper, 64.8 × 49.8 cm. National Portrait Gallery, Smithsonian Institution/Art Resource, NY. Reproduced by permission of Derek L. Spratley, Esquire, Court Appointed Administrator of The Estate of Beauford Delaney.

including in Switzerland, Turkey, and France. So it is understandable that he has a reputation as an estranged writer and thinker with few fellow travelers.

Yet, far from the image of him as isolated artist in retreat, Baldwin was actually at the very center of mid-twentieth century debates over the meaning and intersection of art, race, and politics. This *Companion* seeks that fuller rendering of Baldwin, one that captures his many rich contradictions: as an artist who rejected the notion of art as propaganda but believed artists should be "disturbers of the peace"[5]; as the author of *Giovanni's Room* (1955), often celebrated as foundational within black queer studies, although his rejection of most vocabularies of identity and politics (refusing even the label, "civil rights activist"[6]) positions him uneasily within that field of study; as a writer singularly renowned as an essayist and novelist but who also promiscuously experimented with many other genres and frequently collaborated with other artists. With that recognition, this *Companion* examines Baldwin's classic novels and essays as well as his exciting work across many lesser-examined domains – poetry, music, theatre, sermon, photo-text, children's literature, public media, comedy, and artistic collaboration. In doing so, the *Companion* seeks to capture the power and influence of his work during the civil rights era as well as his relevance in the "post-race" transnational twenty-first century, when his prescient questioning of the boundaries of race, sex, love, leadership, and country assume new urgency.

Beyond the Bad Boy: Baldwin in Literary History

Baldwin's feature cover on *Time* magazine in 1963 (Fig 1.2) – with the banner "The Negro's Push for Equality" – marks for many when he became the face of black America. On the one hand, his presence on the cover soon after the publication of *The Fire Next Time* signaled his rising influence as a writer and thinker across the color line. His powerful, eloquent prose quickly became part of the early intellectual ferment animating the Civil Rights Movement. Yet some of Dr. Martin Luther King's advisors were so uncomfortable with the sexual orientation of this newly hailed spokesman for the race that he was abruptly pulled at a late hour from the speakers' list for the historic 1963 March on Washington for Jobs and Freedom.[7] Indeed, he was racially, sexually, and politically suspect in the eyes of both blacks and whites: the Federal Bureau of Investigation's extensive file on him, more than 1,800 pages long, frets over what investigators saw as both his homosexual and communist inclinations – even though the FBI had trouble slotting him into any camp or affiliation.

Perhaps, then, it is understandable that scholarship similarly often characterizes Baldwin as not occasionally out of step with his contemporaries but also ill-fit within the literary historical paradigms and aesthetic criteria that guide curricula. A renowned author of more than twenty works of fiction and nonfiction, honored with many distinguished awards and distinctions including a Guggenheim Fellowship, Baldwin has by most measures achieved canonical status.[8] But in recent years, Baldwin has been taught less frequently in classrooms across the country.[9] Unlike in the 1960s and 1970s, when a wide variety of his essays, short stories, and novels were assigned, students in the early twenty-first century often encounter only Baldwin's story, "Sonny's Blues" (1957), and maybe anthologized excerpts from *Giovanni's Room*.[10] Baldwin's diminished presence in the classroom may be, in part, due to his inability to be comfortably housed in the traditional narrative tropes and aesthetic conventions of realism, naturalism, modernism, or protest literature; he slips between the categories and periodizations that so often structure literary surveys, anthologies, and disciplinary territories.

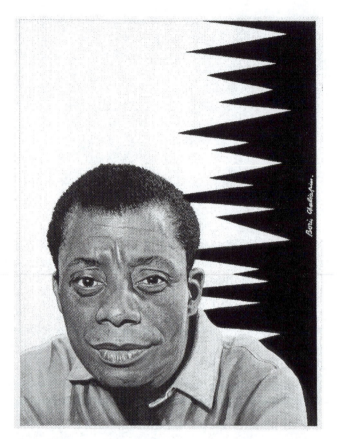

Figure 1.2. Boris Chaliapin (1904–1979), *American Writer James Baldwin (1924–1987)*. Painting used on the cover of Time Magazine Vol. LXXXI No. 20, May 17, 1963. Watercolor and pencil on board. Gift of Time Magazine at the National Portrait Gallery, Smithsonian Institution. Reproduced by permission of Art Resource, NY.

As Jacqueline Goldsby, Meta DuEwa Jones, and Brian Norman elaborate in their essays in this *Companion*, Baldwin's oeuvre continues to unsettle critical interpretation and expectation in its transgression of cultural norms and aesthetic covenants. Some of his work, for instance, exceeds the sociopolitical themes and racial characterizations expected in black expressive writing in the 1960s and 1970s. Baldwin was "anomalous,"[11] as Gene Jarrett terms it, most notably when he dared represent interracial, homosexual romance at a time when the characters' crossing of both sex and color lines were doubly taboo and, in many places, illegal. Furthermore, the novel's strategies of focalization through a white protagonist drew criticism from those who felt that presenting much of the narrative from a putatively white perspective made it less of a "black novel."

When he does appear in literary histories, Baldwin is often cast in a scripted role as contender for the throne. His critique of literary colleague and early supporter, Richard Wright, in "Everybody's Protest Novel" (1949) and "Many Thousands Gone" (1951) was interpreted as exemplary proof of the idea that literary history is defined by generational arguments between great men, and in the case of black writers, over how (and who best) to represent the race. Indeed, in his review of Baldwin in *Dissent*, influential literary and social critic Irving Howe paints his subject as an ingrate of lesser talent, part of a postwar "generation of intellectuals soured on the tradition of protest but suspecting they might be pygmies in comparison to the writers who had protested."[12] For Howe, Baldwin's challenge to Wright's approach to literature amounted to a common adolescent gesture, the result of an "anxiety of influence"[13] that he suggests defines the arc of literary history itself:

> Like all attacks launched by young writers against their famous elders, Baldwin's essays were also a kind of announcement of his own intentions...Baldwin's rebellion against the older Negro novelist who had served him as a model and had helped launch his career was not, of course, an unprecedented event. The history of literature is full of such painful ruptures.... he tries to break from his rebellious dependency upon Wright, but he remains tied to the memory of the older man.[14]

In fact, just as the younger W. E. B. Du Bois and more senior Booker T. Washington are cast as battling giants at the last fin de siècle, Baldwin and Wright (and Ralph Ellison) are frequently framed as literary gladiators of the mid-twentieth century. Baldwin himself rejected the idea that the "literary father must be killed,"[15] and, as I have been suggesting, he cannot be understood so simply as an artist in agonistic relation to his "elders," nor defined as estranged from the world around him. Such approaches miscast or outcast Baldwin in literary history and overlook just how deeply collaborative and socially engaged were his vision and craft.

In touch with the most important civil rights political figures – from Malcolm X to Martin Luther King, Jr. – and with celebrities of all colors – from Harry Belafonte to Sidney Poitier, and from Charleton Heston to Marlon Brando – Baldwin was also, importantly, deeply engaged with black women writers and activists, including Angela Davis, Toni Morrison, Maya Angelou, Nikki Giovanni, Betty Shabazz, Nina Simone, and Suzan-Lori Parks.[16] In fact, Baldwin himself was a charismatic "political celebrity," as Erica Edwards notes in her essay in this *Companion* – keenly responsive to his audiences and strategic in capitalizing on the period's new media.[17] He created a cogent presence as one of the first black public intellectuals of the postwar period,[18] and his many televised public speeches and talks – including his 1965 Cambridge University debate with William F. Buckley,[19]

his appearance on the Dick Cavett Show in 1968, his talk at the University
of California at Berkeley in 1979 – reveal a passionate, often sharply witty
speaker, poised to take excellent advantage of the fact that "the black freedom struggle 'went live' on the evening news."[20] Baldwin understood well
the transformative potential of public performance, schooled as he was in
the church, first by his stepfather preacher, and then as a child preacher himself. The rhetorical cadences of the Bible and the social rituals of the black
church inform both his writing and his speaking, as do – as Danielle Heard's
essay in this *Companion*, "Baldwin's Humor," explains – the political wit
and comic timing of Dick Gregory.

Baldwin was in many ways a crucible for nearly all the cultural and
artistic frictions of the mid-twentieth century. Many of these tensions and
debates revolved directly or indirectly around the politics of art and the art
of politics. "Art and sociology are not one and the same,"[21] he famously
stated, rejecting an instrumentalist approach in which art was used merely
in the service of a cause. But his understanding of the relationship between
artistic creation and social reality is much more complex than his comment
suggests, for he had a rich appreciation of literature as a distinctive form of
social engagement. The entwining of the form and content in his work can
be productively viewed as part of a long dialogue within African-American
expressive traditions, for instance, about whether there is a distinctive
black aesthetic, as Langston Hughes argued in "The Negro Artist and the
Racial Mountain" (1926), or whether the African-American was, as George
Schuyler put it in the "Negro Art Hokum" (1926), merely a "lampblacked
Anglo-Saxon"[22] whose art and sensibilities are no different than white
people's. I foreground Hughes here because he, like Baldwin, calls for the
embrace of racial experience as grist for art. For both Hughes and Baldwin,
this experience was keenly voiced in blues and jazz, as "one of the inherent expressions of Negro life in America; the eternal tom-tom beating in
the Negro soul – the tom-tom of revolt against weariness in a white world,
a world of subway trains, and work, work, work; the tom-tom of joy and
laughter, and pain swallowed in a smile."[23] Despite the metaphysical language of the "inherent" and the "eternal," Hughes's "Negro soul" here is
based not in essence but in social experience – in the shared "weariness," the
grinding commute, the endless labor, the donning of the facade that, as Paul
Laurence Dunbar puts it in "We Wear the Mask," "grins and lies."[24]

Race in the Making

Hughes's – and Baldwin's – sense of racial identity derives not from the
fetish of blood, then, but rather the metronome of the "tom-tom," which is

the pulse to a lived and living experience. It is this experience that informs the "we" of Dunbar's title. Dunbar's "we" exists somewhere on a continuum between poetic creation and social truth, highlighting the fact that all identities are not merely neutral designations but fraught ascriptions, inventions, projections, wish fulfillments. Significantly, in Hughes's and Dunbar's poetry, an "imagined community"[25] is created through its doing. That is, the "we" is not a static entity; rather, it emerges through the ongoing iteration of acts and behaviors, and to that extent references more generally the ways such communities are always in the making.[26]

Elaborated similarly and even more powerfully in Baldwin's work is the notion that race, rather than inhering within as a trait or feature, exists as a social dynamic and interpersonal negotiation. It is an insight that presciently anticipates contemporary considerations of race as constructed, or perhaps more specifically, as performative.[27] Baldwin takes as a given that race is not an a priori characteristic, and therefore both his fiction and nonfiction rarely describe race in terms of physical features or innate characteristics. Instead, his writings represent how race is a phenomenon performed, enacted, and maintained not only by social structures and institutions but also through the everyday actions and interactions often invisibly informed by them. As he explains in the 1965 Cambridge debate with Buckley, whether one is a "white South African or a Mississippi sharecropper or a Mississippi sheriff or a white Frenchman driven out of Algeria," people act and interact based on "one's system of reality" as he put it, an always racialized sense of reality and one's place within it that "depends on assumptions held so deeply as to be scarcely aware of them."[28] This conception allows Baldwin to explore the ways race is at once historical and embedded in social structures and yet continually renewed and remade in the moment, between people.

His attentiveness in both his fiction and his critical essays to the iterative and interpersonal nature of this process allows him both to diagnose the persistence of racism and to imagine the potential for social change. For although he is often arguing that social justice can occur only when Americans truly confront their history, the recognition that race is also a daily formation – renewed or resisted in the smallest, most mundane exchanges between people – leads him to conclude that the "challenge is in the moment, the time is always now."[29] This appreciation of the urgency of the everyday deeply informs Baldwin's complex aesthetic: his love, for example, of Henry James, master of finding social revelation in the quotidian, as well as his attraction to blues and jazz, which locate humanity in the commonplace. As Radiclani Clytus explores in his essay for this *Companion*, Baldwin's frequent references to these musical forms in his fiction and essays create a refrain foregrounding an existential principal that runs throughout all his writings: the ethical potency of human and humane connection as the basis for social transformation.

Baldwin in the Backstage Alley

In Baldwin's work, valuing human connection extends also to an appreciation of the artist's dynamic relation to communities. This view of the artist runs pointedly counter to the notion of "art for art's sake," mentioned at the outset of this Introduction, in which an artist answers to none, a notion that Baldwin dismisses with his parody of the Romantic contemplative in "The Creative Process" (1962). The artist, he insists, is not "meant to bring to mind merely a rustic musing beside some silver lake"; his goal is "to make clear the nature of the artist's responsibility to his society."[30] His comments join him, as I suggested earlier, to an ongoing dialogue within African-American arts and letters that dates at least to Frederick Douglass – a critical self-reflection and ongoing inquiry that asks: What is "black" art? What is it for? Who is it for?

The nature and poignancy of artistic responsibility is perhaps best, and most touchingly, illustrated in "Sweet Lorraine" (1969), Baldwin's memorial tribute to the playwright and his dear friend Lorraine Hansberry. In it, Baldwin suggests that an artist's "responsibility" is not about beholding to a burdensome commitment to "represent the race," nor about subordinating one's vision to others' approval and valuation. It is about refusing what Baldwin saw as the fatal tendency to "isolate the artist from the people."[31] After the 1959 opening performance of Hansberry's play *A Raisin in the Sun* – in which, according to Baldwin, "never in the history of American theatre had so much of the truth of black people's lives been seen on stage"[32] – Baldwin and Hansberry left the theatre into a backstage alley, where she was "immediately mobbed" by those wanting her autograph:

> I watched the people, who loved Lorraine for what she had brought to them; and I watched Lorraine, who loved the people for what they had brought her. It was not, for her, a matter of being admired. She was being corroborated and confirmed. She was wise enough and honest enough to recognize that black American artists are in a very special case. One is not merely an artist and one is not judged merely as an artist. The black people crowding around Lorraine, whether or not they considered her an artist, assuredly considered her a witness.[33]

Bearing witness is key to Baldwin's ethics and aesthetics. His notion of witnessing comes from the church, from publically testifying to experience.[34] Hansberry is beloved for what she brought to people, but also, Baldwin emphasizes, she loves what people brought her. In that sense, witnessing is

8

not simply a private testament but a social event in which artist and audience mutually recognize one another as members of a congregation of sorts. This shared acknowledgment is part of a distinct racial aesthetic, Baldwin makes clear: like all African-American artists, he argues, Hansberry is what he calls a "special case" in that she witnesses a "black" experience that is in important ways continuous with, even if not identical to, so many others'. As he put it in an interview: "Your self and your people are indistinguishable from each other, really, in spite of the quarrels you may have, and your people are all people."[35]

The backstage alley with "the people" that Baldwin recalls is a scene and an exchange that runs throughout African-American literature. Sterling Brown's vernacular poem, "Ma Rainey" (1932), for instance, imagines a nearly identical moment of intimacy between artist and audience. The poem concludes when, after a moving performance of "Backwater Blues," the renowned singer Ma Rainey – familiarly claimed by her audience here as "Ma" – joins and becomes one with "de folks" who have come from far and wide to hear her:

> An' den de folks, dey natchally bowed dey heads an' cried,
> Bowed dey heavy heads, shet dey moufs up tight an' cried,
> An' Ma lef' de stage, an' followed some de folks outside."
> Dere wasn't much more de fellow say:
> She jes' gits hold of us dataway.[36]

Rainey's stepping down from the stage and mingling with those gathered is a recognition of art as a transformative social event – and to the extent that that relationship is enacted through the poem, the event is extended, as well, to readers of Brown's poem. As with Hansberry, Ma's moment is not about a luminary greeting her fans, but about an artist's communion with the people who share in and vouchsafe her art. Both Brown and Baldwin suggest that in this way audiences can be active participants in the making and meaning of art. And although this moving experience – getting hold of each other "dataway" – does not move its audience to specific political action, for Baldwin, such examples of palpable human connection always spoke to its possibility.

Acting History, Acts of Love

The political possibilities that emerge from art's ability to bear witness inform Baldwin's view, central to so many of his essays and fiction, that individuals can only realize the full potential of themselves and others by coming to terms with histories that cross the color line. For it is this imbricated, interracial history, Baldwin claims, that often invisibly but powerfully animates our day-to-day experiences and interactions: "If history were past, history wouldn't matter. History is the present... You and I are history. We carry our history. We act our history."[37]

To recognize this fact that history is ever-present is not to concede historical determinism, he argues, but to overcome it. And, Baldwin insists, to overcome it means facing it and oneself, for those who insist they are "masters of their destiny" can only believe themselves so "by becoming specialists in self-deception."[38] Fully recognizing American's interracial history, he argues in "Stranger in the Village" (1955), means robbing "the white man of the jewel of his naiveté" – that is, the historical amnesia of whites who "keep the black man at a certain human remove" so that a white person might not be "called to account for the crimes committed by his forefathers, or his neighbors."[39] Baldwin presciently anticipates that the change of mind and heart required to acknowledge the full humanity of their darker brethren and fellow citizens will be a "very charged and difficult moment, for there is a great deal of will power involved in the white man's naiveté."[40] As he argues in *The Fire Next Time*, "It is the innocence which constitutes the crime."[41] This recognition that "innocence" is not a prepubescent or prelapsarian condition but a fortressed state of mind is one of his most pointed critiques of whites.

For Baldwin, the redress this crime of innocence requires an accounting of the past. But we cannot, he warns, underestimate history's living presence, for "the great force of history comes from the fact that we carry it within us, are unconsciously controlled by it in many ways... [H]istory is literally present in all that we do. It could scarcely be otherwise, since it is to history that we owe our frames of reference, our identities, and our aspirations." Only by engaging history can one effect any kind of personal or social change, and only in this way – sometimes in "great pain and terror," as the individual "begins to assess the history which has placed one where one is and formed one's point of view" – can a person attempt to "recreate oneself according to a principle more humane and liberating." Only then can one "attempt to achieve a level of personal maturity and freedom which robs history of its tyrannical power, and changes history."[42] For Baldwin, that "personal maturity" necessary for social change is what defines "love."

As he explains in *The Fire Next Time* (1963), love is not a sentimental experience but a bracing charge:

> Love takes off the masks that we fear we cannot live without and know we cannot live within. I use the word "love" here not merely in the personal sense but as a state of being, or a state of grace – not in the infantile American

sense of being made happy but in the tough and universal sense of quest and daring and growth.[43]

As Christopher Freeburg in his essay in this *Companion* points out, Baldwin is constantly talking about the necessity of this kind of mature, questing love, and it is crucial to understanding both his politics and his fiction. Love for Baldwin compels the recognition that we exist on a continuum with others – especially with others we might most wish to hold at bay. In *Another Country* (1962), for instance, the failure to love and to be loved reflects both a denial of the characters' responsibility to each other and the fruitless denial of their mutual vulnerability. In the opening pages, the narrator describes the tenuous line that separates the loved from the "beloved," the influential from the outcast, the lucky from the "fallen": "Entirely alone, and dying of it, [Rufus] was part of an unprecedented multitude. There were boys and girls drinking coffee at the drugstore counters who were held back from his condition by barriers as perishable as their dwindling cigarettes."[44] Such scenes illustrate his keen insight that the barriers between people's "conditions" (economic, social, racial) are far more "perishable" than most can see let alone admit. For Baldwin, it is literature's unique ability to prompt a loving and ethical reimagining of self and other – of the other *as* self – that enables social change.

Art and Our Better Angels

This belief in the unique efficacy of art is why, in "Nobody Knows My Name" (1954), Baldwin insists that "It is the writer, not the statesmen, who is our strongest arm. Though we do not wholly believe it yet, the interior life is a real life, and the intangible dreams of people have a tangible effect on the world."[45] Passionate about the "tangible effect" of "interior life," he nonetheless resisted calls to the dogmatic or the prescriptive. His recognition that writers are the "strongest arm," that "real life" extends to "intangible dreams," echoed some of the calls in the late 1960s and 1970s by Black Arts artists and intellectuals for a more muscular aesthetic.

But he lacked the militancy of those like Larry Neal who wished for "poems that shoot guns."[46] Indeed, Baldwin was viewed as artistically impotent and politically ambivalent by many of those in the Black Panther Party as well. In his *Soul on Ice* (1968), Eldridge Cleaver, the Party's Minister of Information, scathingly dismissed Baldwin for the "racial death-wish" that he believed his homosexuality represented. Others distrusted what they perceived as political "skepticism and hesitancy"; his "vague position," was in "sharp contrast to the others who were very much together on what to do and how to do it."[47] Similarly, Baldwin's dismissiveness of certain aspects of gay culture in his fiction, his apology for Cleaver's homophobic remarks about him, combined with what some felt were dissembling claims to bisexuality" – "I've loved some women; I've loved some men"[48] – continue to strike some as a compromising political retreat rather than productive modes of what José Esteban Muñoz called "disidentification."[49]

Many have and will continue to assess and debate the complicated legacy of Baldwin's work for queer studies.[50] His rebuff of political platforms and racial-sexual taxonomies of all kinds might seem to align him with what Ross Posnock sees in Ralph Ellison as the "ludic" dimension to American identity – identity gained through a "playful act of assemblage."[51] But, although Baldwin embraced the creative license to invent (and reinvent) his self, he did not believe one should just "change clothes and go"[52] – that is, temporarily assume a particular performance of identity when socially expedient or commercially beneficial. Baldwin was not opportunistic. His fiction and nonfiction argued explicitly and implicitly for a way of being in the world that was at once free and responsive to others, imaginatively capacious yet socially committed. That Baldwin has been at times accused of lacking political mettle, even as others define his later writing as "failed" because of being *too* political, only speaks to how challenging his project is.

In threading the needle's eye between art and politics, Baldwin preferred the ethical potency of art. As Hortense Spillers notes, "Baldwin was able to make a profound appeal to the 'better angels of our nature,' a summoning towards an individual's 'visionary potential'; this standing in the space of the moral order is precisely the vocation that our politics most usually eschew, but that the world of art sometimes accomplishes."[53] His oeuvre suggests just how willing was his art to appeal to the better angels, to fill the visionary and moral spaces eschewed by politics.

A Look Ahead

In order to appreciate fully Baldwin's "world of art," this *Companion* offers perspectives on Baldwin's aesthetic practice and politics across genre, across gender, across the globe, and across the color line. He is acclaimed as an extraordinarily gifted essayist – one of if not the best of the twentieth century. But in order to understand why he was hailed as "one of the few genuinely indispensable American writers,"[54] it is essential to consider his remarkable and too rarely recognized forays across nearly every genre.

To that end, this volume is structured by two sections, both of which highlight generic forms and modes of craft as integral to his political presence: in an effort to honor Baldwin's rich mélange of genres and the interconnectedness of his literary-social concerns, the first section emphasizes Baldwin's social relation to form; the second section explores his formal relation to society. Part I, "Genres and Mélanges," highlights the interdisciplinary dimensions of Baldwin's most renowned fiction and nonfiction, considering new aspects of his work as it merged with lesser-studied terrains of music, poetry, performance, interview, film, sermon, photo-text, children's literature, public media, and comedy. Part II, "Collaborations and Confluences," considers Baldwin's artistic production in relation to the social and political world around him.

Part I begins with Jacqueline Goldsby's essay, "'Closer to Something Unnameable': Baldwin's Novel Form," which considers the narrative aesthetics in Baldwin's work by looking at both the canonical and the so-called failed late novels, often accused of "formlessness." Focusing on Baldwin's fourth novel, *Tell Me How Long the Train's Been Gone* (1968) as an example of these later texts' form through their putative formlessness, she argues that, to the extent these novels feature artist figures as their protagonists – musicians, actors, painters, sculptors, and novelists – they are also mediations on the status and shape of art itself.

Meta DuEwa Jones's essay, "Baldwin's Poetics," is one of the first essays to offer serious formal analysis of Baldwin's poetics, which is particularly timely with the reissue of his poetry (including some previously unpublished verses) in *Jimmy's Blues and Other Poems* (2014), edited by Nikki Finney. Focusing on Baldwin's interest in poetic time – both the temporal passage of time and the formal measure of it within his poetry – Jones demonstrates how Baldwin "theorized time through the verse lines," as she explains, as a way of understanding both his poetic philosophy and his artistic practice. If few have considered Baldwin's poetry, many more have documented Baldwin's complicated relationship with religious faith. In "Baldwin's Sermonic," Soyica Diggs Colbert analyzes the marshalling of religious expression and political intent. Documenting how the sermon assumes particular force in his plays *The Amen Corner* (1954) and *Blues for Mister Charlie* (1964), Colbert explains how Baldwin "uses the redemptive narrative of the sermon...toward the political aims of the Civil Rights Movement."

Music was also profoundly important to Baldwin as both culturally expressive and politically suggestive. Although Baldwin insisted he knew little about music, blues and jazz refrains and references punctuate nearly all his writings. Radiclani Clytus's essay, "Paying Dues and Playing the Blues: Baldwin's Existential Jazz," considers "Sonny's Blues" (1957) in the context of Sartrean existentialism and links Baldwin's musical representations to the metaphysical condition of being black in America.

E. Patrick Johnson's "Baldwin's Theatre" explores his deep interest in drama as a particularly powerful vehicle to explore this racial condition. Analyzing *The Amen Corner* (1954) and *Blues for Mister Charlie* (1964), Johnson demonstrates how Baldwin appreciated plays as forms of social ritual that effect both group cohesion and critical self-reflection. These plays, Johnson contends, even suggest a challenge to ritual itself – especially the more oppressive ritualistic practices of the state and the church. Johnson notes that Baldwin always had a dramatic flair himself, a distinctive performative affect. Danielle Heard in "Baldwin's Humor" takes seriously the subversive potential of his affect, his tonal registers, his gestural moves. She examines the wickedly rebellious comic sensibility of Baldwin in her study of the complex performances (both on the page and through his person) of his laughter, his accent, his camp, his timing, and his facial expressions, seeing these work within, and occasionally against, traditions of African-American humor.

Nicholas Boggs's "Baldwin and Yoran Cazac's 'Child's Story for Adults' " considers another aspect of Baldwin – his juvenile fiction – that might be overlooked as merely lighthearted or for the light of heart. Boggs sees Baldwin's representations of childhood in this picture book, a collaboration with the artist Yoran Cazac, as a fierce critique of the kind of unseeing "innocence" about inequality that he so despised in American culture. Analyzing both text and illustrations, Boggs argues that innocence is upended in this children's story, a primer which teaches its readers to lose their innocence by taking "look again" – in the words of the artist Beauford Delaney to Baldwin – at the world around them.

Baldwin's partnership with Cazac was by no means his only collaboration. Part II opens with Brian Norman's provocative examination of Baldwin's collaborative ethos across many different people and genres throughout his lifetime. Looking at collaboration as a social process rather than a formal product, Norman suggests why so many of Baldwin's collaborations did not seem to achieve (nor did they necessarily intend to) a synthesis, consensus, or closure. Baldwin's many collaborations emphasize the creation of art as a social process rather than a solo act, raising questions not only about intellectual property rights but also about the nature of authorship itself. If collaboration is often posed as labor between equals, Erica Edwards's "Baldwin and Black Leadership" examines Baldwin – hailed as a "race leader" – within the hierarchies of black leadership. Edwards goes beyond the usual questions about the politics of representation, of who gets to represent whom, to suggest that Baldwin critiques the enterprise of leadership itself. Looking at figurations of the prophet across three texts in Baldwin's oeuvre - the short story "The Death of the Prophet" (1950), the autobiographical essay *No Name in the Street* (1972), and *One Day When I Was Lost* (1972) (Baldwin's screenplay adaptation of *The Autobiography of Malcolm X*) – Edwards considers the political rise, psychic costs, and commercial losses of those who would lead in Baldwin's works.

Baldwin was often disappointed when he looked to individual political leaders as the stewards for social change[55]; he more often called for a broader conversion of the national soul that usually slipped the noose of partisanship and grandstanding. As Aliyyah I. Abdur-Rahman notes in "'As Though a Metaphor were Tangible': Baldwin's Identities," Baldwin's conception of self also tended to escape traditional categories. Focusing on *Giovanni's Room* (1956) and "Going to Meet the Man" (1965), she argues that Baldwin posits an identity that is represented not as static nor necessarily even internally coherent, but rather "relational, contextual, processual, and contingent."

If, as Abdur-Rahman argues, Baldwin appreciated the ways in which identity is socially negotiated, then love, in Baldwin's terms, is the ultimate negotiation of self with other. As Christopher Freeburg elaborates in "Baldwin and the Occasion of Love," love for Baldwin is at once intensely personal and yet socially transformative, in its highest sense – a holding-to-account of people to each other. The epigraph to Freeburg's essay – cited from James Baldwin, "A Letter to my Nephew," which later became part of *The Fire Next Time* (1963) – suggests the fortitude this kind of "hard" loving can offer in a world that loves not: "To be loved, baby, hard, at once, and forever, to strengthen you against the loveless world." That "loveless world" Baldwin mentions included the Federal Bureau of Investigation, which conducted extensive surveillance and harassment of him over many years. Douglas Field, in "Baldwin's FBI Files as Political Biography," offers close readings of many of those files – some only recently released – suggesting that they reveal more about the FBI than about the target of their investigations. Treating the files as both literary documents and cultural artifacts, Field turns the FBI's surveilling eye back on itself.

Magdalena Zaborowska's concluding essay, "Domesticating Baldwin's Global Imagination," returns the gaze to Baldwin in her intimate look at the last place he called home – a house in St. Paul-de-Vence, France, that, Zaborowska argues, Baldwin viewed as, in his own words, a "space to be manipulated" – a creative and generative abode that framed the writer's last decade and enabled his late works. This private space also functioned, simultaneously, as a social event – not so much a haven for an expatriate recluse as a literary salon staged for the many friends, intellectuals, and celebrities Baldwin knew and welcomed to his table, nearly up to the day of his "home-going."

"A New Confrontation with Reality"

The essays in this *Companion* seek to present Baldwin at this communal table. His work is brought into full and vivid relief only when seen in the mix, as it were: in the colorful mix of genres with which Baldwin experimented, in the heterogeneous mix of people with whom he collaborated, in the mix of social relations and political kinships that animated his art. I had the occasion to talk to people of many walks of life, professions, ages, and backgrounds in my research for this volume of essays, aided by the fact that the preparation of this *Companion* has occurred during the year when Baldwin would have turned ninety. That 2014 anniversary occasioned much feting – a street was named for him, a postage stamp bearing his likeness went into circulation, New York Live Arts dedicated a twelve-month city-wide festival of arts and study grandly called "The Year of James Baldwin," devoted solely to the study and celebration of him.[56] During this process, I discovered that there is something poignantly different about the way people speak about Baldwin. For so many, he is not simply a canonical figure from the past who wrote a few important essays or books that one "should" read. Rather, he is profoundly transformational. Again and again, I heard the expression, "his works changed my life" – always said with a kind of heartfelt intensity that would make even the most cynical among us pause. For so many, Baldwin is associated with a coming of age – sexually, racially, politically, spiritually. Like Brown's Ma Rainey, whose public concert becomes part-revival, Baldwin, too, "jes' gits hold of us some dataway." Baldwin's "hold of us" is not just a deeply felt experience; it is a call to action.

I began this Introduction discussing how critics have imagined Baldwin through a consideration of Delaney's portrait. Let me conclude with a meditation on how Baldwin, in turn, saw the world through Delaney: "I learned about light from Beauford Delaney, the light contained in every thing, every surface, every face.... [His] work leads the inner and the outer eye, directly and inexorably, to a new confrontation with reality."[57] Baldwin here encourages us to see the world with both "eyes," to see in art the possibility to explore the human interior as well as the potential to challenge the political exterior that shapes our experience. This double vision – the sight and insight that compel revelation, that require a "new confrontation with reality" – realizes the higher possibilities in W. E. B. Du Bois's notion of double-consciousness. As Du Bois put it, the aim in overcoming the tension between being black and being American is "to merge his double self into a better and truer self...to be a co-worker in the kingdom of culture."[58] It is fitting that this way of seeing, for both Baldwin and Du Bois, is at once an aesthetic and political illumination. Baldwin writes of the ability to see "the light contained in every thing, every surface, every face." With this double vision – or more accurately, doubled vision – we might see the "light contained" in Baldwin's face in that Delaney portrait. It is a face outward-looking; it is a face gazing back at the light that is also contained in ours.

NOTES

1 So Amiri Baraka calls Baldwin's eyes in his memorial speech at Baldwin's funeral. Karen Thorsen, et al. *James Baldwin: The Price of the Ticket.* (San Francisco: California Newsreel, 1989).
2 Quoted in the documentary *The Price of the Ticket.*
3 See James Campbell, *Talking at the Gates: A Life of James Baldwin, with New Afterward edition* (Berkeley: University of California Press, 2002).
4 James Baldwin, *Giovanni's Room* (New York: Dell Publishing, 1956), p. 62.
5 From "An interview with James Baldwin" (1961) with Studs Terkel. reprinted in *Conversations with James Baldwin* (Jackson and London: University Press of Mississippi, 1989).
6 As he explains in his speech at Wheeler Hall at the University of California at Berkeley (January 15, 1979), the expression, "civil rights activist," implies that one must agitate for rights that any citizen should already have. http://www.c-spanvideo.org/videoLibrary/mobilevideo.php?progid=174206. Accessed June 2014.
7 This discomfort with Baldwin among King's advisors – for example, Clarence Jones – extended also to Bayard Rustin, also gay. Although he was the principal organizer for the March and a close confidante to King, Rustin did not receive full public recognition for his work because some felt his sexual orientation tainted him.
8 See Fred L. Standley and Nancy V. Burt (eds.), *Critical Essays on James Baldwin* (Boston: G.K. Hall & Co., 1988), for a useful collection of early reviews and scholarly reactions to his work.
9 Felicia Lee, "Trying to Bring Baldwin's Complex Voice Back to the Classroom," *The New York Times* (April 24, 2014).
10 Rich Blint, associate director in the Office of Community Outreach and Education at Columbia University School of the Arts, speculated whether Baldwin's increasing absence from syllabi is because contemporary readers may simply find his views on race, sex, and American life "incendiary and…inflammatory." Quoted in Lee, "Trying to Bring Baldwin's Complex Voice Back to the Classroom." Choreographer Bill T. Jones and Blint also raised the question about whether persistent homophobia is to blame at "Baldwin's Capacious Imagination & Influence" (New York Live Arts, April 23, 2014), a public session that was part of "The Year of James Baldwin," a year-long multidisciplinary festival on Baldwin sponsored by a consortium of organizations across New York City, including New York Live Arts, Harlem Stage, Columbia University School of the Arts, New York University, New York School's Vera list Center for Art and Politics and the School of Writing, The Poetry Society of America, The James Baldwin School, and others.

11 See Gene Jarrett, *African American Literature Beyond Race: An Alternative Reader* (New York: New York University Press), 2006. See also Jarrett, *Deans and Truants: Race and Realism in African American Realism* (Philadelphia: University of Pennsylvania Press, 2006).

12 Irving Howe, "Black Boys and Native Sons," *Dissent* 10 (Autumn 1963), 353–68. Although Howe finds Baldwin a failed novelist who has produced only "minor" works, in the same article he argues that he is "one of the two or three greatest essayists this country has ever produced."

13 Harold Bloom's *The Anxiety of Influence: A Theory of Poetry* (Oxford: Oxford University Press, 1973) argues that poets, seeking an original vision but always necessarily informed by influential literary forbearers, always exist in tension with these precursors to whom they recognize a debt but from whom they must distance themselves in order to create.

14 Howe, p. 353.

15 See Julius Lester's interview with Baldwin, "Reflections of a Maverick," *The New York Times* (May 27, 1984), in which he questions Baldwin about his response to Richard Wright and Eldridge Cleaver's criticism of him. http://www.nytimes.com/books/98/03/29/specials/baldwin-reflections.html

16 As Nigel Hatton argues in his MLA 2014 paper, "Dear Sister: Deconstruction in in the Collaborative Spirit of Baldwin and African American Women Artists," Baldwin's influence extends to a generation of younger artists such as Jewel Gomez, Nikki Finney, and Sharifa Rhodes-Pitts.

17 It is important to note that Baldwin himself did not claim to be either a spokesperson (he identified himself as a "witness") nor a "celebrity," which as he suggests in interviews with Julius Lester, to the extent the celebrity lacks self-awareness: "The celebrity never sees himself. I have some idea what I'm doing on that stage; above all, I have some idea what sustains me on that stage. But the celebrity is not exactly Jimmy, though he comes out of Jimmy and Jimmy nourishes that, too. I can see now, with hindsight, that I would've had to become a celebrity in order to survive. A boy like me with all his handicaps, real and fancied, could not have survived in obscurity. I can say that it would have had to happen this way, though I could not see it coming." In "James Baldwin: Reflections of a Maverick," *The New York Times* (May 27, 1984).

18 Baldwin came of age among the so-called New York Intellectuals: mostly Jewish, mostly male, and mostly politically left-leaning (socialist but not communist) writers and literary critics, who rose in prominence in the 1930s and 1940s. Associated with the journals *Commentary* and *Partisan Review*, in particular, Irving Howe, Nathan Glazer, Daniel Bell, and Irving Kristol, among others, became influential cultural commentators.

19 "Debate: James Baldwin and William F. Buckley." Sponsored by the Cambridge Union Society, Cambridge University, 1965. http://vimeo.com/18413741. Baldwin's remarks garnered him a standing ovation – the television announcer suggests it is the first in the history of the Cambridge debates.

20 See Erica R. Edwards, *Charisma and the Fictions of Black Leadership, Difference Incorporated* (Minneapolis: University of Minnesota Press, 2012); Sasha Torres, *Black, White, and in Color: Television and Black Civil Rights* (Princeton: Princeton University Press, 2003).

21 James Baldwin, "Everybody's Protest Novel" (1948), in Toni Morrison (ed.), *James Baldwin: Collected Essays* (New York: The Library of America, 1998), p. 15.

22 George Schuyler, "The Negro Art Hokum" (1926) in Henry Louis Gates, Jr. et al (eds.), *The Norton Anthology of African American Literature*, second edition (New York: W. W. Norton & Co. 2004), p. 1222.

23 Langston Hughes, "The Negro Artist and the Racial Mountain" (1926), in Gates (ed.), *The Norton Anthology of African American Literature*, pp. 1311, 1314. I am arguing for a literary not a biographical connection between the two. Baldwin admits he came late to an appreciation of Hughes. Hughes suggested Baldwin's fiction did not live up to the potential of his essays in his 1958 *New York Times* review: http://www.nytimes.com/books/98/03/29/specials/baldwin-native.html

24 Paul Laurence Dunbar, "We Wear the Mask" (1895), in Gates (ed.), *The Norton Anthology of African American Literature*, p. 918.

25 In Benedict Anderson's *Imagined Communities: Reflections on the Origin and Spread of Nationalism* (London: Verso, 1983), he argues that all political communities are cultural artifacts, creations that are made, not found.

26 In the case of these works, these acts constituting community – masking, for instance – are portrayed as both representative (common modes of survival) and aspirational (models for "revolt against weariness in a white world"). It is important to note that Baldwin never bought into the prescriptive models of performing blackness that became more codified and rigid during the Black Arts and Black Power movements.

27 On the idea that race is made and maintained through iterated processes and social interaction, see, for instance, Hazel Markus and Paula Moya (eds.), *Doing Race: 21 Essays for the 21st Century* (New York: Norton & Co., 2010) and Michael Omi and Howard Winant, *Racial Formation in the United States: From the 1960s to the 1990s*, third edition (New York: Routledge, 2014).

28 Quoted from the televised debate between James Baldwin and William F. Buckley.

29 "Nobody Knows My Name" (1954), in Morrison (ed.), *Collected Essays*, p. 214.

30 James Baldwin, "The Creative Process" (1962), in Morrison (ed.), *Collected Essays*, pp. 669, 670.

31 James Baldwin, "Sweet Lorraine" (1969), in Morrison (ed.), *Collected Essays*, p. 758.

32 Ibid., p. 728.

33 Ibid., p. 758.

34 From "An interview with James Baldwin" (1961) with Studs Terkel, reprinted in *Conversations with James Baldwin* (1989).

35 Interview with James Elgrably, "James Baldwin. The Art of Fiction No. 78," *Paris Review* 91 (Spring 1984). http://www.theparisreview.org/interviews/2994/the-art-of-fiction-no-78-james-baldwin. Accessed July 2014.

36 Sterling Brown, "Ma Rainey" (1932), in Gates (ed.), *The Norton Anthology of African American Literature*, p. 1259.

37 James Baldwin and Margaret Mead, *A Rap on Race* (Philadelphia: Lippincott, 1971).

38 So David argues in *Giovanni's Room*, p. 21.

39 James Baldwin, "Stranger in the Village" (1955), in Morrison (ed.), *Collected Essays*, p. 122.

40 Ibid.

41 James Baldwin, *The Fire Next Time* (originally published 1962), (New York: Vintage, 1993), p. 6.

42 James Baldwin, "A White Man's Guilt" (originally published in *Ebony* magazine, August 1965), in *The Price of the Ticket: Collected Nonfiction, 1948–1985* (New York: St. Martin's Press, 1985), p. 140.

43 Baldwin, *The Fire Next Time*, p. 95.

44 James Baldwin, *Another Country* (originally published 1962) (New York: Vintage Press, 1993), p. 4.

45 James Baldwin, "Nobody Knows My Name" (1954), in Morrison (ed.), *Collected Essays*, p. 142.

46 Larry Neal "The Black Arts Movement," *Drama Review* 12 (Summer 1968), 29–39.

47 James Campbell, *Talking at the Gates: A Life of James Baldwin* (London: Faber and Faber, 1991), pp. 218–19.

48 Quoted in the documentary *The Price of the Ticket*.

49 In *Disidentifications: Queers of Color and the Performance of Politics* (St. Paul: University of Minnesota, 1999), Muñoz argues that "disidentifying" enables a complex model of minority survival and activism that involves working within majority culture to critique and transform it.

50 See Matt Brim, *James Baldwin and the Queer Imagination* (Ann Arbor: University of Michigan Press, 2014).

51 Ross Posnock, "Introduction: Ellison's Joking," in Ross Posnock (ed.), *The Cambridge Companion to Ralph Ellison* (Cambridge: Cambridge University Press, 2005), p. 7.

52 For an in-depth exploration of this phenomenon, see Harry J. Elam Jr., "Change Clothes and Go: A Postscript to Blackness," in Harry J. Elam, Jr. and Kennell Jackson (eds.), *Black Cultural Traffic: Crossroads in Global Performance and Popular Culture* (Ann Arbor: University of Michigan Press, 2005), pp. 379–98.

53 Hortense Spillers, "Afterward," in Cora Kaplan and Bill Schwartz (eds.), *James Baldwin: America and Beyond* (Ann Arbor: University of Michigan Press, 2011), p. 242.

54 From *Saturday Review*, quoted on back jacket of *Another Country*.

55 He expressed great frustration and disappointment at his highly publicized, but by all accounts ineffective, meeting with Attorney General Robert Kennedy in May 1963 meant to help improve race relations.

56 The 2014 "Year of James Baldwin," sponsored by New York Live Arts in collaboration with many arts organizations and universities, represents the artistic reach of Baldwin that this *Companion* seeks to capture as well in its outreach to musicians, artists, dancers, visual artists, playwrights, and others. As described by one of its many university sponsors, Columbia University: "Among the highlights of the festival are the world premiere of the theater work *Nothing Personal*, based on the 1964 collaborative book by James Baldwin and Richard Avedon, directed by Patricia McGregor and starring Colman Domingo; a preview of Carl Hancock Rux's play *Stranger on Earth*, featuring vocalist Marcelle

Davies Lashley; a preview of award-winning composer STEW's *Notes of a Native Song*; the New York premiere of choreographer Charles O. Anderson's *Restless Natives*; and the world premiere of choreographer Dianne McIntyre's *Time Is Time*. Also featured during the festival are an original video installation, inspired by the writings of Baldwin, by contemporary visual artist Hank Willis Thomas; and the speaking program 'Jimmy at High Noon,' featuring poet Yusef Komunyakaa, critic, essayist and memoirist Hilton Als, playwright and actor Tarell McCraney and others reading Baldwin's work and discussing its impact. Collaborators include the Richard Avedon Foundation; The New School and its Vera List Center for Art and Politics and the School of Writing; NYU and others." http://arts.columbia.edu/coe/news/2014/year-of-james-baldwin. Accessed June 18, 2014.

57 Baldwin, "On the Painter Beauford Delaney," in Morrison (ed.), *Collected Essays*, pp. 720–1.

58 W. E. B. Du Bois, "Of Our Spiritual Strivings," *The Souls of Black Folk* (1903).

PART I

Genres and Mélanges

I

JACQUELINE GOLDSBY

"Closer to Something Unnameable": Baldwin's Novel Form

Finding Form in Baldwin's Late Prose

Critics largely agree that James Baldwin's early novels and essay collections represent his "best," most trenchant writing, given their decisive interventions into the Civil Rights Movement and the literary developments of the mid-twentieth century.[1] By comparison, Baldwin's "late" novels – *Another Country* (1962), *Tell Me How Long the Train's Been Gone* (1968), *If Beale Street Could Talk* (1974), and *Just Above My Head* (1978) – have been scorned by critics for their "lack of narrative control," structural "confusion," and political "bitterness."[2] Even his biographers, who are sympathetic to Baldwin's "rage" against America (how could he not be distressed by the Civil Rights Movement's apparent collapse?), castigate the late fiction as formally weak, attributing the decline to Baldwin's life in exile and the lures of celebrity. For David Leeming and James Campbell, writing on the move and in the media's constant limelight sapped Baldwin's aesthetic strengths. Staying in perpetual motion and packaging his language into consumable sound bites, Baldwin diffused the creative discipline that novel-writing demands. Consequently, these critics lament, the late novels lacked the rigor of the earlier works.[3]

Did the craft-minded Baldwin relinquish his long-standing commitment to advancing the novel's aesthetic form? Starting with his infamous attack on sentimentalism, "Everybody's Protest Novel" (1948), Baldwin persistently reflected on the challenges posed by the genre. In subsequent essays such as "The Discovery of What It Means to Be American" (1959), "Notes for a Hypothetical Novel" (1960), and "The Creative Process" (1962), he posed vigorous claims about the virtues and limits of plot, character, temporality, history, and ethics as special domains through which novel-writing could engage public life.[4] Given his penchant to theorize his practice, we should not assume Baldwin's late fiction constitutes a betrayal of his novel-writing interests or talents.

Rather, we should follow the lead of scholar Lynn Scott, who argues that American racism's protean forms demanded that Baldwin experiment in his efforts to bear witness to it.[5] The historical traumas and flux that characterized American life in the late 1960s and 1970s – the assassinations of Medgar Evers, Malcolm X, and Martin Luther King, Jr.; the war in Vietnam; the emergence of Black Power, feminism, gay liberation, free speech, and flower power movements – gave rise to a telling trope in Baldwin's late fiction, Scott observes. Novelists, musicians, actors, and sculptors serve as protagonists of these works, and their struggles for freedom in a "deforming" world can be read allegorically. What should the artist's role be in a broken, unhinged society? For Scott, that Baldwin asks but does not resolve this question explains his novels' "open-ended" form.[6]

Critic Robert Reid-Pharr's compelling account of the late fiction confronts the virulent homophobia Baldwin endured from African-American readers. At apparent odds with the Black Arts Movement's veneration of black heterosexuality and patriarchal authority as cultural ideals, Baldwin's slackened control over his novels' form was maligned as evidence of his queer "depravity" and its distorting effects on his interests in more properly "black" subjects.[7] Reid-Pharr argues that the "breadth and coarseness" of the late novels counteract the critiques of Baldwin's detractors. Those works' focus on same-sex love between black men whose artistry stems from African-American traditions (gospel, jazz, and blues music) "disrupt[s] the often precious manner in which we think about black and American identity," Reid-Pharr contends. Because this "homosexual funkiness" imagines uncharted possibilities for black subjectivity and the novel form itself, the unruly shapes of Baldwin's late fiction reconfigure our ideas of what a body of work – and the black self's body – might look like and mean.[8]

As Reid-Pharr and Scott demonstrate, Baldwin was engaged in deliberate aesthetic tests that aimed to enlarge the scope of his novels' functions and meanings in the world. Building on these scholars' insights, I contend that the late fiction's *formlessness* elicits another concern: What are the expressive and ethical limits of aesthetic mediums as such?[9] This, for instance, is how I approach Hall's narration of his brother Arthur Montana's career as a gospel singer in *Just Above My Head* (1978). Why does gospel music move its performers and listeners to states of spiritual ecstasy? Can storytelling through the medium of the novel produce a comparable rapport between writer and reader? Likewise, considering that Fonny, a central character in *If Beale Street Could Talk* (1974), is a sculptor, one might ask how his carvings of faces and tables out of wood could be akin to the narrator Tish's summoning of words into characters, scenes, and events on a page. Can sculpture's three-dimensionality be realized in the novel's form? That is how I regard the ellipses and other odd punctuation styles that turn reading this novel into a more tactile, touch-oriented exercise.

By placing artists at the center of his late fiction, Baldwin juxtaposes those characters' expressive mediums to that of the novel, inviting readers to speculate about why art forms function the way they do. Moreover, by freeing these artist-types to be openly queer – by letting his protagonists explore unpredictable ranges of human attraction, desire, and even disgust – Baldwin unbinds the novel from norms of theme and content.[10] With queer black folk and multiple aesthetic mediums sharing the novel's discursive space – allowing for their touch, play, contact, and repulsion in close but unregulated quarters – Baldwin's late fiction gives birth to novels whose formlessness does not betray their author's skills. These works urge readers to interrogate their own investments in how art makes meaning in the world. Unseated from its presumed predominance, the novel – in Baldwin's late style of it – re-forms itself in coexistence with other aesthetic practices, as a medium made by and obligated to its cultural surroundings.

I propose this paradigm for interpreting Baldwin's late novels and apply it to one representative text, *Tell Me How Long the Train's Been Gone* (1968).[11] Narrated as a first-person memoir, the novel recounts Leo Proudhammer's tumultuous career as an African-American stage actor during the early 1940s and post–World War II decades, which he reflects on while recovering from a near-fatal heart attack. Having written and staged two dramas of his own by 1968, *The Amen Corner* (published in 1954; first staged in 1955) and *Blues for Mr. Charlie* (published and first staged in 1964), Baldwin infuses *Train* with telling details about the craft of acting and the culture of mid-twentieth-century American theatre. Indeed, Leo's mega-success, along with his sober scrutiny of fame's taxing effects on his health and intimate relationships, invites us to analyze the novel as a roman à clef about Baldwin's own career as a playwright and his struggles under publicity's spotlight.[12]

Though Baldwin's fame and stage-based work surely matter to the discussion I develop here, this essay does not treat either his biography or productions of his playscripts.[13] Rather, by juxtaposing *Train*'s account of stage performance with its strategies of prose narration on the page, I ask: How does the novel posit theatre's formal claims on actors and audiences in relation to the parallel obligation of novel-writing and novel-reading through the medium of printed books? If we read Leo's recollection of his career as a theory about theatrical aesthetics, does his prose activate comparable expressive forms to elicit analogous relationships between himself and the reader? If so, are those strategies comparable to those of Leo's stagecraft?

As I show, the formless shape with which *Train* poses these questions invites readers to recognize the novel's specificities as an art medium and how, when read in relation to the conventions of stage performance, literature seeks to liberate the imagination fully.

The "Salt" of Stage Performance

When *Train* opens, its unsubtly named protagonist is struck down while performing a play in San Francisco:

> I came offstage at the end of the second act. I felt hot and I was having trouble catching my breath. But I knew that I was tired. I went to my dressing room and poured myself a drink and put my feet up. Then I felt better. I knew I had about twenty-five minutes before I was due onstage. I felt very bitterly nauseous and I went to the bathroom but nothing happened. Then I began to be afraid, rather, to sit or lie down again and I poured myself another drink and left my dressing room to stand in the wings. I had begun to sweat and I was freezing cold. The nausea came back, making me feel that my belly was about to rise to the roof of my head. (3)

The reader is forced to relive Leo Proudhammer's feeling of danger, almost experiencing the short bursts of his heart's pounding and swelling within him. We "begin to be afraid" as his nausea roars forth and then quells; our bellies "rise" when "nothing happen[s]." While the theatre's audience relishes his absence because it heightens the suspense of his return ("when will the play's star come back?" viewers wonder during Leo's time offstage), the reader endures Leo's presence as a prolonged state of dread because his writing functions as a symbolic curtain behind which the reader witnesses the heart attack as an act without seeming end.

Fusing these scenes of art-making (Leo's stage-acting and memoir-writing), Baldwin establishes their distinction from and relation to one another in ways that allow *Train*'s readers to discern the medium-specific properties of each. First, as if to underscore the reader's anxieties, Leo shapes his sentences into short, declarative phrases. The dull thump of his frequent but irregular "I" visually marks the beats of his failing heart, mapping onto the page the time he spends offstage. Leo's use of the simple past heightens the effect of simultaneity, illuminating his body's seizures as an event that *Train*'s readers witness as if they are watching theatre. And yet readers experience this opening scene in a register particular to novel-reading, given the time-space lag inherent to the inscription of prose narration on the page.

That Leo writes and we read this passage after the heart attack emphasizes the solitary nature of novel-writing and novel-reading, in contrast to the communalism of putting on a play. Likewise, novel-reading often occurs in solitude, while theatre-going is a public, collective affair. That these comparisons resonate between the lines of *Train*'s opening scene urges its readers to speculate: How might novel-writing and novel-reading encourage the collectivity and now-ness that theatre requires for its medium to work? By intertwining novel-writing's techniques with those of the stage, *Train* suggests how liveness and communalism are achieved through each medium and explores what purposes those effects might achieve.

Yet as alluring as they may be, theatre's powers of presence cannot be taken for granted. To make this point, Baldwin activates the plot-making resources of the novel in ways that clarify what he defines as the sterile and regenerative modes of theatrical practice. An example of barren acting nearly traumatizes Leo into leaving the profession, not least because it occurs in bucolic upstate New York during a seemingly idyllic summer, in what appeared to be a lucky first break for a twenty-something Negro actor invited to attend "The Actors' Means Workshop." When Leo first arrives at this artistic colony, he is bewildered by the technologies and seeming banalities that organize stage work. A childhood fan of cinema, he was shielded by movies from the artifice that stage performance requires. He writes, "Our first week, we did a great deal of demolishing – of walls, doors, panels – and a great deal of carting and burning.... We made an inventory of the props, which were piled helter-skelter, covered with dust, in the attic of the theater." Classifying the dust-coated props according to "PERIOD, TOLSTOIAN, MODERN, NORTH AMERICA, AND CONTEMPORARY VIENNA" strikes Leo as "peculiarly pretentious" (135) until he realizes what these remains actually symbolize:

> [T]hese uniforms of Czarist generals, of Civil War soldiers, the shawls and dresses of Lorca heroines, the patched jackets of Steinbeck peasants, of Odets insurgents, these buckles, shoes, boots, pumps, bonnets, rugged shirts and ruffled shirts...so deeply drenched in human salt that sometimes shredded at a touch, so icily trapped in time's indifference that they chilled the hand, spoke of the reality, operating relentlessly every hour, which would one day overtake me and all my styles and poses and uniforms. These garments had been worn – by real people; real music had been played for them, and they had moved in a genuine light; they had put their hands on their hearts and delivered their vows, and the curtain had come down. These costumes were like their dispersed, indifferent bones, and the attic always reminded me of Ezekiel's valley, and Ezekiel's question: Oh, Lord, can these bones live? (136)

Yet Leo's ideal of theatrical realism – mobilizing artifice to tell truths that are not delimited by empirical, material reality – depends on the difference it asserts from the truth-seeking plot of the *bildungsroman*, which the Workshop idyll invokes. Thus, as he sorts these ordinary props, Leo rejects "the styles and poses and uniforms" of *status quo* classifications. However, this refusal of normative order – and the deeper, more profound truth that sustains it – gains greater clarity as Leo trains according to The Actors' Means Workshop's approach to its medium.

To begin with, the Workshop's social organization reveals theatre's life-affirming purpose, as Leo begins to understand it. Located at a visible remove from the local community that surrounds it, the Workshop segregates itself from accountability to its cultural context, and the married couple that directs the troupe (whose surname, San Marquand, suggests the French imperial court rather than American democracy), rule the camp as a dictatorship. A hierarchy exists, and their power determines everyone's fate. The arbitrary ways in which the duo dispense attention create rivalries not only among the actors, but throughout the town as well. The residents' frustration and powerlessness lead them to project their resentments on Leo, whose race distracts them from recognizing Saul and Lola San Marquand's power over them all.

Leo, of course, exercises no real sway in this situation. The domestic labor he performs – from cleaning and organizing props to serving as a chauffeur and fetching food for the performers – pegs him not simply as an apprentice, but as specifically "black." Struggling to maintain his artistic ambition, Leo seeks other avenues to channel his confidence. For instance, he works as a nude model for a "Life Art" class in town, yet the white female students' interest in his physique stems from prurient racist stereotypes (157–9). Heaping injury upon insult, the town's white men suspect Leo's every move and summon police to arrest him on the flimsiest of pretexts. These race rituals place Leo in physical jeopardy and humiliate him before his Workshop peers. Subject to racial harassment from the lowbrow townies, the racialized erotic fantasies of middlebrow matrons, and Saul and Lola's highbrow disdain for the cultural tensions their power engenders, Leo "disrupt[s] the town's emotional economy" (166), making the Actors' Means Workshop an unfree space where theatre's potential cannot be realized.

The Workshop's corrupting force finds its fullest, worst expression as Leo prepares for his summer audition, a reading of Clifford Odets's *Waiting for Lefty* (1935). Together with Barbara King, his colleague and would-be lover-turned-lifelong-friend, Leo selects this play in open defiance of Saul and Lola's reign. Since Leo did not want to restrict himself to an all-black script, such as *All God's Chillun Got Wings* (1925), and Barbara refused to typecast herself as a spoiled Southern heiress by reading from August Strindberg's *Miss Julie* (1888),[14] the pair instead picks Odets's drama of doomed working-class love: "The young hack, Sid, and his girl, Florrie, can't marry because it's the depression and they don't have money and this is the scene where they give each other up" (138), Leo explains. However, would "the liberal San Marquands" accept an interracial reading of Odets's script? How might race, in addition to the class tensions that drive the lovers apart, make Sid and Florrie's love impossible? The answers to these questions recall Leo's epiphany among the props he organizes: "I had not known make-believe could be so painful, and, indeed, I now began to learn something about make-believe" (138–9).

As if on perverse cue, Leo and Barbara finally receive their audition call immediately following the summer's most brutal racist attack. Having finally consummated their real-life attraction to one another, the couple giddily heads to the Workshop only to be met by the "hostile, staring, gathering town" (281). Clusters of white mobs trail them to the theatre, hurling awful, ruthless epithets – "nigger," "white slut" (283) – along the way. This violent, pain-filled encounter could be seen as informing Leo and Barbara's "method" to prepare their roles.[15] Racism – which this incident unmasks as its own kind of depression, its own special poverty – would likely (and sadly) wedge Sid and Florrie apart. However, Leo refuses to use that idea as a resource: "'Let's not talk about it, ever'" (284) he insists to Barbara. Nonetheless, the repressed event returns: as their performance unfolds, Leo "hits it" (293) and, drawing upon the deep anger he feels, infuses Sid's "propagandistic" (294) lines with the full fury the mob's assault unleashed upon and within him.

Crucially, though, Saul demeans the uses to which Leo puts this experience. Indeed, the director specifically denies history's relation to the "execution" or making of art, a claim he asserts during his evaluation of Leo and Barbara's performances (296–300). For Saul, "personal motives" (296) have no place in an actor's repertoire of techniques. This puritanical streak extends to his most puzzling and damning observation: "'an actor's instrument is his body, is himself'" (300). This claim makes even less sense once Saul racializes it by regarding Leo's dancing with the uncritical primitivism so often invoked to characterize black expressivity. Applauding Leo's dancing, Saul condescends: "'[t]hen you seemed free and, so to say, joyous and boyish. We found it your very best moment'" (300). Saul's theory of acting is both fallacious and insidious, marked by both flawed logic and racism. His dictum about the "actor's instrument" conflates form – the actor's body – with medium, because the body is not, properly, the "self." Rather, actors invent *personae* that amalgamate their personal histories and experiences with those they imagine in the lives of their characters. These distinctions between body and self, form and medium – which Saul refuses or fails to acknowledge – comprise, for Leo, the basis of his more complex aspirations for theatre's craft. During his epiphany among the costumes (discussed earlier), Leo sees the salt-stained clothes as evidence of theatre's special freedom, wherein human imagination, intelligence, and desire authenticate stagecraft as a meaningful expression, rather than mere embodiment, of life. At the same time, the physical labors of acting, preserved in those "bones" of white sweat, render "make-believe" (138) a tangible reality whose consequences can be seen, touched, tasted, and felt in the actual world. Understood Leo's way, history makes art possible. In turn, art makes life legible. Thus, through the medium and mechanisms of embodied exchange, theatre allows actors and audiences to "break through to each other…and to accept each other's presence" (169).

Scripting Freedom

The occasion that enables Leo to attain artistic fulfillment occurs not at The Actors' Means Workshop but in a low-budget, off-off-off Broadway revival of *The Corn is Green*.[16] The institutional matrix in which this opportunity arises is no small coincidence, because the play's contexts point toward the transformative potential that Leo (and Baldwin) seeks to activate by aligning theatre's aesthetic and social enterprise with those of novel-writing and novel-reading. Crucially, Leo's break happens in the city, not the rural countryside. This symbolic geography matters not because Baldwin implies an essentializing privilege for New York City *per se*; that would be a Saul-style logical error. Rather, the densities of city living demand that Leo not separate his theatre work from his life. In Manhattan, he cannot abandon his social obligations without consequences. For instance, he has to work at the West Village Caribbean restaurant or else he cannot pay his rent (while the barter system that sustains The Actors' Means Workshop allowed Leo to ditch his duties when he felt like it), and he has to balance long hours on the job with the time he needs to learn his lines and attend rehearsals. Prioritizing those obligations over visits with his family in Harlem leads Leo's oldest brother Caleb to chastise him for neglecting their parents, especially their ailing mother. Yet that is precisely Baldwin's point: the living art of theatre demands that artists attend to difficult choices.

Importantly, Leo's theories about theatre "come alive" (387) in the two distinctive features of his being cast in *The Corn Is Green* (1941): Leo is cast against racial type, and the director is not Anglo-American (the reason for this casting choice). A recent immigrant to the United States, Konstantin, or "Connie," Rafaelto justifies his "experiment" of relocating the play from its original British setting among white working-class miners to black farm laborers in the U.S. South because he harbors no preconceived ideas of "the place of black people in this strange place" (412). Arguing against both racial sentimentalism and color-blind casting, Connie explains why reversing racial roles enriches the aesthetic and ethical value of the play-script.[17] In his view, the class oppression of British miners sheds light on the fate of African-American sharecroppers (and vice versa) to the degree that both cultural contexts are recognized. Thus, the protagonist's quest for education – whether played as a white British coal miner or a black American field hand – enlarges the meanings of the character's struggle, either by spotlighting the singular setting (America or Britain) or through the tacit comparisons that the adaptation implies. Staking out this ground, Connie's directorial vision and ethics stand in stark contrast to Saul's. On Connie's stage, "personal motives" can inform an actor's execution of character; art serves as a workshop where life might be better understood. It is no wonder, then, that acting in *The Corn Is Green* makes Leo "come alive" and not feel "alone" (387).

Importantly, theatre's redemptive power crystallizes in this account of Leo's crucial breakthrough during rehearsals with Connie. Like the salt that stained the costumes he organized at the Actors Means Workshop, Leo's words on the page leave the traces of a deeply human encounter:

> That morning, while [Connie] was talking to me, he looked me directly in the eye and he was much too involved in what he was trying to say to me to have energy left over to hand me any shit. He wasn't trying to impress me, and he wasn't blackmailed by my color. He talked to me as one artisan to another, concerning a project which he hoped we would be able to execute together. This was a profound shock, he couldn't have known how profound, and it was a great relief. No one in the theater had ever talked to me like that.
>
> (414)

Baldwin could have chosen to stage this moment in dialogue (like he treats Saul's dictums about acting on the page). Notably, however, Leo describes this epiphany in a long, steady stream of exposition. By dispensing with verbatim transcription, Baldwin leverages the *durée* of reading for *Train*'s audience to approximate Leo's experience of recognition as a textual event. As readers thread through the pages of this moment word by word, line by line, paragraph by paragraph, page by page, we undergo our own version of Connie's call to craftsmanship: "as one artisan to another, concerning a project…to execute together." Conjoining the resources of novel-writing and theatre in this way, Baldwin urges the reader to recognize ourselves as sharing Leo's journey, which we can – and must – if we are to discern the distinctions between aesthetic mediums as liberating knowledge-space.

In yet another gesture that fuses the art of theatre and the novel into a shared but unnamed domain, Leo maps this terrain through his depictions of silence. For instance, when he reads Sid's speech from *Waiting for Lefty*,

33

he describes Saul watching quietly, "alone in the center of [that] vast, high room, [with] students sit[ting] around and behind him" (285). This "tension," Leo recalls, "contained no possibility of release" (292). By contrast, waiting to sing the overture for *The Corn Is Green*, Leo is engulfed by "an incredible silence" (432), which he breaks by entering the stage sonically – in music, as voice. Thus, his first appearance defies corporeal notions of body and self. In this space – which contradicts Saul's theory of the actor's medium – Leo discovers that reciprocity constitutes his bond with the audience:

> When the curtain came up, I knew I was going to vomit, right here, in front of all these people. The moment I delivered my first line, "No, miss," I knew I was going to be all right. And you can tell, from the other actors and from the audience...I played that scene for all that was in it, for all that was in me, and for all the colored kids in the audience – who held their breath, they really did, it was the unmistakable silence in which you and the audience re-create each other – and for the vanished little Leo, and for my mother and father, and all the hope and pain that were in me. For the very first time, the very first time, I realized the fabulous extent of my luck: I could, I *could*, if I kept the faith, transform my sorrow into life and joy. I might live in sorrow and pain forever, but, if I kept the faith, I could do for others what I felt had not been done for me, and if I could do that, if I could give, I could live.
>
> (433; emphases in original)

This passage heralds an extraordinary annunciation about the birth of art and its publics: in "the unmistakable silence [...the artist] and the audience re-create each other," Leo realizes. As this message comes through the medium of a book – which we hold alone, in our hands – *Train*'s readers, too, must question our bonds to this moment: Is the silence of novel-reading the same as the silence of viewing a stage performance? And if fiction bears within it "unmistakable silences," how do the novelist and reader "re-create each other" in those spaces; moreover, where might those spaces be? However, if theatre's reciprocity depends on dread and physical threat – note that Leo connects to his audience by beating back the compulsion to vomit at the curtain's rise (itself a reprise of *Train*'s opening scene) – what kinds of narrative "nausea" might provide such moments of risk and release through novel-writing and novel-reading? Toward what goals and ends?

Narrative Nausea; or, Staging Flashbacks in *Train*

In all of Baldwin's novels, flashbacks stage the type of intimacy Leo aspires to experience in the theatre.[18] For instance, Gabriel Grimes's unmerciful anger toward his family becomes explicable, though not forgivable, when readers learn his backstory in the chapter devoted to him in *Go Tell It on the Mountain* (1953). Likewise, David's confessional reveries account for, but do not free him from, the prison of his guilt after denying Giovanni's love in *Giovanni's Room* (1956). As these examples suggest, flashbacks equip the novel to forge bonds between readers and texts. More precisely, they function as a medium of social history and ethical consciousness – to a certain degree, at least, as the device of the flashback serves to redeem characters from the legacies of their "bad" acts. Indeed, because the technique literally renders Gabriel's rage and David's guilt into legible form – with a taut, almost algebraic linearity that distinguishes Baldwin's early use of this device in both of these novels – social order is distorted and restored at once. With the knowledge that flashbacks provide in the early novels, we can comprehend the damage that men like Gabriel and David unleash in the world; at the same time, we have reason to hope for predictable change at the close of each text: we sense that John Grimes will escape his father's dominion; we suspect we will mourn Giovanni's unjust execution.

In *Train*, flashbacks breach this structural logic. To begin with, they do not have fixed start and end points. They loop, elongate, and embed themselves inside one another to the point where they make the basic fundamental units of a novel – story and plot – indistinguishable from one another. This (dis) organization characterizes the first three chapters (or "books," as Baldwin calls them), which chronicle Leo's theatrical training at the Workshop and for *The Corn Is Green*. Flashbacks derail these sections of the novel with the complex and tangled love relationships Leo pursues with his brother Caleb and his colleague Barbara. Ostensibly, these affairs of the heart should be narrated for readers because they comprise the star's biography: if the loves of Leo's life make him the man and actor he is, and if these experiences of love enrich his craft on the stage, then these stories are not mere gossip, nor are they disposable digressions. That is, if we accept Connie's method of acting over Saul's, these recollections are imperative for readers to know.

However, Leo's love for Caleb and Barbara violates social norms, and by staging those encounters as flashbacks, the novel dares readers not to speak those affections' names. After Leo spends an enjoyable evening carousing with his Workshop friends in two local taverns (one Italian, the other black; the racial difference affects the significance of the evening's joy), he spends the night with a fellow actress, Madeleine. When he awakens, Leo is startled to recall himself "curled up against Caleb, in our narrow bed" (189). A stunning forty-six pages are devoted to this flashback of incestuous intimacy between the brothers (199–245). Then, this flashback wends forward in Leo's lifetime (but still backward from the novel's present) to recount his first sexual liaison with Barbara, which occurs after Leo is arrested for "trespassing" into Madeleine's apartment but before Leo and Barbara perform their scene from *Waiting for Lefty*, the event whose staging is the proper climax of this very long chapter's plot. If that summary is hard to follow, that is the point of the flashback's formlessness. The atemporal relation between these elements unbinds the sutures that linear plotting provides. Stranded inside Leo's loops and bends of memory, readers are left without the comforts of logical flows of time, cause, and action. Here, then, narrative "nausea" begins. Recounting his lovemaking with Barbara in the same flashback in which he recalls his erotic contact with Caleb, Leo positions these events as not merely parallel, but comparable to one another. And to emphasize their (de)stabilizing weight, Baldwin uses the rules of grammar in acutely transgressive ways.

When the brothers caress, Leo's sentence reads like mutual masturbation might, with the commas and strategically placed colon allowing his words to glide across the sentence's surface structure. The use of punctuation in this passage draws the reader into Leo's time and space where, "to be present" in his brother's body is the only "journey" we can make, too:

> We were doing nothing very adventurous, really, we were only using our hands and, of course, I had already done this by myself and I had done it with other boys: but it had not been like this because there had been no agony in it, I had not been trying to give, I had not even been trying to take, and I had not felt myself, as I did now, to be present in the body of another person, had not felt his breath in mine, his sighs and moans, his quivering and shaking as mine, his journey as mine.
>
> (211)

Likewise, Leo's use of declarative sentences – precisely, his use of periods to stop the flow of action – ironizes the social mores and laws which criminalize his intimacy with Barbara[19]:

> Perhaps it could only have happened as it happened. I don't know. I had, then, to suspend judgment, and I suspend judgment now. We had no choice. We really had no choice. I had to warm my girl, my freezing girl. I covered her with my body, and I took off her robe. I covered her, I covered her, she held me, and I entered her. And we rejoiced. Sorrow, what have we not known of sorrow! But, that morning, we rejoiced. And yet, it must be said, there was a shrinking in me when it was over. *Love, honor, and protect.*
>
> (272; emphases in original)

Reading these scenes is not unlike the vertigo Leo experiences as the curtain rises on *The Corn Is Green*'s opening night. A chasm opens before *Train*'s readers: we may very well "vomit, right here, in front of all these people" (433); our hearts could leap in shocked surprise. How are we to understand the relation between these two events? Each is socially tabooed. Indeed, incest and miscegenation – individually or both together – may frighten or disgust us. As if to demand that we confront the precipice, Leo dares readers not to contemplate such connections: he calls Barbara "sister" after their lovemaking. Is their interracial heterosexual intimacy familial the same as Leo's filial love with Caleb? On what grounds can we accept them as integral to Leo's growth: through their *difference from* one another, or based on their *relation to* one another? Or would we deny these as growth-making experiences at all? In reference to what norms or standards? If it unsettles readers that these flashbacks impose such questions and demand answers that the novel itself does not give, the visceral nature of our discomfort stresses how, for Baldwin, novel-writing and novel-reading might strive to provoke the openness and reciprocity that theatre aims to foster through the medium of radical, embodied presence.

Formlessness as Late Style

Testing temporal and ethical limits in ways that Baldwin's early novels do not, *Train*'s formless flashbacks enact what Leo experiences on stage: "life, and life is many things, but it is, above all, the touch of another. The touch of another: no matter how transient, at no matter what price" (316). To be sure, Baldwin asks readers of his late fiction to pay a steep price for inhabiting the worlds he envisions. In *Train*, achieving a "human connection" (313) entails accepting relationships – human, temporal, causal – that may strain one's sense of normalcy and order.

That price extends to the value we place on aesthetic mediums, and to the expressive boundaries we expect art forms to generate, organize, and maintain in the name of delivering a "satisfying" or "pleasing" experience. Through this framework, my reading of *Train* can serve as a paradigm for readers to return to Baldwin's late novels and reconsider the complaints against their supposed artlessness in new ways. After all, as Edward Said reminds us, we tend to harbor limited definitions of artists' "late style":

> [W]hat [if we understand] artistic lateness not as harmony and resolution but as intransigence, difficulty, and unresolved contradiction? What if age and ill health don't produce the serenity that "ripeness is all"? [What about] final works [that] tear apart the career and the artist's craft and reopen the questions of meaning, success, and progress that the artist's late period is supposed to move beyond [?][20]

By placing fiction's mediums in dialogue with theatre and other art forms, Baldwin does not lose the control that defined his early works of fiction.

Rather, his late novels reopen what the work of art can be, do, and mean in the world because their complexities refuse the "tricks which would never help one come closer to life" (346).

NOTES

1 Karen Thorsen et al., *James Baldwin: The Price of the Ticket* (San Francisco: California Newsreel, 1989). This documentary succinctly outlines this phase of Baldwin's career, as do these biographies: David Leeming, *James Baldwin: A Biography* (New York: Henry Holt, 1994) and James Campbell 1991, *Talking at the Gates: A Life of James Baldwin* (London: Faber & Faber, 2008). Historian David W. Blight focuses on the 1960s as the zenith of Baldwin's clout as a public intellectual in *American Oracle: The Civil War in the Civil Rights Era* (Cambridge, MA: Belknap Press of Harvard University, 2011), esp. pp. 193–240.

2 Thorsen's *Price of the Ticket* surveys this negative critique. The most comprehensive account of the late fiction's contested reception can be found in Lynn Orilla Scott, *James Baldwin's Later Fiction: Witness to the Journey* (East Lansing: Michigan State University Press, 2002).

3 Novelist Caryl Phillips critiques Baldwin's rootless cosmopolitanism in "The Price of the Ticket," *The Guardian* (July 13, 2007). http://www.theguardian.com/books/2007/jul/14/fiction.jamesbaldwin. December 24, 2013. David Blight describes the psychic strains of Baldwin's traveling; see *American Oracle*, 204–6. However, a new perspective is coming to regard Baldwin's life in exile as creatively productive: see essays on Baldwin's transatlantic crossings collected in Dwight A. McBride (ed.), *James Baldwin Now* (New York: New York University Press, 1999); Magdalena Zaborowska, *James Baldwin's Turkish Decade: Erotics of Exile* (Durham: Duke University Press, 2010); and Cora Kaplan and Bill Schwarz (eds.), *James Baldwin: America and Beyond* (Ann Arbor: University of Michigan Press, 2011).

4 James Baldwin, *The Price of the Ticket: Collected Essays, 1948–1985* (New York: St. Martin's Press, 1985). See also Randall Kenan (ed.), *The Cross of Redemption: Uncollected Writings* (New York: Pantheon, 2010).

5 Scott, *James Baldwin's Later Fiction*, p. xiv.

6 Ibid., p. xiv. For Baldwin's own testimony about these crises – and to see how the social flux of the post–civil rights era altered Baldwin's prose style – compare 1972's *No Name in the Street* to the early essay "Notes of a Native Son" (1955).

7 Black Panther member Eldridge Cleaver disparaged Baldwin's sexuality in his 1968 memoir, *Soul on Ice*. On this controversy, see Scott, *James Baldwin's Later Fiction*, pp. 12–13. On this and other affronts from black literary nationalists see James Campbell, *Talking at the Gates*, pp. 205, 218–19, 264–5.

8 Robert Reid-Pharr, *Once You Go Black: Choice, Desire, and the Black American Intellectual* (New York: New York University Press, 2007), esp. pp. 108, 113.

9 My approach has been influenced by Scott and Reid-Pharr, and by two other accounts of experimental writing: Ross Chambers, *Loiterature* (Lincoln:University of Nebraska Press, 1999) and Judith Halberstam, *The Queer Art of Failure* (Durham: Duke University Press, 2011).

10 I use the term "queer" to mean more than "gay" or same-sex erotic/romantic identifications, to refer to nonnormative affections, identifications, and behaviors. Importantly, Baldwin himself refused either term to describe his own sexual identity or relationships.

11 I rely on the 1998 Vintage edition of *Train* and will abbreviate the title to *Train* and cite page numbers parenthetically from here on.

12 Scott carefully illuminates these themes; see *James Baldwin's Later Fiction*, chapter 2. As Magdalena Zaborowska notes, the novel is also centrally concerned with "sexuality and the erotic" (*James Baldwin's Turkish Decade*, 73). Other thematic dimensions include the protagonist's diaspora genealogy (Leo's father hails from the West Indies and his mother from New Orleans) and the critique of evangelical Pentecostalism. *Train*'s message overload contributed to the novel's alleged incoherence; for a representative example of this complaint, see Campbell, *Talking at the Gates*, pp. 226–8.

13 Baldwin discusses distinctions of genre and medium in an interview with Mel Watkins; see "James Baldwin Writing and Talking," *New York Times Book Review* (September 23, 1979), 1.

14 *All God's Chillun Got Wings*, Eugene O'Neill's version of doomed interracial love, starred Paul Robeson when it premiered in 1924. *Miss Julie* (1888) is a canonical work by August Strindberg about a rich heiress who seeks freedom by socializing with the servant class. *Waiting for Lefty* presents a series of vignettes about cab drivers on the eve of a labor strike. The Depression-era play was first staged in 1936 by the Group Theater, the New York City troupe that first practiced Method acting. For background on Odets's play, see Melissa Barton, "Staging Liberation: Race, Representation, and Forms of American Theater, 1934–65," PhD dissertation, University of Chicago (2012), chapters 1 and 4.

15 "Method" acting refers to a dramatic technique that encourages actors to draw upon their own life experience to forge emotional identifications with the characters they portray. The technique was introduced to the American stage with the translation of Konstantin Stanislavski's *An Actor Prepares* (1936). Its most famous instructors included Lee Strasberg, Stella Adler, and Elia Kazan, all of whom Baldwin encountered during his efforts to have his plays staged in New York City as early as 1956. See Leeming, *James Baldwin*, pp. 148–56; Campbell, *Talking at the Gates*, pp. 125–7, 190–9, 233–6; and Barton's analysis of Baldwin's engagements with the Method approach in "Staging Liberation," pp. 164–9, 182–206.

16 Like *Waiting for Lefty*, Emylyn Williams's *The Corn Is Green* is a 1930s stage drama about working-class struggles and aspirations. The play debuted in London in 1938, had a Broadway run in 1940, and was adapted into a film starring Bette Davis in 1945.

17 Connie's dramaturgy recapitulates Baldwin's central claims in "Everybody's Protest Novel." Barton explicates these allusions to suggest how Baldwin reclaims Method acting to explore characters' interiorities in his novels; see "Staging Liberation," 182–206. My interest in medium rather than specific novel-writing techniques distinguishes my approach to Leo's exchanges with Connie.

18 See Barton, "Staging Liberation," 187–204 for a differently emphasized reading of Baldwin's flashbacks in *Another Country*. Her discussion of *Train*'s use

of this device (203–6) does not deal with the issues of (homo)eroticism, reader response, and medium treated here.

19 Even though the U.S. Supreme Court's 1967 ruling in *Loving v. Virginia* struck down state laws forbidding interracial marriage, Leo's relationship with the white Southern heiress Barbara would have been both socially tabooed and legally prohibited during the 1950s and early 1960s, the decades of their early romance.

20 Edward Said, *On Late Style: Music and Literature against the Grain* (New York: Vintage Books, 2007), p. 7.

2

META DUEWA JONES

Baldwin's Poetics

The Time of Poetry

By the 1983 publication of *Jimmy's Blues: Selected Poems*, James "Jimmy" Baldwin had entered his sixth decade. His collection of nineteen poems comprised nearly, and neatly, as many pages as Baldwin counted years. And how did Mr. Baldwin count the years? Carefully. He took meticulous – and metaphorical – inventory of the passage of time. Baldwin noted, in his poetry and prose, the limits of mortal time: death. As he avowed prophetically, "I think a person is in sight of his or her death around the age of forty .... You are struck by the fact of your mortality, that it is unlikely you'll live another forty years. So time alters you, actually becoming either an enemy or a friend."[1] These remarks illustrate Baldwin's thinking about time, often connected to his ideas about aging and death. In this essay, I will demonstrate why a temporal frame enables us to better understand Baldwin's poetics.

This essay assesses Baldwin's poetry, since readers have not invested sufficient time and critical attention in this aspect of Baldwin's publishing career. Baldwin possessed an imagination that was as poetic as it was political, as countless critics have shown. However, when most scholars and writers invoke "poetics" in Baldwin, they are referencing the sensitivity, insight, and elegance with words that grace the pages of his prose. Yet despite "his own dismissal" of the quality of his poetry "early in his career," "Baldwin wrote throughout his life" and "saw himself more poet than anything else."[2]

This essay is dedicated to the memory of Robert Charles Beasley, historian, teacher, and beloved friend, who shared Baldwin's birthday of August 2; who shared Baldwin's expansively humanistic vision of love; who "confronted with passion" and joy, as Baldwin himself urged, "the conundrum of life"; who died prematurely during the research and writing of this essay; who is cherished for all times.

Thanks to my colleagues Michele Elam, Walton Muyumba, and Daina Ramey Berry for clarifying insights and commentary on Baldwin that benefited the arguments made in this essay. Thanks also to Alice Underwood and Michael Fuller for additional editorial assistance.

This assertion might seem incongruous with the bulk of "the 6,895 pages of [Baldwin's] published work" that exists in prose form: in essays, reviews, novels, and plays.³ In fact, *Jimmy's Blues* was Baldwin's first commercially published full-length collection of poems – and he died just four years after its publication.

Baldwin's late-in-life verse publication, and his persistence in publishing it despite his publisher's initial rejection, provides compelling grounds to consider – if not categorize, given Baldwin's eschewing of labels – "James Baldwin, as poet."⁴ Extant Baldwin scholarship tends to compare his work to that of novelists such as Richard Wright, Chester Himes, or Toni Morrison⁵; by contrast, I contend it is vital to place Baldwin's poetics in relationship with other African-American poets, specifically his predecessors and successors. The major themes and forms of *Jimmy's Blues* also compel questions: Why did Baldwin turn, or return, to poetry, in the twilight of his career? What did poetry do for Baldwin temporally, and what did it do formally? Baldwin was not only an astute theorist of time; he was a time formalist, too. He used time as a motif, a metaphor, and a measurement throughout his poetry. My primary purpose here is to provide a formal analysis that assesses Baldwin's temporal measurement in multiple ways.⁶

Temporal markers mark the scope of *Jimmy's Blues*. Seven of the nineteen poems, more than one-third of the volume, highlight a specific day, time of day, season, year, or age. Many poems evoke linear time, *chronos*, measurable by the minute or the hour. The word "time" is also accounted for numerically; it appears thirty-eight times in a book that numbers fewer than seventy pages total – that is, on slightly more than half of the volume's page-scape. The percentage increases to nearly 70 percent, with more than fifty references to "time," when the variant "sometimes" is tallied. The point of counting for time by text-mining Baldwin's poems is to emphasize that Baldwin possessed a heightened time-consciousness. His formal rendering of time through the use of poetic and rhetorical devices demonstrated an awareness of time's revelations and time's limitations.

Apprenticeship, Age, and Poetry for the Future

Time has taken care of the tendency to ignore Baldwin's poetry. This essay's focus on Baldwin's poetics heralds the recent reissue of *Jimmy's Blues*, along with poems from *Gypsy*, a limited-edition chapbook, by Beacon Press.⁷ The poet Sonia Sanchez proclaimed on the book jacket, "These poems are morning stars to be inhaled everyday as we strip search our eyes for new memory."⁸ Sanchez echoed lines from Baldwin's poem "Song": "we must be…the guiding star…. Our children are / the morning star."⁹ These celestial metaphors reference points in time and point toward the reproductive future. Significantly, James Baldwin's "own death would inspire the future" of African-American poetry, as his funeral inaugurated the Dark Room Collective, the Boston-based black writers group, cofounded by poets Thomas Sayers Ellis and Sharan Strange. As the poet Kevin Young recalls: "we only wished that Baldwin was beside us, but in a way, through his writing and his vision, he was and still is."[10] In other words, Baldwin may have been limited by mortal time, yet his prophetic oeuvre is timeless. Baldwin's investment in poetry reflected a need for affiliation at key temporal transitions such as birth or death, in his life, or in the lives of others.

Baldwin "read many plays and a lot of poetry as a kind of apprenticeship."[11] Who did he read? He confessed that he was "addicted to" reading Gwendolyn Brooks.[12] And he was drawn to Emily Dickinson as well, admiring her "use of language," "style of solitude," and humor.[13] Baldwin also engaged many younger poets and writers active in the Black Aesthetic and Black Arts Movements, such as Ed Bullins, LeRoi Jones (Later Amiri Baraka), and Nikki Giovanni.[14] By the early 1970s, poetry networks provided Baldwin, at midlife, an elder statesman's authority – a generational distinction earned by the time he spent paying his dues as a black writer and activist. In a "dialogue" with Giovanni, he professed being "'very proud' of her and her youthful cohort for what they have achieved in the black freedom struggle." And he focused on Giovanni's role as a poet, stating that African-Americans "have survived the roughest game in the history of the world…and you're a poet precisely because you are beginning to apprehend [this] and put it into a form which will be useful for your kid and his kid and for the world."[15] His high regard for Giovanni's poetry for future generations did not mitigate his discomfort with "being slotted" by Giovanni "as an elder before his fiftieth birthday."[16] When she told Baldwin that she was only six when his essay "Everybody's Protest Novel," was published in 1948, he replied, tongue in cheek: "Oh, Jesus."[17] Toward the end of his life, however, more than a decade later, Baldwin had embraced the mantle of "older brother" to writers like Baraka.[18]

Temporal Transformations: Baldwin Banishes Hughes's Blues Form

Baldwin also turned to poetry at signal moments of transformation and maturation. For instance, he wrote about masculinity and coming of age in poems such as "Song":

> I see you, somehow,
> about the age of ten,
> determined to enter the world of men,

> yet not too far from your mother's lap,
> wearing your stunning
> baseball cap.
>
> …
>
> Then take it all
> and use it well
> this manhood, calculating
> through this hell.[19]

The rhyme scheme for the initial sestet is "a-b-b-c-d-c." Significantly, the rhyme pairs in lines 2, 3, 4, and 6 of the stanza – "ten" / "men" and "lap"/ "cap" – are called "masculine endings," each of these words are single syllables that are stressed at the end of the verse line. The monosyllabic "all," "well," and "hell," shows that Baldwin used full, partial, and consonantal rhyme[20] and syncopated rhythm in "Song," effectively resembling the sing-song qualities of sounds often found in children's books. Baldwin's use of rhyme illustrates how he merged his thematic exploration of the rites of time's passage with an adept formalism.

Although "poetry provided an emotional release" and connection for Baldwin, it also served as a site of alienation and anxiety, especially during adolescence.[21] "Shortly after [he] turned sixteen," Baldwin experienced his first significant relationship with a "Harlem racketeer" more than twice his age. He exclaimed, "I will be grateful to that man until the day I die. I showed him all my poetry, because I had no one else in Harlem to show it to."[22] It is not apparent if Baldwin shared these poems with his lover before giving them to the poet Countee Cullen, his high school French teacher, for review. But Baldwin later recalled that Cullen read his verse and told him it was "too much like Langston Hughes." Baldwin "never showed [Cullen] anything again."[23] This early critique by a leading poet of the Harlem Renaissance suggests that Baldwin may have been exorcising his own demons in his infamously harsh review of Hughes's *Selected Poems*. He wrote that Hughes's "book contains a great deal which a more disciplined poet would have thrown into the waste-basket."[24] He further salted the wound by singling out for censure Hughes's prize-winning poem: Baldwin carped, "I do not like all of 'The Weary Blues,' which copies, rather than exploits, the cadence of the blues."[25]

Baldwin's disapproval of Hughes's use of blues cadence is pertinent. In poetry, cadence involves the "rhythmic shape made by a flow of words."[26] In music, cadence can refer to a "stylized close" at the end of a composition, and to the division of the music into periods, or particular time frames.[27] Examining the time-based terms of Baldwin's disaffiliation with Hughes's poetry is key to understanding Baldwin's formal choices in *Jimmy's Blues*. Baldwin's verses are not structured based on the eight- or twelve-bar blues in music, or its analogous poetic form, in which a statement is made in the first verse line, the thought is repeated with slight variation in the second line, and the third line resolves, extends, or reverses the thought.[28] The kind of stanza patterns most often found in blues lyrics or poems are tercets, comprised of three lines, and quatrains, comprised of four; both are scarcely present in *Jimmy's Blues*. Baldwin divested his poems of the traditional blues forms of repetition with variance, of the "changing same," in order to distinguish his poetry from Hughes and to level any charge that he might be repeating him.[29] Baldwin's verses countered metrical conventions by reflecting the blues more "as a structure of feeling rather than a particular musical genre."[30] One notable exception is Baldwin's adaptation of a refrain from the blues song "I'm Gonna Tell God How You Treat Me"; yet he spreads the excerpted lyric across five verse lines and does not repeat the line.[31] The other caveat concerning his use of blues form is the last poem in *Jimmy's Blues,* "Amen," which includes one blues stanza form and will be examined at the essay's conclusion.

No Nostalgia: Staggerlee Wanders through Time Past

Even though *Jimmy's Blues* does not slavishly imitate blues forms or structure, Baldwin opens his poetry collection with a persona poem, written in the voice of Lee Shelton, who was mythologized in blues music, African-American folklore, and poetry as Stagolee, Stack O' Lee, or Staggerlee.[32] By opening *Jimmy's Blues* with Staggerlee speaking, Baldwin continued his connection to the vernacular expressive traditions, particularly the African-American tradition of testifying through song. Baldwin's use of Staggerlee's personae to frame *Jimmy's Blues* also initiated links to an earlier African-American poetic tradition, since Shelton's "outlaw" characteristics, or bad-man personality, became rewritten as a legend of oppositional resistance to white power in poems by black poets such as Margaret Walker in the 1930s and 1940s.[33]

"Staggerlee Wonders," the first and longest poem in the collection, is a whopping 419 lines, partitioned into thirty-eight stanzas and four sections. Its expansive, epic, long-poem form takes up sixteen pages – nearly one quarter of the entire book. As Nikki Finney writes in the introduction to *Jimmy's Blues*, the poem "sets the tone and temperature for everything else in this volume, as well as the sound and sense found throughout Badwin's *oeuvre*."[34] Many of the verses read more like prose passages than like the short rhyming lyric poems included in the rest of *Jimmy's Blues*. The sprawling lines of "Staggerlee Wonders" suit Baldwin's use of poetry as a form of "apprenticeship," as a pathway to aesthetic and technical development within his prose craft.[35] In fact, Baldwin read segments of the poem aloud to the novelist and folklorist Cecil Brown when he visited him at his home in St. Paul-De-Vence, France, and had even planned to write a Staggerlee novel.[36]

The final section of "Staggerlee Wonders" focuses on the contrast and conflict between time and history, rendered allegorically. The poem's speaker apostrophizes:

> Lord, History is weary
> Of her unspeakable liaison with Time,
> For Time and History
> Have never seen eye to eye:
> Time laughs at History
> And time and time and time again
> Time traps History in a lie."[37]

The repetition in this septet, or seven-line stanza, is aggravating. And that is a deliberate rhetorical strategy by Baldwin that marks this stanza as being tired of the tussle between Time and History over accurate representation. The word "history," appears four times; the word "time," by comparison, is nearly double that amount: time is that which "traps" History. The end consonantal and slant assonantal rhymes "wea-ry" and "histo-ry" underscore and envelop the stanza's content. The so-called "true," or "full" rhyme words "eye" and "lie" make evident the irony: what you see or read in mainstream history is not true at all. As Staggerlee indicates in a subsequent stanza, "Time warned us to ask for our money back, / and disagreed with History / as concerns colours white and black."[38]

"Staggerlee Wonders" also focuses on white western power brokers' continually supremacist and imperialist approaches to nation-states throughout the globe. Baldwin begins the poem in the time of always, meaning, for all time:

> I always wonder
> what they think the niggers are doing
> while they, the pink and alabaster pragmatists,
> are containing
> Russia
> and defining and re-defining and re-aligning
> China[39]

Baldwin's geography of these poetic lines places each country in visually and politically parallel containment and alignment: Russia and China hold the weight of the verse line alone. The lines in this stanza undulate, connecting the spatial shifts between long and short lines with temporal shifts. I stated that Staggerlee begins with the time of *always*; he later moves into the time of *again*. He repeats his critique of the containment of "Russia" and "China," expanding the terrain to an accounting of colonialists that are "patronizing / Africa / and calculating / the Caribbean plunder."[40] Staggerlee begins by wondering in perpetual time. Fittingly, Baldwin repeatedly uses participles, especially the "– ing" form, in both passages, for the resonance of both rhyme and time.

Staggerlee skewers those "pink and alabaster pragmatists" who are "containing" and:

> nobly restraining themselves, meanwhile,
> from blowing up that earth
> which they have already
> blasphemed into dung:
> the gentle, wide-eyed, cheerful
> ladies, and their men,
> nostalgic for the noble cause of Vietnam,
> nostalgic for noble causes,
> aching, nobly, to wade through the blood of savages –
> ah –![41]

The adverbs "while," "meanwhile" and "already" mark the duration of time present and time past. "Already" also signals impatience. The exclamation point punctuating the poem's first sentence points to Staggerlee's ironic, exasperated utterance, an interjection: "ah!" Staggerlee's wondering aloud – presented in the poem as a meditation – is rhetorically aggressive. As Miller observes, Staggerlee is not "simply musing about America...he is delivering a prophetic sermon": he "knows because he can see."[42] What does Staggerlee see? He sees the past.

Baldwin is particularly reproachful toward nostalgia as a sentimental approach to events in time past, proclaiming: "No Nostalgia."[43] If nostalgia reflects a relation to history and memory, "a purposive construction of a past filled with golden virtues, golden men, and sterling events," then Baldwin's truth-telling reveals the romanticized histories of American elites' warmongering to be patently false.[44] Instead, he counters such false reminiscences through Staggerlee's sardonic tone and sharp critique. Baldwin's critical approach to time past is tonal, temporal, and formal. For instance, he employs alliteration – the repetition of a consonant at the beginning of a word – and anaphora – the repetition of a phrase at the beginning of successive clauses – with the repeated "n," and with the line "nostalgic for the noble cause." The emphasis provided by verbal repetition here serves to negate, rather than enhance, the connotation of words such as "noble," especially because the repeated prefix sounds like a resounding "no-." Baldwin's critique of a politically motivated nostalgia can be understood as a cautionary tale against looking backward in time through the myopic lens of a white supremacist worldview.

By contrast, as a prophetic writer, Baldwin envisioned what lay ahead instead of focusing on what lies behind. We can read the end-times as the warning wand Baldwin waved often in "Song." His apocalyptic admonition resonates in temporal terms. The days, and the dream, may be deferred, but not for long, and not forever. The poem begins conversationally:

> I believe, my brother
> that some are haunted by a song,
> all day, and all the midnight long:
> *I'm gonna tell*
> *God*
> *how you've treated*
> *me*
> *One of these days.*[45]

The poem's speaker then indirectly addresses "the authors of the blasphemy / of our chains," thereby invoking slavery's legacy in verse and in the lyrics of a song recorded by blues guitarists and vocalists Brownie McGhee, Sonny Terry, and Big Bill Broonzy.[46] "Song" concludes its penultimate stanza with an aphoristic couplet: "Those who required, of us, a song/ know that their hour is not long."[47] The poem suggests, as Baldwin frequently forecasted, that the reckoning hour for racial justice is imminent.

"Song" also figures time allegorically and literally. Baldwin repeats, then negates, the hackneyed phrase, "Time is money"; the changes in the refrain are formally subtle and self-reflexive. For example, in the first instance, Baldwin writes:

> Time is not money.
> *Time*
> *is*
> *time.*

In the subsequent appearances of the phrase, the lines are compacted: "Time is not money. / Time is time," and again: "Time is not money: / time is time." Each of these subtle formal shifts yields a poetic sense of time that renders its duration paradoxically literal. For example, in the first instance, indenting each line with one word of the phrase yields a visual representation in which time is spaced out through the absence of the sign, of words. The abundance of white space before and after each of the three short words that make up the tautology "time is time" enact its subject. Furthermore, the movement from a period, an end-stop, to a colon, and the lowercase "t" in "time" that follows, also remind us of the colon's dramatic pause and the use of the colon to signal both break and continuum, representing another temporal register that punctuation marks. This repetition, with slight variation, of "time" in "Song" shows how time is made textual through the use of white space as a background canvas that becomes foregrounded. Time is also made textural through the chime of "rime riche" – French for rich rhyme, meaning "rhyme made up of words that are pronounced or spelled the same."[48]

Smashing Cages and Jazz Tempo: Slavery, Syllables, Syncopation

In a poem that references a different kind of song and different forms of repetition, called "Le sporting-club de Monte Carlo (For Lena Horne)," Baldwin changes the accentual stress pattern, the number of syllables, and the type of rhyme to alter the perception of the aesthetics and politics of jazz time. He thereby renders Horne's presence and performance within the poem as a sonic and lyric form of radical and radial black power. As Amiri Baraka eloquently asserts, "Jimmy Baldwin created 'contemporary American speech...so we could speak to each other at unimaginable intensities of feeling, so we could make sense to each other at yet higher and higher tempos."[49] Baraka suggests that Baldwin's use of language leads to clear communication, paradoxically, by heightening the perception of the speed of speech within time.

Baldwin begins "Le sporting-club" with the title of a 1930s Broadway show tune that Horne performed frequently with jazz accompaniment: "The lady is a tramp."[50] He then riffs on the word "tramp" to springboard into a series of monosyllable "perfect" rhymes presumably describing Horne's virtuosic stage presence:

> The lady is a tramp
> a camp
> a lamp.
> The lady is a sight
> a might
> a light.[51]
> the lady devastated
> an alley or two
> reverberated through the valley
> which leads to me, and you[52]

The similarities between the synonyms "lamp" and "light" in the first two stanzas capture the nuance in Horne's vocal jazz phrasing. The lines that immediately follow introduce polysyllabic rhyming words, such as "devastated" and "reverberated." Baldwin's cross-placement of such words at the beginning and the end of verse lines – and the addition of a consonant, building the rhyme "up" from the "alley" to the "valley" – creates a syncopated rhythm. This sense of jazzed – or perhaps, jagged – time is enhanced based on the spatial shift from vertically centered verse lines to the left-margin alignment after the word "light." Baldwin's use of sound, rhyme, and sight here highlights an aspect of "temporality," *tempo,* as musical and metrical pace, arranged on the page as visual space.

Baldwin describes Horne in rhyme and a syncopated rhythm in the poem's final stanza:

> the lady is a wonder
> daughter of the thunder
> smashing cages
> legislating rages
> with the voice of ages
> singing us through.[53]

Rhythmic play with syllables and stress involves the manipulation of meter and therefore tempo. In other words, metrical play potentially influences the reader's sense of time. This shifting perception of time occurs through Baldwin's use of iambic meter, which is a line of verse with an unstressed syllable followed by a stressed syllable, such as in "a camp" "a lamp," or, in the verse abundant with open vowel sounds, "the lady is a wonder." The metrical pattern shifts to trochaic meter, which is a line of verse with a stressed syllable followed by an unstressed syllable, such as in "daughter of the thunder" or "smashing cages" – this reverses the metrical pull already established in the poem's opening line, with three feet iambs, or iambic tetrameter: "the lady is a tramp." The "association of trochaic meter with abandon and play ... is probably why we most often encounter this meter in songs," explains the poet Carl Phillips.[54] Yet the penultimate couplet in "Le sporting-club," "smashing cages / legislating rages," underscores the gravity of Baldwin's metrical play.

"Cage" is a "mascon" word, in the scholar Stephen Henderson's phrasing. Such words within African-American poetry reflect a "massive concentration of black experiential energy" and heightened historical, literary, and cultural significance.[55] "Cage" brings to mind Paul Lawrence Dunbar's poem "Sympathy" with its haunting refrain, "I know why the caged bird sings"; it also evokes Maya Angelou's autobiography of the same title – which she recalled that Baldwin "set the stage for [her] to write."[56] "Cage" also recalls slavery and the racial disparity in rates of incarceration, both of which render racialized experiences of time. The cage-smashing tempo of "Le sporting-club de Monte Carlo" obliquely evokes the historical origins of jazz music in slavery. Baldwin asserts that "black American music…begins on the auction block."[57] Yet Lena Horne keeps "singing us through" to the present, triumphantly breaking the shackles that engendered the sorrow songs. In spirituals, jazz, and blues, the "[m]usic is our witness, and our ally," Baldwin insists; the "'beat' is the confession which recognizes, changes, and conquers time."[58] Baldwin lyrically translates Horne's sonic power, suggesting that she possesses the capacity to transcend temporal and formal boundaries. Horne's "voice of ages," her timelessness, "smashes the cage" of the compressed tercet and sestet, the three- and six-line stanza forms. Ultimately, Baldwin's verse and Horne's voice both beat and conquer time.

"The Brightest Hour / Before We Cease": Baldwin's Untimely Death

Although time may be figuratively conquered, death cannot literally be beat. Death as an enduring temporal limit is a persistent theme of *Jimmy's Blues*. Several poems in the volume deal with death temporarily – that is, "for the time being" – and temporally, for the nature of time's being. For instance, one of the shortest poems in the collection begins with the cliché, "The darkest hour / is just before the dawn." Yet it ends with a more nuanced sense of darkness, light, time, and being: "the brightest hour / we will ever see / occurs just before we cease / to be."[59]

In these very short lines, Baldwin uses alliteration, assonance, and rhyme to embody his point about the moment just before death. The consonants "s" and "w" are tripled, "see," "cea-*se*," "we," "will," "we," and the long vowel "e" sound occurs six times in only four lines. This temporal instance before death is both the "brightest" and the most sonically rich; the perception of sight and sound is intensified. In "The darkest hour," Baldwin's use of enjambment separates the infinitive, "to be," so that it seems to insist on infinite existence; it contradicts the meaning and the stop-time of the penultimate line, "we cease."

"Amen" also revisits the moment of meeting death, but then dismisses it, as the poem's speaker exclaims:

> No, I don't feel death coming.
> I feel death going:
> having thrown up his hands,
> for the moment.[60]

The first stanza is a blues quatrain. In four short lines, the speaker sings, "I don't feel death;" then he echoes the opposite, "I feel death." The rhyming use of the "–ing" suffix creates a chiming sound that is cut short by the irres-olution in the couplet: death has given up, at least for a short time.

"Death is easy," Baldwin's speaker stoically remarks in another epony-mous poem. The speaker compels the reader "to understand / that moment / which, anyway, occurs / over and over and over."[61] Death is a temporal affair; it is relentless in its repetition. But Baldwin's poems are not resigned to death's certainty. Instead, he urges, "one ought to rejoice in the fact of death." How? By "confronting with passion…the conundrum of life."[62] Baldwin's detached attitude comes from a perspective steeped in the blues ethos. As Albert Murray indicates, despite its "preoccupation with the most disturbing aspects of life," blues music aims "to generate a disposition that is both elegantly playful and heroic in its nonchalance."[63] The poems "The Darkest Hour," "Death Is Easy," and "Amen," each contain short lyrics that exude blues insouciance in the face of death as an inevitable fact of life.

Baldwin used poetry as a vehicle for voicing affiliation across temporal divides: he crossed generational and gender lines to dialogue with youn-ger and older poets and musicians. By indicating how Baldwin's poems fit within the tradition of black poetics, this essay secures a place for Baldwin in the literary history of black poetry. Baldwin theorized time *through* the verse line, poetically, "measure for measure" – to pun on Shakespeare, the writer Baldwin called "the greatest poet of the English language."[64] The musical concept of "measure," as a formal organization of sound patterns within time, best suits Baldwin's poetics, since this essay has revealed how Baldwin's poetry was deeply informed by variations in the tempos of black music and black speech.

Jimmy's Blues reflects the temporality of life. As Toni Morrison wrote, "[Baldwin's] life refuses summation."[65] In fact, one of the conundrums of his life involved the contrast between his vitality and endurance as a writer and his frequent ailments. He faced his mortality, courageously battling cancer at the same time that he wrote some of the poems addressed in this essay. As "Amen," the final poem in *Jimmy's Blues* suggests, death may depart for *a* while, yet it will return *after* a while. Death returned to meet Baldwin on December 1, 1987, when he was only sixty-three years old. As Baldwin him-self said, "Unless a writer is extremely old when he dies…his death must always seem untimely."[66]

NOTES

1 Jordan Elgrably and George Plimpton, "The Art of Fiction LXXVIII: James Baldwin," in *The Paris Review*. Reprinted in Fred L. Standley and Louis H. Pratt (eds.), *Conversations with James Baldwin* (Jackson: University Press of Mississippi, 1989) p. 250.

2 D. Quentin Miller, "James Baldwin, Poet," in D. Quentin Miller (ed.), *Re-Viewing James Baldwin: Things Not Seen* (Philadelphia: Temple University Press, 2000), p. 236. See also Nikky Finney, Introduction, "Playing By Ear, Praying for Rain: The Poetry of James Baldwin," in *Jimmy's Blues and Other Poems* (Boston: Beacon Press, 2014), pp. xi, xvi.

3 Toni Morrison, "James Baldwin: His Voice Remembered; Life in His Language," *New York Times Book Review Desk* (December 20, 1987), Section 7, 27.

4 See Miller, "James Baldwin, Poet," in Miller, pp. 234–5; and Finney, "Introduction: Playing By Ear," in *Jimmy's Blues*, p. xiii.

5 See Lovalerie King and Lynn Orilla Scott (eds.), *James Baldwin and Toni Morrison: Comparative Critical and Theoretical Essays* (New York: Palgrave Macmillan, 2006); see also Marlon Ross, "White Fantasies of Desire: Baldwin and the Racial Identities of Sexuality," in Dwight McBride (ed.), *James Baldwin Now!* (New York: New York University Press, 1999), pp. 13–55.

6 See Daylanne English, *Each Hour Redeem: Time and Justice in African American Literature* (Minneapolis: University of Minnesota Press, 2013), and José Muñoz, *Cruising Utopia: The Then and There of Queer Futurity* (New York: New York University Press, 2009) for connections between contemporary time studies and race, gender, and sexuality pertinent to Baldwin's time consciousness.

7 James Baldwin, *Jimmy's Blues and Other Poems* (originally published 1985), (Boston: Beacon Press, 2014).

8 Sonia Sanchez, "About Jimmy's Blues and Other Poems," *Jimmy's Blues and Other Poems*, book jacket.

9 James Baldwin, "Song" (1983), in *Jimmy's Blues* (New York: St. Martin's Press, 1985), pp. 26, 29. All remaining quotations from Baldwin's poems will be dated and cited from this edition.

10 Kevin Young, "How Not to Be A Slave," in *The Grey Album: On the Blackness of Blackness*, (St. Paul: Greywolf Press, 2012), p. 51.

11 Elgrably, "The Art of Fiction LXXVIII: James Baldwin," in Standley and Pratt, p. 248.

12 Wolfgang Binder, "James Baldwin: An Interview" (1980), in Standley and Pratt, p. 207.

13 Elgrably, "The Art of Fiction LXXVIII: James Baldwin," in Standley and Pratt, pp. 248–9.

14 See Quincy Troupe, "Last Testament: An Interview with James Baldwin," in *Village Voice* (January 12, 1988), 36. Reprinted in Standley and Pratt, pp. 281–6. See also Binder, "James Baldwin: An Interview," in Standley and Pratt, p. 207.

15 James Baldwin and Nikki Giovanni, *A Dialogue* (Philadelphia: J. P. Lippincott, 1972), p. 34. The dialogue is an edited version of the transcript of the two-episode television interview on Soul!, WNET Channel 13, New York, Dist. National Education Television, Dec. 15 and 22, 1971.

16 See Gayle Wald: *"It's Been Beautiful"*: Soul! *and Black Power TV*, unpublished manuscript, Durham (Duke University Press, forthcoming), cited by permission of the author.

17 Baldwin, *A Dialogue*, p. 15.

18 Amiri Baraka, "We Carry Him as Us," *The New York Times* (December 20, 1987), 27. Reprinted as "Jimmy!" in William J. Harris (ed.), *The Leroi*

Jones / Amiri Baraka Reader (originally published 1991), (New York: Basic Books, 2009), p. 451.

19 Baldwin, "Song," in *Jimmy's Blues*, p. 27. See Yasmin DeGout's discussion of Baldwin's rewriting of coming-of-age narratives to "revise notions of maturity and masculinity" in "Masculinity and (Im)maturity: 'The Man Child and Other Stories in Baldwin's Gender Studies Enterpise," in Miller, *Re-Viewing James Baldwin*, pp. 148–9.

20 "Types of Rhyme," in John Drury (ed.), *The Poetry Dictionary* (Cincinatti: Writer's Digest Books, 2006), pp. 253–4.

21 David Leeming, *James Baldwin: A Biography* (New York: Knopf, 1994), p. 360.

22 James Baldwin, "Freaks and the American Ideal of Manhood," in Toni Morrison (ed.), *James Baldwin: Collected Essays* (New York: Library of America, 1998), p. 818.

23 Baldwin, quoted in "James Baldwin, Poet," in Miller, *Re-Viewing Baldwin*, p. 236. In Quincy Troupe, *James Baldwin: A Legacy* (New York: Simon and Schuster, 1989), p. 58.

24 Baldwin, "Sermons and Blues," Review of *Selected Poems* by Langston Hughes, *New York Times* (March 29, 1959).

25 Ibid.

26 "Cadence," in Drury, *The Poetry Dictionary*, p. 48.

27 "Cadence." *Music Dictionary*. Web. Jun. 5, 2014. http://dictionary.onmusic.org/terms/558-cadence

28 This form is often referred to as AAB; the verses in music, and the end rhyme in blues poems typically follow this pattern. See Stephen C. Tracy, *Langston Hughes and the Blues* (Urbana-Champaign: University of Illinois Press, 1988), p. 76.

29 See Amiri Baraka, "The Changing Same: R&B Music," in Harris (ed.), *The Leroi Jones / Amiri Baraka Reader*, pp. 186–209.

30 See Alexander G. Weheliye, "Post-Integration Blues: Black Geeks and Afro-Diasporic Humanism," in Lovalerie King and Shirley Moody-Turner (eds.), *Contemporary African American Literature: The Living Canon* (Bloomington: Indiana University Press, 2013), p. 213.

31 Baldwin, "Song," in *Jimmy's Blues*, p. 24.

32 See Cecil Brown, *Stagolee Shot Billy* (Cambridge: Harvard University Press, 2004) for an extensive discussion of this figure.

33 See Margaret Walker, "Bad Man Stagolee," in *This Is My Century: New and Selected Poems* (Athens: University of Georgia Press, 1989), p. 28.

34 Finney, "Introduction: Playing by Ear," in *Jimmy's Blues*, p. xiv.

35 Elgrably, "The Art of Fiction LXXVIII: James Baldwin," in Standley and Pratt, p. 248.

36 Leeming, *Baldwin: A Biography*, p. 360. Ironically, Cecil Brown eventually wrote such a novel. See *I, Stagolee* (Berkeley, CA: North Atlantic Books, 2006).

37 Baldwin, "Staggerlee Wonders," in *Jimmy's Blues*, p. 20.

38 Baldwin, Ibid., p. 16.

39 Baldwin, Ibid., p. 7.

40 Baldwin, Ibid., p. 16.

41 Baldwin, Ibid., p. 7.

42 Miller, "James Baldwin, Poet," in Miller, pp. 240, 243.

43 Elgrably, "The Art of Fiction LXXVIII: James Baldwin," in Standley and Pratt, p. 250.

44 Houston Baker, "Critical Memory and the Black Public Sphere," in *The Black Public Sphere: A Public Culture Book* (Chicago: The University of Chicago Press, 1995), p. 7.

45 Baldwin, "Song," in *Jimmy's Blues*, p. 24.

46 "I'm Gonna Tell God How You Treat Me," in *Blues with Big Bill Broonzy, Sonny Terry, Brownie McGhee*. Smithsonian / Folkways Records, 1959. CD.

47 Baldwin, "Song," in *Jimmy's Blues*, pp. 26–9.

48 "Rime Riche," in Drury, *The Poetry Dictionary*, p. 258.

49 Baraka, "Jimmy!," in Harris, *The Leroi Jones / Amiri Baraka Reader*, p. 452.

50 Richard Rodgers and Lorenz Hart (composers). "The Lady is a Tramp." 1937. See also Lena Horne. "The Lady is a Tramp." *Words and Music*. Metro-Goldyn-Mayer, 1948. Web. May 14, 2014. https://www.youtube.com/watch?v=BLwREAX4d2A.

51 Baldwin, "Le sporting-club De Monte Carlo," in *Jimmy's Blues*, p. 44.

52 Ibid., p. 44.

53 Ibid., p. 44.

54 Carl Phillips, "Running With Abandon: Some Notes on Trochaic Meter," in Annie Finch and Katherine Varnes (eds.), *Exaltation of Forms: Contemporary Poets Celebrate the Diversity of Their Art* (Ann Arbor: University of Michigan Press, 2005), p. 60.

55 See Stephen Henderson, "Introduction: The Forms of Things Unknown" in *Understanding the New Black Poetry* (New York: William and Morrow, 1973), pp. 44, 46, 49. See also "Mascon Words," in *The Columbia Dictionary of Modern Literary and Cultural Criticism* (New York: Columbia University Press, 1995), p. 179.

56 See Paul Laurence Dunbar, "Sympathy." *Poetry Foundation*, 2004. Web June 5, 2014. http://www.poetryfoundation.org/poem/175756; Maya Angelou, "James Baldwin: His Voice Remembered; A Brother's Love," *New York Times Book Review Desk* (December 20, 1987), Section 7, p. 29; See also: Maya Angelou, *I Know Why the Caged Bird Sings* (originally published 1969), (New York: Ballantine Books, 2009).

57 Baldwin "Of the Sorrow Songs: The Cross of Redemption" (originally published 1979), in Randall Kenan (ed.), *The Cross of Redemption: Uncollected Writings* (New York: Pantheon Books, 2010), p. 124.

58 Baldwin, Ibid., p. 124.

59 Baldwin, "The Darkest Hour," in *Jimmy's Blues*, p. 36.

60 Baldwin, "Amen," in *Jimmy's Blues*, p. 75.

61 Baldwin, "Death is Easy," in *Jimmy's Blues*, p. 59.

62 Baldwin, *The Fire Next Time* (originally published 1963), (New York: Modern Library Edition, 1995), pp. 90–1.

63 Albert Murray, *Stomping the Blues* (Cambridge, MA: DaCapo Press, 1976), p. 45.

64 Baldwin, "Why I Stopped Hating Shakespeare," in Kenan, *The Cross of Redemption*, p. 56.

65 Morrison, "Life in His Language," p. 27.

66 Baldwin, "Alas, Poor Richard," in Morrison, *James Baldwin: Collected Essays*, p. 247.

3

SOYICA DIGGS COLBERT

Go Tell It on the Mountain: Baldwin's Sermonic

Being in the pulpit was like being in the theatre; I was behind the scenes and knew how the illusion was worked.
  – James Baldwin, *The Fire Next Time*[1]

I'd been a boy preacher for three years. Those three years really in a sense, those three years in the pulpit, I didn't realize it then, that is what turned me into a writer really dealing with all that anguish and that despair and that beauty for those three years.
  – James Baldwin, *The Price of the Ticket*[2]

Baldwin has in common with the black preacher a passion for the dramatic, a taste for the exuberant, a genius for the melody of words and details of scene.
  – Hortense Spillers, *Fabrics of History*[3]

Context is everything. Context transforms an act from injurious in one setting to enabling in another. Context also explains James Baldwin's simultaneous romance with the practices of the Pentecostal church – the sermon, music, and rituals – and disenchantment with it as an institution. This chapter considers how the sermon – as a practice central to many faith traditions – informs three foundational Baldwin texts: *Go Tell It on the Mountain*, *Blues for Mister Charlie*, and *The Fire Next Time*. In Baldwin's use, the sermon functions to disrupt the power of institutions (such as the church and the government via the court and the police) and to bear witness to the conditions of the politically disenfranchised. In content and form, Baldwin revises and differentiates the traditional deployment of the structure of the sermon.[4] Customarily, the Christian sermon aims toward the expansion of the church and the cultivation of the soul. Instead, Baldwin uses the structure of the sermon to create collectivity, and by extension political agency, through bearing witness to shared experiences of disenfranchisement. And he uses the redemptive narrative of the sermon, its content, toward the political aims of the Civil Rights Movement. Rather than deploying the sermon toward religious ends, Baldwin uses the sermon to further secular goals.

While Baldwin often questioned the church as an institution, he was strongly invested in the rhetoric of sacrificial love at the heart of Christianity and in "the Biblical 'rhythm' – its overwhelming restorative sense."[5] This chapter examines how Baldwin deploys the qualities of the sermonic as a disruptive force of witnessing. In Baldwin's work, religious performance traditions of the sermon (praise, refrain, repetition) direct the disruptive force toward the political aims of the Civil Rights Movement to expand the experience of democracy. Although my examination dovetails with considerations of Baldwin's critiques of the church as an institution, I focus on the sermon and its manifestation from the perspective of witness, because it is as a witness that Baldwin's work cultivates human connections that are central to his understanding of the beloved community and to the restorative nature of his work.[6] Baldwin's first play, *The Amen Corner* (1955), depicts how disruption relates to a method of healing and community formation:

> I knew that out of the ritual of the church, historically speaking, comes the act of the theatre, the communion which is the theatre. And I knew that what I wanted to do in the theatre was to recreate moments I remembered as a boy preacher, to involve people, even against their will, to shake them up, and, hopefully, to change them.[7]

These functions of the sermon as a catalyst for the cultivation of collectivity and change emerge not only in the theater community of *The Amen Corner*, but also out of the confluence of events depicted in his essay "Notes of a Native Son," through the disorderly force of the riots, the loss of his father, and the birth of his youngest sister. By means of the sermon, the communal and familial structures are altered, opening up space for Baldwin to bear witness to the racism that plagues America in the 1950s.

For Baldwin, the Christian church serves as a source of inspiration for his writing, both through the sermon and through offering a space of escape. As he explains in *The Fire Next Time*,

> Every Negro boy – in my situation during those years, at least – who reaches this point realizes, at once, profoundly, because he wants to live, that he stands in great peril and must find, with speed, a "thing," a gimmick, to lift him out, to start him on his way.... It was this last realization that terrified me and...helped to hurl me into the church.[8]

Baldwin notes that the church functioned not only as a place to seek refuge from the dangers that beset black men and boys living in Harlem during World War II; it also contributed significantly, and perhaps singularly, to his development as a writer. In the documentary *The Price of the Ticket*, he recalls, "I'd been a boy preacher for three years. Those three years really in a sense, those three years in the pulpit, I didn't realize it then, that is what turned me into a writer really dealing with all that anguish and that despair and that beauty for those three years."[9] Baldwin makes a similar assertion in *Notes of a Native Son*, writing, "I hazard that the King James Bible, the rhetoric of the storefront church, something ironic and violent and perpetually understood in Negro speech – and something of Dickens' love for bravura – have something to do with me today."[10] Although Baldwin finds limitations in the church as an institution, the distinctive characteristics of the sermon – the rhetoric, rhythms, drama, and hope in a season of sorrow (to borrow a phrase from Baldwin's dear friend Lorraine Hansberry) – shape his writing. His time as a preacher also teach him how to disentangle practice from structure, the liberating potential of the sermon from the institution of the church.

The language, narrative content, and structure of the sermons that Baldwin experienced and performed, then, became a blueprint for his writing. Eddie Glaude has argued persuasively that exodus typology particularizes the nature of the black experience of striving to get by in the United States.[11] In the biblical exodus narrative based on Moses' experiences as the leader of the Israelites, the trajectory from slavery to freedom depends on progression toward a promised land, which is seen as a gift that awaits the enslaved and is based on both the benevolence of an outside force and the leadership of a chosen figure designated to guide others to the land of milk and honey.[12] The sense of a sojourn toward triumph enables the coexistence of "agony and joy"[13]: "All that anguish and that despair and that beauty" coexist in harmony due to an understanding of life predicated on sacrifice and ultimate reward. The exodus narrative is foundational to the content of the black sermonic tradition, offering a blueprint for uplift. Putting a twist on the exodus plot, Baldwin's writing presents the reward as appearing in political possibilities of the present and not heavenly rewards of the future.

Exodus typology, along with the cornerstone narrative of the fall, impacts Baldwin's understanding of the sermonic. The thrust of Baldwin's message, as Hortense Spillers details, "harks back to Old Testament drama with its extraordinary deeds and awakenings. This sensitivity to the 'awful' and extraordinary in human affairs is also a feature of the black sermon tradition and makes up the chief emotional issue of *Go Tell it on the Mountain*."[14] While Baldwin references the long tradition of exodus typology in black culture, his work also draws attention to the limitations of the narrative structure of deliverance in the afterlife, focusing instead on how individuals may intercede on their own behalf. *The Fire Next Time* draws from the biblical imagery of apocalypse to discuss race relations in the United States but contends that individual citizens, not God, must intercede on the nation's behalf to achieve a more democratic state. He warns, "Everything now, we must assume, is in our hands; we have no right to assume otherwise.... we – and now I mean the relatively conscious whites and the relatively conscious blacks," must "end the racial nightmare, and achieve our country, and change the history of the world."[15] Baldwin's work consistently draws from the aims of the sermon, yet reconfigures the outcomes, focusing on political, cultural, social, and communal change.

It was not only the content of the sermon that attracted Baldwin; he was also impacted by the rhetorical flair of its delivery. According to Spillers, "The Biblical 'rhythm' – its overwhelming restorative sense – presented an appealing contrast to the realities of oppression."[16] Repetition, refrain, rhyme, call and response, and the expression of familiar phrases are some of the sermonic devices that produce the rhythm of the sermon in Baldwin's work. The rhythm, as in a good dance song, invites participation, either routine or improvised. As a form, the sermon has a communal function that preachers traditionally deploy toward building the church but that Baldwin uses to bolster the Civil Rights Movement, as evidenced in his closing call for action to *The Fire Next Time*. In order to grow either the church or the movement, the sermon must have a transformative quality that comes from engaging and disorienting the audience.

Demonstrating the sermon's ability to enact disruption and change in *Go Tell It on the Mountain*, the much-maligned father figure Gabriel Grimes delivers a sermon that reorients the dynamic of a revival meeting featuring twenty-four preachers. As Gabriel is the most junior of the speakers, his sermon functions as his introduction to a larger community and audience. Filled with anxiety about "his performance – the most important of his career so far, and on which so much depended –" Gabriel fasts and prays.[17] Gabriel is aware of the choreography of the service, remembering his first sermon as a "performance." The theatrical nature of the service intensifies when he enters the venue – "the great, lighted lodge hall that had but lately held a dance band, and that the saints had rented for the duration of the revival." As he recalls it, the members of the dais "smiled and nodded as he mounted the pulpit steps; and one of them said, nodding toward the congregation, which was as spirited as any evangelist could wish: 'Just getting them folks warmed up for you, boy. Want to see you make them *holler* tonight.' "[18] Stunned by their "ease in the holy place, and a levity, that made *his* soul uneasy," Gabriel refuses the implicit stage directions of his performance.[19]

All of the cues point toward the well-known script, which governs the service in general and the sermon in particular. The novel reveals that the revival takes place in a lodge hall that most recently showcased a dance band. Just as a band has a set playlist, so too do the evangelists have a set order of events that, when accomplished, result in making the congregation *holler*. The sonic expression of exultation affirms the excellence of execution. The novel also suggests that practice overshadows content, producing "ease in the holy place" and "levity." The members of the dais, so familiar with how events will unfold, express no urgency or unease with what has become routine. Gabriel, conversely, knowing that the function of the sermon is to produce disquiet and to challenge the monotony of the quotidian, finds the demeanor of his fellow clergy disturbing.

Intent upon shifting the dynamic of the service, instead of beginning with a rousing song or a personal and inspiring testimony, Gabriel opens with a scripture reading that leads to a cry rather than a holler. Taking Isaiah 6:5 as the scriptural basis for his sermon, Gabriel describes the prophet as a chosen figure who, even while enacting his ordained position, cries out for mercy when confronted with the magnitude of God. Gabriel recounts:

These words have been uttered by the prophet Isaiah, who had been called the Eagle-eyed because he had looked down the dark centuries and foreseen the birth of Christ.... This was a man whom God had raised in righteousness, whom God had chosen to do many mighty works, yet this man, beholding the vision of God's glory, had cried out: 'Woe is me!'[20]

Questioning the idea of the chosen, Gabriel describes how "the vision of God's glory" rendered one of the prophets awestruck. The idea of being chosen suggests a more intimate relationship with God than that of the average believer. Gabriel's sermon renders all believers, however, prostrate, vulnerable, and overwhelmed by God.[21] As such he undermines the implicit hierarchies of the church as expressed in the ordering of the dais and the service. Although participating in the traditional function of the sermon as part of a church service, *Go Tell It on the Mountain* demonstrates how Baldwin's writing engages the sermonic, troubling the power dynamics of the proceeding and reconfiguring the space to liberate all participants, not just the chosen few.

Baldwin's implicit critique of the limitations of the church as an institution foreshadows his critique in *The Fire Next Time*, his civil rights manifesto – that the church functions through fear instead of liberation. His depiction of church leadership in *Go Tell It on the Mountain* also anticipates his questioning of church leader as civil rights leader in *Blues for Mister Charlie*. Although the scene from *Go Tell It on the Mountain* is not set during the Civil Rights Movement period, it does demonstrate some of the institutional limitations of the church, which, as Baldwin suggests in *Blues for Mister Charlie*, limit the effectiveness of civil rights activism. Nevertheless, Baldwin depicts religious performance as providing a basis for liberating political practices because they provide a non-discriminating path to transformation.

The cry "Woe is me!" communicates that humility is necessary for one to partake in the loving relationship modeled by God's intimate connection to the church. The notions of vulnerability and awe function as essential doctrine in Baldwin's critical imagination, driving both his writing and his political activity. The cry expresses a state of becoming, communicating the sense that work has been done and yet remains incomplete. The cry "Woe is me" also punctuates Gabriel's sermon, serving as a refrain. The musical device of this refrain helps to establish the rhythm of Gabriel's address, making use of repetition, a fundamental aspect of the black sermonic tradition.[22] The sermon functions as a mode of performance. Performance facilitates affective connections, as in the cry "Woe is me," and participates in self-fashioning (for example, Gabriel becomes a preacher in this scene, but not the kind of preacher the service scripts him to be). In so doing, the performance may either affirm or challenge ongoing power dynamics between the preacher and the congregation.

In Baldwin's writing, the transformative power of the sermon evokes affective dynamics that secure political coalitions. He acknowledges the power of sensuality produced in black culture more generally:

> The word 'sensual' is not intended to bring to mind quivering dusky maidens or priapic black studs. I am referring to something much simpler and much less fanciful. To be sensual, I think, is to respect and rejoice in the force of life, of life itself, and to be *present* in all that one does, from the effort of loving to the breaking of bread.[23]

Baldwin also depicts the sensual as sacred in *Go Tell It on the Mountain* when he describes women in dance halls as "twisting their bodies into lewd hallelujahs"; along similar lines, the narrator of *Another Country* says, "The act of love is a confession;" finally, in *The Fire Next Time*, he writes that black and white Americans must come together "like lovers" to address racial inequality.[24] Placing religious expressions and rituals in secular contexts, Baldwin activates the power of sensuality in his writing to inspire "a kind of intelligence of hope."[25] He presents hope as a future-oriented desire actualized in present action.

Blues for Mister Charlie explores the possibility of structuring affective communities on love and humility in the face of personal and familial sacrifice. Unlike *Go Tell It on the Mountain*, the play does not feature a traditional sermon in the context of a religious gathering. The play does depict, however, how the juridical practice of testifying gives way to the sermonic function of bearing witness to the conditions of the politically disenfranchised; the black sermonic tradition, then, counteracts the erasure of black suffering through the practice of witnessing. As Baldwin explains in "Notes for *Blues*," two deaths inspired the play: those of Medgar Evers and Emmett Till. Evers and Till became civil rights icons in part because of the tragic nature of their deaths. The first was a veteran, father, husband, and field secretary for the NAACP who was brutally murdered in his driveway for advocating for desegregation. The second was a fourteen-year-old boy lynched for allegedly whistling at a white woman. Both cases present sympathetic victims, due to social station in the former case and age in the latter. Additionally, both figures evince a historical narrative of unwarranted violence against upstanding and innocent black people. *Blues for Mister Charlie*, conversely, presents a flawed character who evokes fears of violence (he carries a gun) and miscegenation (he brags about sleeping with white women in the North). Richard seems an unlikely character to recollect Evers and Till unless one considers the function of witnessing to expose the underlying causes of violence, terror, and fear. The disruptive quality of witnessing works toward social healing and communion. Therefore, witnessing must reveal what ails the community and motivates acts of gratuitous violence. The play suggests that until America deals with the threat Richard poses, the racial nightmare will continue.

The central character of *Blues for Mister Charlie* inspires the practice of witness central to the sermon and to Baldwin's writing, as he shifts the course of history. In Baldwin's civil rights drama, the black characters confront the impossible choice to reaffirm the order of things – to remain disenfranchised and dehumanized, silent and subjugated – or to defy the violent force of history, risking life and limb to disturb the peace. The death of the protagonist, Richard Henry, which opens the play, serves as a warning of what will happen to disturbers of the peace. Mourning the death of his wife and son, Meridian, Richard's father and the minister of the black community opens the play as a representative of moderation. By the end of the play, Meridian's act of witness changes his perspective on the direct action activists must exercise to achieve freedom.

To tell Richard's story, the play calls forth the multiple meanings of witness – to proclaim, to testify, and to reveal forgotten histories – and demands that Meridian reconsider his role within the community. As *Blues for Mister Charlie* opens with Richard's death, all the scenes that include Richard are acts of memory, functioning as flashbacks. This is clear in the final act, which depicts the trial of Lyle Britten, the white storeowner who killed Richard. Its background consists in Richard's return to his small Southern hometown – after the promising musician and recovering drug addict had migrated to New York – and finding himself looking down the barrel of Lyle's gun. All the characters in the play know that Lyle murdered Richard for "sassing" his wife, Jo Britten; the trial scene, then, functions not as a site of potential justice, but instead as one of instruction for the characters and the audience, focusing on the histories that must be witnessed for America more fully to realize its democratic promise. Baldwin stages the drama, like many of the battles of the Civil Rights Movement, in a courtroom. And as the playwright learns (and details in *The Fire Next Time*) in comparing the practices of the Christian church of his youth to that of the Nation of Islam, the role of the civil rights leader must be to call for the fulfillment of democracy by offering a truthful depiction of living conditions. Confronted with the death of his son and the mocking acquittal of a murderer, Meridian becomes a witness in the play.

Once again displacing the sermon from the church pulpit (it appears in a dance hall in *Go Tell It on the Mountain*), Baldwin combines church and courthouse in the final scene of the play to suggest how the sermonic tradition of witnessing can inform, and perhaps recoup, a central site of the democratic process. The stage directions read, "The witness stand is downstage, in the same place, and at the same angle as the pulpit in Acts I and II."[26] The replacement of the pulpit with the witness stand suggests the possible convergence of the visionary practice of the sermon from the pulpit and the truth-telling that emerges from the witness stand. The scene features testimony from all the play's central figures save Richard, whose testimony takes place after the acquittal: Juanita (Richard's childhood friend and former lover), Meridian, Parnell (the white liberal who presses for Lyle's arrest and acquittal), and Lyle, as well as some secondary characters. In each testimony, the characters try to come to terms with the forces that required Richard's death. In the first act, Meridian states and then exclaims "No witnesses"; this is an anticipatory excuse for Lyle's acquittal and represents yet another denial of justice, and consequently, of the black characters' rights as citizens to protection against violence.

Drawing from the rhetorical practice of repetition central to the sermon, the second iteration of "No witnesses" shifts the scene to a flashback of Richard. The flashback suggests that the characters must come to terms with the protagonist as a disruptive force to the social dynamic of their town and to the linear structure of the play. Richard's memory alters Meridian's testimony into an act of witness, and the scenes that feature Richard shift the present time of the play into the past. Richard's acts of interference in the play – affecting both content and structure – serve a similar function as the cry "Woe is me" in *Go Tell It on the Mountain*, which alters the form and content of Gabriel's sermon.

While Meridian is a preacher, the other characters, I suggest, engage with the sermon as a form of witness not only to acknowledge Richard as a haunting presence in the community, but also to reveal the function of grace. In this case, grace means the ability to accept another person regardless of his or her limitations and faults, as Baldwin encourages his nephew to do in "My Dungeon Shook." Accepting the inherent lack of reciprocity, Baldwin explains, "There is no reason for you to try to become like white people and there is no basis whatever for their impertinent assumption that *they* must accept *you*. The really terrible thing, old buddy, is that *you* must accept *them*. And I mean that very seriously. You must accept them and accept them with love."[27] While Evers and Till function as martyrs, *Blues for Mister Charlie* questions the logics that make vigilante justice (even the killing of a gun-carrying, haughty, black junkie) acceptable.

Richard's death sparks a series of protests that the play references in the opening scene and the final act, and the testimonies of Richard's friends Lorenzo and Juanita draws from the function of the sermon in Baldwin's writing to create political agency. Juanita and Lorenzo display the physical costs of disturbing the peace: prior to his testimony, Lorenzo remembers being beaten in jail and the sound of his fellow protestor Pete screaming in pain. Although the prosecution attempts to get Lorenzo to confirm the depiction of Richard as a womanizing drug addict, Lorenzo refuses to validate the state's accusations. Conversely, the witness asserts, "They been asking me about photographs they say he was carrying and they been asking about a gun I never saw. No. It wasn't like that. He was a beautiful cat, and they killed him. That's all. That's *all*."[28] While Lorenzo believes that Lyle shot Richard, his choice of the pronoun "they" suggests a larger cultural condition that enabled the death of his friend. The plural pronoun indicts a group of individuals for Richard's death, suggesting that a collectivity be held accountable for the murder. Additionally, while the prosecution attempts to besmirch Richard's reputation, Lorenzo describes the victim in human terms, based not on what he did but who he was. This shift in focus recalibrates the emphasis on the right to life as universal. Lorenzo's testimony seeks to establish what qualifies as a life worth protecting.

Lorenzo's testimony, echoing *The Fire Next Time*, points to the cultural cancer that ails the United States: although Lyle pulled the trigger, the structural inequality that enables the murder of a black man to go unpunished speaks to a larger set of social inequalities. Moreover, challenging the notion that such inequalities may be addressed through the courts, Lorenzo shifts focus from the inadequacies of due process to how such unevenness determines who qualifies as human and who does not. Depicting Richard's murder as a human rights violation demonstrates the inadequacy of the court as a site of adjudication or repair.

The play further comments on juridical notions of who qualifies as human by depicting what qualifies or disqualifies a witness as reliable: the state attempts to sully not only Richard's reputation, but also Juanita's in order to disqualify her as a witness. The defense intimates that Juanita has had several sexual partners, which she denies. Nevertheless, based on the implicit culture of sexism, the suggestion that she is not a virgin serves to undermine her reliability as a witness. Notably, the same state-authorized rubrics that disqualify Juanita as a witness render her fit to bear witness and disturb the peace because she is able to describe her experience of the limited function of democracy.

Compounding the issue of gender dynamics, Juanita's testimony ends with a flashback that reveals Richard's radical choice to live in the shadow of death. Although Juanita tries to convince Richard to leave town with her after his confrontation with Lyle, he contends that in order to be a man he must remain in the South. His choice to stay and face probable death explains why Richard willingly goes with Lyle in the moments leading to his murder. Juanita refuses in her testimony to challenge the cultural cache of a respectable lady – a startling choice given her acknowledgment in the flashback of Richard's willingness to die to protect his notion of heteronormative masculinity. Together, the choices demonstrate a shared cultural logic of misogyny that debilitates the community as a whole.

The function of Meridian's testimony differs from Lorenzo's and Juanita's because of his position as a minister and as Richard's father. Meridian's role as a leader in the church serves a particular cultural purpose: as Spillers describes "the black preacher has been called upon historically to serve his community in a versatile way – leader/prophet, interpreter/hierophant, orator/actor, symbolist/healer."[29] The multiple roles of the black preacher create ample room for variation, as each actor may emphasize one feature over another. While Meridian serves as a spiritual and political leader in his community, he also advocates participation in nonviolent protest, even in the midst of vigilante justice.

After Richard's murder, Meridian measures the wisdom of self-protection against the imperative to diminish violence. Given Meridian's moral quagmire, it is curious that he testifies, "But you cannot consider my son's death to have been tragic. For you, it would have been tragic if he had lived."[30] The tragedy is understood as being either Richard's constant urge to fall within the dictates of society or his perpetual disruption of cultural norms. Yet even as Meridian attempts to give voice to the cultural realities that enabled Richard's murder, he concludes, "The truth cannot be heard in this dreadful place."[31] The intractable presumption of Lyle's innocence magnifies the sense that the courtroom is a charade of justice and leads Meridian, in the final scene, to place Richard's gun in the pulpit, which, significantly, stands where the witness stand once stood. Meridian's testimony does not change the dynamics of the courtroom but it does transform his role as the spiritual leader of his community, no longer exclusively an advocate of nonviolent means of protest. Its ability to break through seemingly impenetrable structures (juridical, social, religious) demonstrates both the power and the function of the sermon. To make audible through musical and poetic forms of rhythm, repetition, and figurative language the ghostly narratives of the politically and socially disenfranchised, Baldwin uses the sermonic form to witness.

Throughout Baldwin's work, the sermon functions within and outside of the church to build human connections as a form of witness. In a 1979 interview with Kalamu ya Salaam entitled "Looking Toward the Eighties," Baldwin said, "The role of the writer is to write, but this is a cryptic statement.... His function is very particular and so is his responsibility. After all, to write, if taken seriously, is to be subversive. To disturb the peace."[32] As Joshua Miller details in his consideration of "the term *witness* in the dynamic context of the cold war culture," "Baldwin transforms the already deeply ingrained cold war notion of the witness, testifying for or against the West in it absolute struggle with the Soviet Union, into that of a truth seeker observing his own society."[33] Just as Miller situates his analysis within the context of the Cold War, my argument assumes the importance of the role of witness to the Civil Rights Movement as a social justice movement seeking to disrupt the force of history and shift the distribution of political power. As Clarence E. Hardy III argues, "Baldwin renders judgment on American society not through the invocation of a brooding Christian god, but through the blind inexorability of history that will undo white racial identities that are just as fluid as black identities."[34] The witness serves to bolster the force of history, drawing attention to narratives that may otherwise be forgotten.

In Baldwin's writing, the shifting location of the sermon, from pulpit to courtroom, demonstrates the force of that mode of address toward the democratization of secular institutions and power structures. The sermon, in content and form, reconfigures the dynamics of its site of articulation (for example, the courtroom in *Blues for Mister Charlie*) to enact change. As Baldwin illustrates in *The Fire Next Time*, describing an impromptu sermon he overhears while walking in Harlem, "I paid very little attention to what I heard, because the burden of the message did not strike me as being very original; I had been hearing variations of it all my life."[35] What does give

Baldwin pause is the Nation of Islam's ability to shift the power dynamics that structure the message; the key is not what is being articulated on the corner of 125th Street, but how the moment of articulation draws attention to an ongoing set of negotiations between the Nation of Islam and the police. Instead of dragging the speaker from his platform and dispersing the crowd, the police did nothing "because they were under orders and because they were afraid."[36] The Nation of Islam's ability to coopt power from the police and evoke "silent intensity" from the crowd demands Baldwin's attention as well.[37] A familiar message becomes a moment of political and personal instruction because of the context in which it occurs.

As the scene that Baldwin's witnessing demonstrates, the individual act of delivering a sermon cannot be understood outside of the context of prior acts in terms of how it shapes the speaker, the audience, or the Nation of Islam. As Baldwin explains, although he is struck by the distinctive nature of the Nation of Islam's show of force, the street preacher's ability to occupy and command the public space reflects an ongoing relationship between the police and the religious organization. The singular act of street preaching draws force from prior acts. Judith Butler demonstrates how the constitutive nature of an actor's performance works in relationship to the role he or she plays and the site of the performance, whether a stage or a street corner.[38] As discussed in the scene from *Go Tell It on the Mountain*, Gabriel Grimes must negotiate what his audience expects from a preacher – to make them holler – even as he strives to distinguish himself from the other men on the dais. Performance constitutes the actor, as it renders the individual answerable to the nature of the role he or she inhabits and the regulatory forces of the environment. Gabriel's ability to forestall the regulatory forces of the revival, like the Nation of Islam's ability to limit the police's regulation of public space, shifts the commonplace role of the preacher and activates the force of witnessing. The messenger speaking on a corner in Harlem becomes recognizable as a preacher – or for Baldwin, initially invisible – based on the familiar setting and content of his message. But the reaction of the police and the crowd alters the constitution of the individual and the role he plays from quotidian to awe-inspiring. A similar force of shock that calls forth the cry of "Woe is me" in *Go Tell It on the Mountain*, then, activates Baldwin's engagement in *The Fire Next Time*.

In each act of witnessing – from the pulpit in *Go Tell It on the Mountain*, from the witness stand in *Blues for Mister Charlie*, and from the street corner in *The Fire Next Time* – the speaker uses the form and content of the sermon to reconfigure power dynamics. The sermon bears witness to disenfranchisement based on social status, race, gender, or religious beliefs in order to incorporate multiple points of view in the historical record. In

Baldwin's rendering, the sermon borrows from the traditional function of the practice to build community and emancipate the listener, but he deploys it toward secular aims that inevitably require disruption of the status quo. Such disruption explains why Baldwin must disentangle the practice of the sermon from the institution of the church: it is the province of the sermon to challenge the fixity of institutions in order to trouble undemocratic imbalances of power.

NOTES

1 James Baldwin, *The Fire Next Time* (New York: Vintage Books, 1993), p. 37.
2 Karen Thorsen, et al. *James Baldwin: The Price of the Ticket* (San Francisco: California Newsreel, 1989).
3 Hortense J. Spillers, "Fabrics of History: Essays on the Black Sermon," doctoral dissertation, University of Michigan (1974), p. 28.
4 See Henry Louis Gates, Jr., *The Signifying Monkey: A Theory of African American Literary Criticism* (New York: Oxford University Press, 1988).
5 Spillers, "Fabrics of History," p. 14.
6 For more analysis of Baldwin's critique of the church, see Clarence E. Hardy III's "James Baldwin as Religious Writer: The Burdens and Gifts of Black Evangelicism," in Douglas Field (ed.), *A Historical Guide to James Baldwin* (Oxford: Oxford University Press, 2009), pp. 61–82; Trudier Harris, "Introduction," *New Essays on Go Tell It on the Mountain* (Cambridge: Cambridge University Press, 1996), pp. 1–28; Michael F. Lynch, "A Glimpse of the Hidden God: Dialectical Vision in Baldwin's *Go Tell It on the Mountain*," in Trudier Harris (ed.), *New Essays on Go Tell It on the Mountain* (Cambridge: Cambridge University Press, 1996), pp. 29–57; Sondra A. O'Neale, "Fathers, Gods, and Religion: Perceptions of Christianity and Ethnic Faith in James Baldwin," in Fred L. Standley and Nancy V. Burt (eds.), *Critical Essays on James Baldwin* (Boston: G. K. Hall, 1988), pp. 125–43; and Peter Kerry Powers, "The Treacherous Body: Isolation, Confession, and Community in James Baldwin," *American Literature* 77.4 (December 2005), 787–813.
7 James Baldwin, *The Amen Corner* (New York: Vintage International, 1998; first published 1968), p. xvi.
8 Baldwin, *The Fire Next Time*, p. 24.
9 James Baldwin in *The Price of the Ticket*, Film.
10 James Baldwin, *Notes of a Native Son* (New York: Beacon Press, 1984), p. 2.
11 Eddie Glaude, *Exodus!: Religion, Race, and Nation in Early Nineteenth-Century Black America* (Chicago: University of Chicago Press, 2000).
12 For more on exodus typology, see Glaude, *Exodus!*
13 Spillers, "Fabrics of History," p. 26.
14 Ibid., pp. 30–1.
15 Baldwin, *The Fire Next Time*, p. 105.
16 Spillers, "Fabrics of History," p. 14.
17 Baldwin, *Go Tell It on the Mountain*, p. 97.
18 Ibid., pp. 97, 98.
19 Ibid., p. 98.

20 Ibid., p. 99.
21 For further analysis of the limitations of the chosen and the aims of the Civil Rights Movement see the introduction of Robert J. Patterson, *Exodus Politics: Civil Rights and Leadership in African American Literature and Culture* (Charlottesville: University of Virginia Press, 2013).
22 See Spillers, "Fabrics of History," p. 29, and Soyica Diggs Colbert, "Black Leadership at the Crossroads: Unfixing Martin Luther King, Jr. in Katori Hall's *the Mountaintop*," *South Atlantic Quarterly* 112.2 (March 2013), 261–83.
23 Baldwin, *The Fire Next Time*, p. 43.
24 Baldwin, *Go Tell It on the Mountain*, p. 135 and *Another Country* (New York: Vintage Books, 1993), p. 212 and *The Fire Next Time*, p. 105.
25 Baldwin, *The Fire Next Time*, p. 49.
26 James Baldwin, *Blues for Mister Charlie*, originally published 1964 (New York: Vintage Books, 1992), p. 81.
27 Ibid., p. 8.
28 Ibid., p. 93.
29 Spillers, "Fabrics of History," pp. 9–10.
30 Baldwin, *Blues for Mister Charlie*, p. 102.
31 Ibid., p. 105.
32 Kalamu ya Salaam, "Interview: James Baldwin: Looking towards the Eighties," in Fred L. Standley and Nancy V. Burt (eds.), *Critical Essays on James Baldwin* (Boston: G. K. Hall & Co.: 1988) pp. 35–42, p. 36.
33 Joshua L. Miller, "The Discovery of What It Means to Be a Witness: James Baldwin's Dialectics of Difference," in Dwight A. McBride (ed.), *James Baldwin Now* (New York: New York University Press, 1999), pp. 331–59, p. 331, 333.
34 Hardy, "James Baldwin as Religious Writer," p. 78.
35 Baldwin, *The Fire Next Time*, p. 47.
36 Ibid., p. 48.
37 Ibid., p. 49.
38 See Judith Butler, *The Psychic Life of Power: Theories in Subjection* (Stanford: Stanford University Press, 1997).

4

RADICLANI CLYTUS

Paying Dues and Playing the Blues: Baldwin's Existential Jazz

"What does the Negro want?" The question betrays a flight from reality which is absolutely unimaginable: if we weren't dealing with what, in the public mind, is a *Negro*, the question could never be asked.... Anyone who asks "What does the Negro want?" is saying, in another way, that he does not wish to be told, is saying that he is afraid to change, is afraid to pay his dues.

　　　　　　　　　　　　　– James Baldwin, "The White Problem" (1964)

Everything a jazzman feels, sees, hears, everything he was and is becomes the source and object of his music. It is a music purchased with dues of hardship, suffering and pain, optimism and love.

　　　　　　　　　　　　　– Roy DeCarava, *The Sound I Saw* (2003)

In the opening to his essay "The Uses of the Blues," James Baldwin – bon vivant of the New York jazz scene as well as acclaimed novelist and cultural critic – emphatically declares: "I don't know anything about music."[1] For those readers acquainted with the author who penned such tunefully inspired titles as *Go Tell It on the Mountain* (1953), *The Amen Corner* (1954), "Sonny's Blues" (1957), *Blues for Mr. Charlie* (1964), and *If Beale Street Could Talk* (1974), it is clear that Baldwin's self-effacement is intended as a rhetorical ploy to enhance the unique musicological insights in his writings. By disavowing competency at the outset of his analysis, Baldwin shifts emphasis away from the technological terrain of music criticism and theory in order to enable his examination of the psychosocial origins of black expressive arts. As he opines in one of his most profound testaments to how black interwar music gave voice and meaning to the "Facts of [Black] Life" (including "work, love, death, floods, lynchings," and so on), Baldwin stresses that his decision to talk about the blues as metaphor is not only "because [the blues] speak of this particular experience of life and this state of being, but because they contain the toughness that manages to make this experience articulate."[2]

And yet, despite his lack of formal musical training, Baldwin recognized the important role that black music would play in mid–twentieth century cultural politics. In both his essays and fiction, his explanation of a self-conscious black musicality suggests a legacy of purposefulness that understands the artist's pursuit for aesthetic perfection as commensurate with the highest principles of moral idealism. Such insight owes partly to the fact that his coming of age coincided with one of the most dynamic transitions in American music, as the era of big band and swing gave way to the intense small combo arrangements of modern jazz and bebop. Furthermore, by Baldwin's adolescence, the status of black music in American cultural life was such that both the blues and jazz had begun to gain credibility as reputable American art forms. Artists such as Bessie Smith, Fats Waller, Billie Holiday, and Paul Robeson, when not being denigrated as social outcasts, sonically signified a black creative ethos that challenged the political status quo and pointed the way toward more liberatory democratic sensibilities.[3] During his lifetime, Baldwin would uphold the integrity of these performers by publicly acknowledging that his aesthetic and cultural registers were largely indebted to the uncompromising humanity of "jazz musicians, dancers, a couple of whores and a few junkies"[4] – an affirmation that indicates his affinity for an embattled black underclass and reflects his belief that black expressive culture was intrinsically relevant to black survival.

In an oft-cited 1961 interview with Studs Terkel, Baldwin would go so far as to assert that it was his time spent considering "where [he] came from and where [he] had been," while communing with a couple of Bessie Smith records in Loèche-les-Bains, Switzerland, that had enabled him to become more attuned to the revelatory expressiveness of the blues and its importance to his literary vocation:

> When I say I was trying to dig back to the way I myself must have spoken when I was little, I realized that…I really had buried myself beneath a whole fantastic image of myself which wasn't mine, but white people's image of me…. I had to find out what I had been like in the beginning, in order, just technically as a writer, to re-create Negro speech. I realized it was a cadence; it was not a question of dropping s's or n's or g's, but a question of the beat…. In that icy wilderness, as far removed from Harlem as anything you can imagine, with Bessie Smith and me…. I began.[5]

Through this recollection, Baldwin's relationship to blues and jazz music garners its most salient autobiographical and creative resonance. As Josh Kun suggests, "Bessie Smith signified a version of American stereotypes [that Baldwin] had yet to confront" in his life. Through her unrepentant blackness, she embodied "all the projected racial and sexual fantasies…and all the externally imposed self-hate" that had "menaced" him before he retreated abroad.[6] Thus the cadence of Smith's music exemplifies more than an autobiographical soundtrack to Baldwin's European exile: implicit in his reminiscence is his long-standing view that "the artist's struggle for…integrity must be considered as a kind of metaphor for the struggle, which is universal and daily, of all human beings on the face of this globe to get to become human beings."[7]

Indeed, as Kun concludes, "Baldwin's identification with both the persona and the voice of Bessie Smith reveals as much about his approach to race as it does about his belief in the possibilities of gay male desire."[8] Consequently, the protracted burden of self-reflection that informs both personhood and musicianship in the above epigraphs not only speaks to the transparency Baldwin locates in Smith's expressive vocality but is also integral to his inclinations as an openly gay black writer. As Baldwin notes in "The Discovery of What It Means to Be an American," the primary role of the novelist is to expose the "hidden laws" and "profound assumptions on the part of the people" so that we might "free ourselves" of such "myth[s]" and "try to find out what is really happening here."[9] In this way, Baldwin's concept of "paying dues," like his use of other pecuniary metaphors (for example, "the price of the ticket"[10] and "the price for the beat"[11]), demonstrates his indebtedness to the Socratic ideal that an unexamined life is not *worth* living.[12]

However, Baldwin and DeCarava's claim that a meaningful existence is only possible through "the dues of hardship, suffering and pain, optimism and love," is hardly unique.[13] As early as 1940, the novelist and cultural critic Ralph Ellison would theorize a jazz-blues aesthetic that encompassed the rigors of self-reflection as a governing motif: "The blues," asserts Ellison, "is an impulse to keep the painful details and episodes of a brutal experience alive in one's aching consciousness, to finger its jagged grain, and to transcend it, not by the consolation of philosophy but by squeezing from it a near-tragic, near-comic lyricism. As a form, the blues is an autobiographical chronicle of personal catastrophe expressed lyrically."[14] Hence, central to the blues, and to jazz for that matter, is a steadfast avowal that the nature of black existence is struggle. In other words, if one pursues one's "entire life in flight from death" and suffering, as Baldwin asserts, one is "also in flight from life."[15]

But while this same desire for fingering the "jagged grain" of life experience operates as a subtext in Baldwin's subtle scrutiny of "What does the Negro want?",[16] his approach to representing the enduring "tale of how we suffer and how we are delighted" has implications beyond the ontology of black life.[17] Through his treatments of blues and jazz culture, and his precise reframing of "The Negro Question" in the opening epigraph – characterized as "The White Problem" – Baldwin achieves a sustained meditation on the tenets of mid-century existentialist thought.[18] His use of the editorial "we" to speak "objectively" (and thus inclusively) about the philosophical significance of self-examination exposes readers to the idea that black subjectivity is essentially a speculative trope in the minds of black and white Americans alike. As he asserts in his analysis of the "Of the Sorrow Songs," what motivates the anxieties surrounding The Negro Question is "nothing more – and nothing less – than the question of identity: *Who am I? And what am I doing here?*"[19] According to Baldwin, not examining who we are to ourselves renders us incapable of confronting the social realities of others.

That Baldwin locates this metaphysical dilemma at "the very heart, and root" of black musical expression reflects a strain of thought that appears in many of his interviews and essays, but especially in his musically inflected short story, "Sonny's Blues." In this modern tale of estrangement, two alienated brothers – one a budding bebop pianist, Sonny, and the other, a middle-class school teacher who narrates and remains unnamed – struggle to understand the persistence of human suffering as their common bond.[20] Through a pronounced degree of symbolism that punctuates the fallibility of language, Baldwin draws a parallel between his protagonists' brooding ruminations on the meaning of life and the type of existential subjectivism popularized by his philosophical contemporary Jean-Paul Sartre. Although the short story's denouement of reconciliation rests entirely upon the two brothers' self-reflective agency, it is the indomitable will of Sonny's jazz performance that facilitates their empathic connection. To the extent that "Sonny's Blues," much like Baldwin's nonfiction, proffers a searing portrait of the alienation inherent to human existence, it also illustrates Baldwin's belief that music is perhaps best suited to illumine our ability to cope with existential suffering. This essay considers the importance of contextualizing Baldwin's identitarian politics in accordance with Sartre's philosophy of existentialism. By doing so, it advances the claim that Baldwin's concept of "dues paying" epitomizes Sartre's revolutionary understanding of sovereign will. While most criticism of "Sonny's Blues" speaks to some aspect of Baldwin's existential ideals, what follows enables the possibility of reading his jazz-related debt motif as a consistent politics across his oeuvre.[21]

The most productive site to reflect on how Baldwin's metaphysics of "dues-paying" is suggestive of the mid-century's philosophical preoccupation with self-awareness occurs in Jean-Paul Sartre's *Existentialism is a Humanism* (1945).[22] In the philosophy of *EH*, Sartre proposes that an individual is capable of willing a sense of self into being, making an argument that predates Baldwin's own struggle to qualify what it means to live (and produce art) with integrity. Composed on the heels of World War II and at the height of third-world colonialism and first-world racial apartheid, *EH* advances a concept of humanity in which one's idea of personhood exists distinctly from that individual's social environment, or the conditions producing that individual. For "Man," declares Sartre, "is nothing other than his own project": "he materializes in the world, encounters himself, and only afterwards defines himself." Sartre posits that since our "existence precedes [our] essence" – suggesting that we arrive in this world with no "true" or innate nature and only later assume those predetermined categories, labels, and types that define us – it is up to the "individual subject to choose what he will be." To this end, man "exists only to the extent that he realizes himself, [and is thus] nothing more than the sum of his actions…responsible for what he is…free…condemned to be free…commit[ing] himself to life."[23] Implied in this radical notion of choice is the possibility that one can choose to behave justly or dishonorably. In either case, Sartre's claim remains steadfast; there is no essential nature to humankind except what is chosen or made. We "make [ourselves] by choosing [our] own morality," and through our "choosing" we declare "the value of what we choose."[24]

Understandably, such a theory of personhood was attractive to many mid-century cultural theorists and artists who witnessed a world overtaken by mass-conformist regimes, whether political, social, or economic.[25] By defining the possibilities of individual sovereignty through self-creation rather than social praxis, Sartrean existentialism shifted the concept of freedom away from structural forces, which were seen as usurping an individual's right to one's very own being. Under Sartre's doctrine it became conceivable that an entire society could remake itself according to the better character of its members and avoid the "recourse to excuses" informed by "deterministic theory."[26]

It is no wonder that a philosophy emphasizing commitment to self-creation as a revolutionary act found its way into Baldwin's writings. Throughout many of his essays on America's race problem, Baldwin affirmed his belief that "the interior life is a real life, and [that] the intangible dreams of people have a tangible effect on the world."[27] In a manner similar to Sartre's idealization of sovereign will, Baldwin's focus on the productive conditions of identity from within substantiates the transformative power of individual personhood. But while there is no material evidence that Baldwin was a disciple of Sartrean existentialism, there are significant parallels between his understanding of the nature of human freedom and those philosophical precepts outlined in Sartre's landmark tome. A number of examples in Baldwin's nonfiction display his awareness and application of Sartre's vision for a more radical view of identity as a recurring process of self-creation, wherein through the act of choosing for oneself, one constructs the only true state of human universality: the freedom to choose.

For example, in Baldwin's 1964 speech "The White Problem," he not only appears to echo Sartre's notion of "perpetual construction" as a condition of actual being, but he also adjusts Sartre's formulation to account for the alienating effects under which he himself continually labored[28]:

> In the life of a woman, in the life of a man, in anybody's life, there are always many elements at work. The crucial element I wish to consider here is the element of a life which we consider to be an identity; the way in which one puts oneself together, what one imagines oneself to be; for one example, the invented reality standing before you now, who is arbitrarily known as Jimmy Baldwin. This invented reality contains a great number of elements, all of them extremely difficult, if not impossible, to name.... The truth, forever, for everybody, is that one is a stranger to oneself, and that one must deal with this stranger day in and day out – that one, in fact, is forced to create, as distinct from invent, oneself.[29]

If, as Sartre asserts, humankind's "real problem is not one of...existence" but that "what man needs is to rediscover himself and to comprehend that nothing can save him from himself," then the above passage more than corroborates his notion that the burden of existential estrangement is the single universality connecting all humankind.[30] But there are, as Baldwin implies rather ambiguously, many different "elements" impacting the "invented reality" of individual identity. While his acknowledgement that "one is a stranger to oneself, and that one must deal with this stranger day in and day out"[31] confirms Sartre's dictum that "man is condemned to be free" and "is responsible for everything he does,"[32] Baldwin's ambivalent portrayal of himself as an arbitrary phenomenon[33] suggests his awareness that one experiences the responsibility of self-creation to varying degrees.

Further, while Sartre's scope of experience was that of a bourgeois intellectual who was relatively integrated into the fabric of metropolitan French life, for Baldwin, the urgency of "perpetual construction"[34] as a black gay writer surely emanated from a greater sense of psychic necessity. "All you are ever told in this country about being black," remarks Baldwin during his interview with Studs Terkel,

> is that it is a terrible, terrible thing to be. Now, in order to survive this, you have to really dig down into yourself and re-create yourself, really, according to no image which yet exists in America. You have to impose, in fact – this may sound very strange – you have to *decide* who you are, and force the world to deal with you, not with its idea of you.[35]

There can be no mistaking that Baldwin's elaboration on choice reflects a particular sense of estrangement that resulted from his being reared in a "Protestant Puritan country, [where...] all the taboos [are] placed on the flesh."[36] So while Baldwin contends during a British television interview that his being "black, impoverished, and homosexual," was tantamount to a literary artist "hit[ing] the jackpot,"[37] it is also indisputable that his radical sense of self-acceptance contributed to moments of mental crisis.[38]

But this is not to say that Baldwin intended to glorify black suffering for a white audience that sometimes looked upon his public display of emotional injuries with a hint of guilty pleasure.[39] Rather, Baldwin's explicitly identitarian concerns align with Sartre's revolutionary campaign to promote greater responsibility toward others:

> I prefer to believe that since a society is created by men, it can be remade by men. The price for this transformation is high. White people will have to ask themselves precisely why they found it necessary to invent the nigger; for the nigger is a white invention, and white people invented him out of the terrible necessities of their own.... Black people will have to do something very hard, too, which is to allow the white citizen his first awkward steps toward maturity.... If we can hang on just a little bit longer, all of us, we may make it. We've got to try.[40]

Significantly, the shared cost that Baldwin describes is emblematic of the dialectical paradigm from which Sartre's humanistic philosophy of self-liberation arises. Rather than viewing the subject as operating beyond social or political context, Sartre qualifies subjecthood as a dynamic, interdependent relation that is duty-bound for the benefit of society:

> [W]e each attain ourselves in the presence of the other, and we are just as certain of the other as we are of ourselves. Therefore the man who becomes aware of himself directly in the *cogito* also perceives all others, and he does so as the condition of his own existence. He realizes that he cannot be anything...unless others acknowledge him as such. I cannot discover any truth whatsoever about myself except through the mediation of another. The other is essential to my existence, as well as to the knowledge I have of myself.[41]

This synthesis of estrangement and reconciliation is not the only theme that these two thinkers share. What makes their dialectical method of transformative morality possible is their belief in humankind's ability to choose a life of integrity over one of social acquiescence. For example, when Baldwin posits that "the really ghastly thing about trying to convey to a white man [that] the reality of the Negro experience has nothing whatever to do with the fact of color, but has to do with this man's relationship to his own life" – concluding that "He will face in your life only what he is willing to face in his"[42] – Baldwin essentially mirrors Sartre's assertion that "in creating the man each of us wills ourselves to be, there is not a single one of our actions that does not at the same time create an image of man as we think he ought to be."[43] While much has been made of Baldwin's incisive analysis of American culture, it is important to remember that his primary objective was always to avail his audience of those "choices" that he insists we have "got to make, for ever and ever and ever, every day."[44]

But it is Baldwin's decision to pit syntax against the expressive musicality of jazz idioms in "Sonny's Blues" that is perhaps his most creative adaptation of Sartre's existential project. Set in Harlem during the early 1950s, "Sonny's Blues" depicts the reconciliation of two estranged brothers who struggle with how to bear the burden of their innate freedom in a society where race delimits the possibilities of personal achievement. Baldwin's unnamed narrator is a character who has internalized the supporting myths of middle-class conformity in order to avoid the terrifying charge of establishing a conception of his own identity. As a high school algebra teacher who marries into a family that is "inclined to be dicty," he judges Sonny's choice to become a jazz musician, a career that he derides as consisting of "good time people" "clowning around on bandstands."[45] However, after reading about Sonny's arrest for the possession of heroin and grappling with the sudden death of his daughter Grace from polio, the narrator becomes better able to reflect upon the nature of Sonny's struggles in light of his own emotional vulnerability. In true existential fashion, it is only when the narrator begins to accept the meaninglessness of Grace's death and his brother's life immersed in jazz that he becomes aware of the inevitability of human suffering and can realize his filial responsibilities anew. While this dramatic shift in perspective leads to their seeming reunion, it also reinforces Sartre's more disconcerting thesis that "the ultimate significance of the actions of men of good faith is the quest of freedom itself." This proposition implies the negation of everything except the concept that we alone are the shapers of our morality, as when Sonny chooses heroin and jazz music over a figurative bourgeois death.[46]

Ironically, Baldwin challenges the integrity of the printed word in his efforts to address the sanctity of personhood and the elusive nature of meaning. At the outset of "Sonny's Blues," the narrator's reaction to the newspaper coverage of Sonny's arrest is offered as a series of bewildering impressions that are clearly intended to highlight the fallibility of language:

> I read about it in the paper, in the subway, on my way to work. I read it, and I couldn't believe it, and I read it again. Then perhaps I just stared at it, at the newsprint spelling out his name, spelling out the story. I stared at it in the swinging lights of the subway car, and in the faces and bodies of the people, and in my own face, trapped in the darkness which roared outside.[47]

Here, the narrator's ambivalence toward Sonny's plight – which is based on the brother he thinks he knows and not the stranger instantiated via newsprint – is scrutinized by Baldwin's systematic use of the third-person pronominal case. Through this cryptic approach, readers are free to surmise what exactly "it" is that Sonny has done; but by doing so, we, of course, enact the very imposition of fiction onto Sonny that is performed by the media's imperfect delineation of his character. For Sonny, as the narrative later reveals, embodies complexities beyond the designation of a mere drug-addicted felon. Additionally, while the narrator tries to find meaning in the facts of Sonny's "name" and his "story," he also begins to recognize his own unintelligible struggle in the physical comportment of his fellow commuters. Their presence on the subway, a vehicular symbol laden with existential angst, characterizes the universality of alienation which Baldwin posits as the condition of our modernity. This theme is underscored by Baldwin's metaphorical use of light and darkness to suggest that suffering is a generative feature in our process of self-creation. That the narrator's image of himself is glimpsed as the light of the subway car is reflected off of the series of windows that open up onto the soot-filled train tunnel symbolically confirms that only the totality of our worldly experiences, both vulgar (darkness) and virtuous (light), can connect us to ourselves and thus to others.

Yet, it is understandable that the narrator would experience such apprehension while trying to respond emotionally to the story of Sonny's arrest. Given the one-dimensional depictions that typically attend newspaper reporting, the motivation behind Sonny's drug use is perhaps beyond the pale of generic representation. Furthermore, when we consider the stereotyping of black jazz musicians as purveyors of pathology in Cold War-era media, it is also conceivable that Baldwin was subtly critiquing the culture industry's gross racial politics by reducing the narrator's reaction to that of confoundment.[48] As Scott Saul demonstrates in his study *Freedom Is, Freedom Ain't: Jazz and the Making of the Sixties* (2003), the radical shift in jazz music toward bop aesthetics was often characterized as "a kind of subcultural delusion for both black and white America." Instead of embracing the innovative experimentation of jazz as the artistic arm of a burgeoning Civil Rights Movement, mainstream cultural critics often evidenced "a neurotic music that symptomatized a larger American disease" of disorder and ruin from the margins of black life.[49]

However, Baldwin's meditation on semantics extends beyond the dictates of genre and race-baiting. Throughout "Sonny's Blues," language also proves to be a barrier as the characters attempt to corroborate a sense of meaningfulness and empathy. This is especially apparent during a chance meeting between the narrator and one of Sonny's unnamed childhood associates, who presumably endures a fate similar to that awaiting Sonny:

"Then they'll let him loose" – he gestured throwing his cigarette into the gutter. "That's all."

"What do you mean that's *all*?"

But I knew what he meant.

"I *mean* that's *all*." He turned his head and looked at me, pulling down the corners of his mouth. "Don't you know what I mean?" he asked softly.

"How the hell *would* I know what you mean?" I almost whispered it, I don't know why.

"That's right," he said to the air, "how would *he* know what I mean?...Listen. They'll let him out and then it'll just start all over again. That's what I mean."

"You mean – they'll let him out. And then he'll just start working his way back in again. You mean he'll never kick the habit. Is that what you mean?"

"That's right," he said, cheerfully. "*You* see what I mean."[50]

Within this rather Beckettian dialogue, the inherent flaws of linguistic signification expose an even greater rift between the narrator and the all-knowing junkie whom he believes to be without "a story of his own, much less a sad one."[51] The repetition, self-referentials, and looming debate over intention not only demonstrate the inability of words to establish definitive meaning but also render each man hermetically sealed off from the other; the narrator leaves the above encounter thinking that he still "wanted to ask...too many things" before concluding that it was "none of his business" and he "could not have borne the answers" to the facts in question.[52] What is more, despite their seemingly mutual confirmation, neither character is able to acknowledge the unspeakable suffering that lies at the root of Sonny's blues.

Such estrangement is as true of the narrator's relationship with Sonny as it is with his anonymous informant. Even during moments of direct communication between the brothers, language remains ill-suited for expressing those complex ideas involving an individual's freedom to choose: "I can't tell you much about how I got here," explains Sonny in his account of the details leading up to his incarceration. "I mean I don't know how to tell you. I guess I was afraid of something or I was trying to escape from something.... I don't want you to think it had anything to do with me being a musician. It's more than that. Or maybe less than that."[53] Accordingly, the struggle for comprehension between Sonny and the narrator is not so much a matter of Sonny's inability to convey his emotions as it is a matter of his expressive needs existing outside the boundaries of speech. For Sonny, who has dedicated his life to jazz, the range of his articulation, as it concerns the essence of his subjectivity, is limited to the realm of musical sound. And this "sound," as the narrator discovers, "didn't make any sense" because "it was as though Sonny were some sort of god or monster...and there wasn't any way to reach him."[54]

Notwithstanding these impasses in communication, Sonny does offer the narrator an intelligible description of his lingering malaise. After he observes an "old-fashion revival meeting" across the street from the narrator's public housing project, they each parse the experience of human suffering on their own terms. For Sonny, who is linked to the performing evangelists both as a musician and because he stood at the edge of their open-air assembly, the impassioned presence of the congregates motivates him to disclose the psychical exigency surrounding his addiction:

> I was all by myself at the bottom of something, stinking and sweating and crying and shaking, and I smelled it, you know? *my* stink, and I thought I'd die if I couldn't get away from it and yet, all the same, I knew that everything I was doing was just locking me in with it. And I didn't know…I didn't know, I still *don't* know, something kept telling me that maybe it was good to smell your own stink, but I didn't think that *that* was what I'd been trying to do – and – who can stand it?[55]

While the concept of stench represents Sonny's physical withdrawal, it also highlights the fortitude that Sartre regards as essential to realizing a "morality of action." By Sartre's logic, if an individual is truly committed to freedom, "he cannot avoid bearing full responsibility for his situation. He must choose without reference to any preestablished values"[56] if he is to attain the integrity necessary to become self-aware, or, as Baldwin would have it, an "artist."[57] Such conviction is exemplified by Sonny's characterization of how his heroin abuse informs his creative ethos, considering "it was actually when [he] was most *out* of the world, [he] felt that [he] was in it, that [he] was *with* it."[58] Indeed, if Sonny's "stink" qualifies his desperation to escape the circumstances of Harlem at whatever cost – that is, to the extent that he would "do *anything* to play"[59] – it also triggers the type of emotional intelligence that jazz music demands of its practitioners. By paying his dues and not forgetting "where [he's] *been*. And *what* [he's] been,"[60] Sonny is released from those mainstream conventions (moral or otherwise) that would inhibit his exploratory initiative.

In keeping with Sartre's notion of "perpetual construction," Sonny's attempts to imbue the piano "with the breath of [his own] life" ultimately allow the two brothers to reach some semblance of empathic bonding.[61] What Sonny cannot clarify through speech, he elucidates during his post-prison debut in a Greenwich Village jazz club. "[A]t the risk of ruin, destruction, madness, and death," it is on stage that Sonny's performance engenders "a common 'inside' space, an 'us' beyond estrangement" that finally becomes "a collective act of introspection"[62]:

> Freedom lurked around us and I understood, at last that [Sonny] could help us to be free if we would only listen, that he would never be free until we did….

I heard what he had gone through, and would continue to go through until
he came to rest in the earth. He made it his:...And he was giving it back as
everything must be given back.... I saw my mother's face again, and felt, for
the first time, how the stones of the road she had walked on must have bruised
her feet....I saw my little girl again...and I felt my own tears begin to rise.[63]

Thus Sonny's blues, his "autobiographical chronicle of personal catastrophe expressed lyrically,"[64] encourages the narrator's empathetic recollection of unmentionable sufferings. Moreover, as Walton Muyumba argues,
Sonny's performance "is the narration of self-reinvention, but the act is also
redemption by improvisation."[65] During the band's "sardonic"[66] cover of
"Am I Blue?", the narrator "shifts from knowing only that 'not many people ever really hear [jazz]' to understanding that jazz musicians must shape
the cacophony emerging from the inaudible void, 'imposing order on it as
it hits the air.'"[67]

But even given such cooperation between musician and listener, Baldwin
maintains a dialectical model of selfhood that begins with the individual
choosing self-awareness. For there is no inherent truth in Sonny's "triumph"
that is not the result of the listener's own making. As the narrator attests,
"what we mainly hear, or hear corroborated" from the bandstand "are personal, private, vanishing evocations." Likewise, if "the man who creates
the music is hearing something else," then Baldwin's statement on listening
reveals how musically inspired reflection is always an order imposed by the
will of the individual.[68] Sonny's playing, as an aural testament to his own
estrangement, only suggests the likelihood of "collective emancipation"[69]
because the narrator accepts responsibility in realizing, "My trouble made
his real."[70] As such, the narrator's empathic morality originates first and
foremost as a cost unto himself. Like Sartre's insistence that our freedom
to choose constitutes our commitment to existential humanism, "Sonny's
Blues" establishes that "We will freedom for freedom's sake through our
individual circumstance. And in thus willing freedom, we discover that
it depends entirely on the freedom of others, and that freedom of others
depends on our own."[71]

NOTES

1 James Baldwin, "The Uses of the Blues," in James Baldwin and Randall Kenan
(ed.), *The Cross of Redemption: Uncollected Writings* (New York: Pantheon
Books, 2010), p. 57.
2 Ibid.
3 Artist-activists of the period include but are not limited to Louis Armstrong,
Edward Kennedy "Duke" Ellington, Marian Anderson, Ralph Ellison, Jacob
Lawrence, Max Roach, Odetta Holmes, Joshua Daniel White, Harry Belafonte,
and Josephine Baker. While these cultural figures were routinely lauded for their

artistic abilities, they were often excoriated by the mainstream press for their progressive political views.

4 James Baldwin, quoted in Saadi A. Simawe, "What is in a Sound: the Metaphysics and Politics of *The Amen Corner*," in D. Quentin Miller (ed.), *Re-Viewing James Baldwin: Things Not Seen* (Philadelphia: Temple University Press, 2000), p. 12.

5 James Baldwin, quoted in "An Interview with James Baldwin," in Fred L. Stanley and Louis H. Pratt (eds.), *Conversations with James Baldwin* (Jackson: University Press of Mississippi, 1989), p. 4.

6 Josh Kun, *Audiotopia: Music, Race and America* (Berkeley: University of California Press, 2005), p. 312.

7 James Baldwin, "The Artist's Struggle for Integrity" in Kenan (ed.), *The Cross of Redemption*, p. 41.

8 Josh Kun, *Audiotopia: Music, Race and America*, p. 309.

9 James Baldwin, "The Discovery of What It Means To Be an American," in Toni Morrison (ed.), *James Baldwin: Collected Essays* (New York: Library of America, 1998), p. 142.

10 James Baldwin, "The Price of the Ticket," in Morrison (ed.), *James Baldwin: Collected Essays*, p. 835.

11 James Baldwin, "Of the Sorrow Songs: The Cross of Redemption," in Kenan (ed.), *The Cross of Redemption*, p. 124.

12 The leitmotif of an American psychical debt (billed as past due) can be found throughout the following essays and speeches: "The Price of the Ticket," "The Artist's Struggle for Integrity," "What Price for Freedom?", "The White Problem," and "Black English: A Dishonest Argument." See Kenan (ed.), *The Cross of Redemption*.

13 Roy DeCarava, *The Sound I Saw* (London: Phaidon, 2003), n.p.

14 Ralph Ellison, "Richard Wright's Blues," in Robert G. O'Meally (ed.), *The Jazz Cadence of American Culture* (New York: Columbia University Press, 1998), p. 553.

15 James Baldwin, "The Uses of the Blues," in Kenan (ed.), *The Cross of Redemption*, p. 65.

16 James Baldwin, "The White Problem," in Kenan (ed.), *The Cross of Redemption*, p. 78.

17 James Baldwin, "Sonny's Blues," in *Going to Meet the Man* (New York: Dial Press, 1965), p. 139.

18 The modern "Negro Question" or "Negro Problem" has its origins in those post-emancipation era debates regarding the enfranchisement of African-American Southerners. By the early twentieth century, this public discussion transformed into a disingenuous concern for the intellectual, moral, and political condition of African Americans writ large. By disregarding the means by which racism structured U.S. social inequality, white commentators primarily framed this dialogue as a consequence of African-American inferiority, hence, the "Negro Problem." For further reference, see Booker T. Washington, *The Negro Problem* (New York: J. Pott & Company, 1903); W. E. B. Du Bois, *The Souls of Black Folk* (Chicago: A. C. McClurg & Co., 1903); and Gunnar Myrdal, *An American Dilemma: The Negro Problem and Modern Democracy* (New York: Harper & Brothers, 1944).

19 James Baldwin, "Of the Sorrow Songs: The Cross of Redemption," in Kenan (ed.), *The Cross of Redemption*, p. 122.
20 Ibid.
21 For a general assessment of existentialism in "Sonny's Blues," see Scott Saul, *Freedom Is, Freedom Ain't: Jazz and the Making of the Sixties* (Cambridge: Harvard University Press, 2003) and Walton Muyumba, *The Shadow and the Act: Black Intellectual Practice, Jazz Improvisation, and Philosophical Pragmatism* (Chicago: University of Chicago Press, 2009). For an analysis of existentialism in Baldwin's nonfiction, see Bruce Lapenson, "Race and Existential Commitment in James Baldwin," *Philosophy and Literature* 37.1 (April 2013), 199–209.
22 It should be noted that Sartre regretted the publication of *EH*, which was based on his extremely successful eponymous lecture in Paris, October 28, 1945. His primary concern was that he oversimplified some of the more salient features of his masterwork *Being and Nothingness* (1943). Owing to the popularity of *EH* in the United States and Paris, I've chosen this publication as a more apt introduction to his philosophy. For Sartre's thorough treatment of existentialism, see Jean-Paul Sartre, *Being and Nothingness* (New York: Washington Square Press, 1993).
23 Jean-Paul Sartre, *Existentialism Is a Humanism*, trans. Carol Macomber (New Haven: Yale University Press, 2007), pp. 10, 22–3, 37, 41.
24 Ibid., pp. 24, 46.
25 As a committed philosophical thinker, Sartre's bold formulations informed the political imagination of Albert Camus, Franz Fanon, Simone de Beauvoir, Andre Malraux, Abe Kôbo, Ralph Ellison, Hannah Arendt, and Steve Bantu Biko, among others.
26 Sartre, *Existentialism Is a Humanism*, p. 47.
27 Baldwin, "The Discovery of What It Means To Be an American," in Kenan (ed.), *The Cross of Redemption*, p. 142.
28 Sartre, *Existentialism Is a Humanism*, p. 43.
29 Baldwin, "The White Problem," in Kenan (ed.), *The Cross of Redemption*, p. 73.
30 Sartre, *Existentialism Is a Humanism*, p. 53.
31 Baldwin, "The White Problem," in Kenan (ed.), *The Cross of Redemption*, p. 73.
32 Sartre, *Existentialism Is a Humanism*, p. 29.
33 Baldwin, "The White Problem," in Kenan (ed.), *The Cross of Redemption*, p. 73.
34 Sartre, *Existentialism Is a Humanism*, p. 43.
35 Baldwin, "An Interview with James Baldwin," in Stanley and Pratt (eds.), *Conversations with James Baldwin*, pp. 5–6.
36 Ibid., pp. 8–9.
37 James Baldwin, quoted in Karen Thorsen, et al. *James Baldwin: The Price of the Ticket* (San Francisco: California Newsreel, 1989).
38 For more on Baldwin's mental health, see James Darsey, "Baldwin's Cosmopolitan Loneliness," in Dwight A. McBride (ed.), *James Baldwin Now* (New York: New York University Press, 1999).
39 During the mid-1960s, black activists such as Amiri Baraka and Eldridge Cleaver attacked Baldwin for his homosexuality and his integrationist critique of the American psyche. Both men viewed his frank expositions on racial and sexual identity as politically outdated and indicative of his desire to appease

white audiences. See Douglas Field (ed.), *A Historical Guide to James Baldwin* (London: Oxford University Press, 2009); Eldridge Cleaver, "Notes on a Native Son," *Ramparts Magazine* (June 1966), 51–7; Amiri Baraka, "Brief Reflections on Two Hot-Shots," in *Home: Social Essays* (New York: William Morrow and Company, Inc., 1966); and David Leeming, *James Baldwin: A Biography* (New York: Alfred A. Knopf, Inc.) p. 304.

40 Baldwin, "The White Problem," in Kenan (ed.), *The Cross of Redemption*, p. 79.
41 Sartre, *Existentialism Is a Humanism*, p. 41.
42 James Baldwin, "The Black Boy Looks at the White Boy," in Morrison (ed.), *James Baldwin: Collected Essays*, p. 272.
43 Sartre, *Existentialism Is a Humanism*, p. 24.
44 Baldwin, "The Artist's Struggle for Integrity," p. 41.
45 Baldwin, "Sonny's Blues," in *Going to Meet the Man*, pp. 120, 122.
46 Sartre, *Existentialism Is a Humanism*, p. 48.
47 Baldwin, "Sonny's Blues," in *Going to Meet the Man*, p. 103.
48 See Scott Saul, *Freedom Is, Freedom Ain't: Jazz and the Making of the Sixties* (Cambridge: Harvard University Press, 2003), and Norman Mailer, *The White Negro* (San Francisco: City Lights Books, 1957).
49 Saul, *Freedom Is, Freedom Ain't*, p. 51.
50 Baldwin, "Sonny's Blues," in *Going to Meet the Man*, pp. 107–8.
51 Ibid., p. 106.
52 Ibid., p. 108.
53 Ibid., p. 109.
54 Ibid., pp. 124–5.
55 Ibid., pp. 134–5.
56 Sartre, *Existentialism Is a Humanism*, pp. 40, 45.
57 Baldwin, "The Artist's Struggle for Integrity," in Kenan (ed.), *The Cross of Redemption*, p. 41.
58 Baldwin, "Sonny's Blues," in *Going to Meet the Man*, p. 134.
59 Ibid., p. 133.
60 Ibid.
61 Ibid., p. 138.
62 Saul, *Freedom Is, Freedom Ain't*, pp. 75, 76.
63 Ibid., p. 140.
64 Ralph Ellison, "Richard Wright's Blues," in O'Meally (ed.), *The Jazz Cadence of American Culture*, p. 553.
65 Walton Muyumba, *The Shadow and the Act: Black Intellectual Practice, Jazz Imporvisation, and Philosophical Pragmatism* (Chicago: University of Chicago Press, 2009), pp. 119–20.
66 Baldwin, "Sonny's Blues," in *Going to Meet the Man*, p. 139.
67 Muyumba, *The Shadow and the Act*, p. 120.
68 Baldwin, "Sonny's Blues," in *Going to Meet the Man*, p. 137.
69 Saul, *Freedom Is, Freedom Ain't*, p. 76. For more on the importance of listening as a collective action in jazz culture, see Josh Kun, *Audiotopia: Music, Race and America* and Walton Muyumba, *The Shadow and the Act: Black Intellectual Practice, Jazz Improvisation, and Philosophical Pragmatism*.
70 Baldwin, "Sonny's Blues," in *Going to Meet the Man*, p. 127.
71 Sartre, *Existentialism Is a Humanism*, p. 48.

5

E. PATRICK JOHNSON

Baldwin's Theatre

Baldwin always had a flair for the dramatic – whether manifesting itself in his highly stylized way of speaking while holding his cigarette just so, through the provocative tone of his soul-stirring essays, or the unforgettable dialogue between the characters in his fiction. Drama, it seems, was part of Baldwin's prerequisite for self-presentation and for his representations of others – whether black, white, or another "self." Yet the drama referenced here does not indicate a formal genre, but more an effect/affect of Baldwin's personality and his art. In other words, Baldwin's unrelenting critique of race and religion is made more powerful through his ability to engage his plays' readers and audiences both effectively and affectively by imbuing them with dramatic tension that potentially alienates or captures them, or else leaves them feeling ambivalent, but never indifferent. Baldwin's appeal to affective response at the expense of adhering to traditional theatre conventions prompt some critics to define Baldwin as a "bad" playwright, failing to understand that it is these very affective tensions in Baldwin's plays and fiction that make them so compelling and relevant across generations.[1] Through analysis of reviews of productions of the plays, critical essays, and adaptations of Baldwin's fiction for the stage, this essay argues that Baldwin's plays are not confined within traditional American theatre conventions – for example, linear plot construction, realist staging, and catharsis through identification – and it is this nontraditional engagement with theatrical form that reinforces their political message – that blacks are not solely victims of racism and whites are not purely evil.[2] The popularity of these plays today, therefore, is not necessarily because they are great plays *as* plays in the traditional sense, but because they capture the historically complex role of racism and religion in the daily lives of U.S. blacks.[3]

Baldwin's Antitheatrical Prejudice

To understand Baldwin's aesthetic choices as a playwright, one must understand how he became attracted to the genre of drama, which, ironically, was initiated through his disappointment in film. Baldwin's biographies and semiautobiographical fiction demonstrate that he was an admirer of film. In Baldwin's first novel, *Go Tell It on the Mountain* (1953), the young John Grimes finds himself at a movie theatre watching a film that stars a Bette Davis-type with whom he identifies.[4] Yet in Baldwin's later essays, particularly "The Devil Finds Work," Baldwin demonstrates his belief that theatre, not film, allows us to see and feel our humanity, what he calls our "flesh and blood." He writes:

> There is an enormous difference between the stage and the screen…the tension in the theater is a very different, and very particular tension: this tension between the real and the imagined *is* theater, and this is why the theater will always remain a necessity. One is not in the shadows, but responding to one's flesh and blood: in the theater, we are recreating each other.[5]

For Baldwin, it is the visceral experience of proximity to the actor and to the audience that distinguishes theatre from film and makes social change possible through what performance theorist Jill Dolan refers to as "utopian performatives." Dolan defines utopian performatives as:

> small but profound moments in which performance calls the attention of the audience in a way that lifts everyone slightly above the present, into a hopeful feeling of what the world might be like if every moment of our lives were as emotionally voluminous, generous, aesthetically striking, and intersubjectively intense…. Utopian performatives, in their doings, make palpable an affective vision of how the world might be better.[6]

What is important to note about Dolan's definition of utopian performatives is that while it suggests a "hopeful" outlook on the world through the medium of theatre, it also suggests that the utopian performative moves audiences to *action* and critical engagement. As I argue later in the essay, Baldwin's facilitation of an "affective vision" in his plays compels audiences to think critically about the world in which they live, but also potentially moves them to action to make it better.

Despite Baldwin believing theatre to be a superior form to film, he also had disdain for it – at least for commercial theatre. In his introduction to *Blues for Mister Charlie* (1964), he writes:

> I did not then, and don't now, have much respect for what goes on in the American Theatre. I am not convinced that it is a Theatre; it seems to me a series, merely, of commercial speculations, stale, repetitious, and timid. I certainly didn't see much future for me in that frame-work, and I was profoundly unwilling to risk my morale and my talent – my life – in endeavors which could only increase a level of frustration already dangerously high.[7]

Baldwin's criticism here reflects both the limitations of the theatrical form and the pandering to and placating of audiences in which commercial theatres must engage in order to stay viable. Fiction and nonfiction, two forms for which Baldwin was most notable, seemingly did not have the same restrictions.

In the introduction to *The Amen Corner* (1954), he similarly suggests that he is above American theatre: "I did not want to enter the theatre on the theatre's terms, but on mine. And I waited. And the fact that *The Amen Corner* took ten years to reach the professional stage says a great deal more about the American theatre than it says about this author."[8] While both of these statements ring of conceit, they actually reflect Baldwin's insecurity about drama as a form; he admits as much in the introduction to *The Amen Corner*: "I knew, for one thing, that very few novelists are able to write plays and I really had no reason to suppose that I could be an exception to this age-old, iron rule."[9] Baldwin would prove to be an exception to this rule, however, as he, unlike other novelists, had an extraordinary gift for dramatizing narrative in such a way that made it easily adaptable for the stage. The unconventional form that his plays embodied made them anathema to the conventions of traditional commercial theatre, particularly within the historical period in which they debuted; nonetheless, the affective response they evoke registers across generations.

Baldwin's Church Theatre: *The Amen Corner*

As Baldwin himself has noted and as his biographers have elaborated on,[10] the church provided a major influence for Baldwin from an early age; he was even called to preach at the age of fourteen. The Pentecostal tradition in which Baldwin grew up is decidedly more "dramatic" than other religious denominations, as the tenets of Pentecostalism encourage the practice of glossolalia (speaking in tongues), holy dancing, charismatic preaching, and the use of musical instruments such as horns, trumpets, tambourines, drums, pianos, and organs to accompany singing. Drawing from the theatricality of his church experiences, Baldwin felt he had received the proper training to write his first play, *The Amen Corner*:

> I was armed, I knew, in attempting to write the play, by the fact that I was born in the church. I knew that out of the ritual of the church, historically speaking, comes the act of the theatre, the *communion* which is the theatre. And I knew that what I wanted to do in the theatre was to recreate moments I remembered as a boy preacher, to involve the people, even against their will, to shake them up, and, hopefully, to change them.[11]

Baldwin's intuition here is correct, for the ritual force of the black church is deeply connected to what anthropologists like Victor Turner have theorized as the interrelatedness of religious ritual and theatre *as* ritual. Even Baldwin's use of the word "communion" relates to Turner's notion of "communitas"; this, in Turner's definition, "tends to characterize relationships between those jointly undergoing ritual transition. The bonds of communitas are anti-structural in the sense that they are undifferentiated, equalitarian, direct, extant, nonrational, existential, I-Thou...relationships."[12] Indeed, the theatricality of the black church, and specifically the black Pentecostal church of which Baldwin was a part, is evoked through ritual performance. Intuitively, Baldwin knew that the ritualistic nature of church service could provide a road map that could capture the attention of a theatre audience "to shake them up...to change them."

Baldwin had already demonstrated his ability to capture the inner workings of the black church, with both its sanctimonious trappings and its social efficacy, in *Go Tell It on the Mountain*, which took him ten years to write. Haunted by his editor's question, "What about all that come-to-Jesus stuff?" posed to him after he turned in *Mountain*, Baldwin felt compelled to try his hand at playwriting; he "knew that [he] had more to say and much, much more to discover than [he] had been able to indicate in *Mountain*."[13] *The Amen Corner*, then, allowed Baldwin to move from the representational to the presentational in order to highlight black religious ritual in a way that would call attention to its contradictions in a visceral way – through the ritual act itself. As Turner notes, during the ritual process, communities are at their most heightened, self-reflexive state, wherein "critique of the events leading up to and composing the 'crisis'" may occur.[14] For Baldwin, the ritual of theatre itself and the ritual processes of the black church reenacted therein provided a space for audiences – and particularly black audiences – to become more meditative and critical about the ways in which organized religion can be as oppressive as it is liberating. Being outside the context of the physical church and within theatre where the audience could see itself reflected on stage, Baldwin believed, offered an opportunity for that audience, as Jill Dolan suggests, to "scrutinize public meanings."[15] Thus, Baldwin drew on ritual to critique ritual.

Critics disagree about the level of effectiveness of ritual employed as a site of critique in *Mountain* and ritual as a site of critique in *The Amen Corner*. Some critics believe that the play levels a harsher critique of the black church than does *Mountain*. Carolyn Sylvander, for example, emphasizes the fact that "No member of the congregation [in *The Amen Corner*] is admirable for any reason. Most are despicable – sex-starved, ambitious, jealous, cruel."[16] Furthermore, according to Barbara K. Olson, in the play "we find no Deborah who loves sacrificially, no Elisha who exudes spiritual enthusiasm and infectious affection, and no Elizabeth who models for her son 'that patience, that endurance, that long suffering, which he read of in the Bible and found so hard to imagine.' "[17] And yet Sylvander believes that in Baldwin's attempt "to recreate the ritual of the black church as he knew it," the role of ritual in the theatre ironically served to lessen Baldwin's critique of the church.[18] David Leeming's review of the 2001 Goodman Theatre production of the play corroborates this reading when Leeming, in a slightly backhanded compliment to director Chuck Smith, states, "Chuck Smith's direction, if depending slightly too much on the gospel singing to keep the audience's attention, perhaps to the detriment of the essentially anti-church message, is sensitive and creative."[19]

The audience response that I witnessed at a production of the play directed by Ranaku Jahi at the Creative Arts Foundation in Chicago in 2012 would support both Sylvander and Leeming in that, while the black church rituals in the play are set in motion on stage in a powerful way, the fact that the audience gets swept up in them – and especially the music – somewhat undermines a critical reading of the church as an institution, namely because the "good feeling" evinced by the music produces the effect of mitigating the fact that the church condemns its own. Olson also suggests that

> The audience's involvement in the enthusiasm and bonding which Pentecostal ritual entails absorbs the impact of the critical message. And the transfiguration Baldwin brings about in his central character Margaret can to such an audience seem nothing short of a miracle: a spiritual transformation quite at odds with Baldwin's expressed criticism about the Holy Ghost's power.[20]

Arguably, the experience of the play becomes one of "going to church" – in the black vernacular sense of that phrase – rather than bearing witness to its hypocrisy and cruelty. Olson suggests that Baldwin's critique of religion in *Mountain* is compromised as well, because the "church idiom renders it as much a vindication of Christianity as an indictment."[21]

As stated earlier, critics will agree or disagree about the effectiveness of ritual as a site of critique depending on the their own aesthetic investments. Part of the issue is the difference between narrative form and dramatic form and the limits of each in terms of representation. In narrative, the exposition of plot happens mostly, though not exclusively, through description. One scene may go on for pages, providing background for how a character has arrived at a particular moment or event, or painting a picture of the place where the scene is taking place. In drama, the plot is moved forward mostly through action and rarely through description, with notable exceptions such as Greek tragedies and Shakespearean soliloquys. Indeed, a common directive to performers is "show, don't tell." When adapting a novel for the stage, or what Michael Bowman refers to as "novelizing the stage,"[22] action and description are not mutually exclusive. Because of Baldwin's own brilliance as a novelist in terms of the way he draws on dramatic form, his novels become highly adaptable for the stage and, in some ways, elide the problems of the audience getting so swept up in the ritual that they are unable to think critically.

In performance studies, adaptation is a common methodology employed to dramatize the relationship between narrators and characters. Though practiced within the discipline of oral interpretation of literature since the late 1950s "chamber theatre," as developed by Robert S. Breen at Northwestern University, became codified as an adaptation practice in the 1970s with the publication of Breen's book on the method. Breen defines chamber theatre accordingly: "Chamber Theatre is dedicated to the proposition that the ideal literary experience is one in which the simultaneity of the drama, representing the illusion of actuality (that is, social and psychological realism), may be profitably combined with the novel's narrative privilege of examining human motivation at the moment of action."[23] In practice, the privileging of the examination of human motivation occurs through chamber theatre's affiliation to Bertolt Brecht's epic theatre, which relies on alienation devices that "[destroy] theatrical illusionism and [interrupt] the pleasures of identification."[24] Such techniques in chamber theatre might include characters narrating their own actions or speaking their own dialogue tags (for example, "Put that down!" Joe screamed from the other room.) Thus, given the tenets of chamber theatre, the possibilities for providing a space for critical distance for an audience become readily available.

To draw on one brief example, I directed a chamber theatre version of "Gabriel's Prayer," Part II of *Mountain*, as a final project for a graduate directing class, focusing on the sermon around which the action of that section pivots. As in *The Amen Corner*, my adaptation of *Mountain* begins with singing. Members of the cast seated in the audience open with the song "Down by the Riverside," encouraging those around them to sing along. During the song, the actor playing Gabriel walks center stage behind a podium meant to be a pulpit, and joins in the singing, motioning for the other cast members to join him onstage. The members of the "congregation" take their seats on either side of Gabriel but face the audience. It is important to note here that the "congregation" is both inside and outside the church. In other words, they do not represent churchgoers who suffer from false consciousness and are fully accepting of religious dogma. Their sitting with and then facing the audience with their backs to Gabriel once onstage signals their "betwixt and between" status. Gabriel, on the other hand, is a synecdoche for the black church. Downstage center, directly opposite Gabriel, a female actress is elevated above the audience on a block; she is meant to represent God, yet her words are often those of Gabriel's sister Florence, arguably the most secular character in the novel, and sometimes those of the novel's omniscient narrator.

After the song ends, Gabriel begins his sermon. "God/Florence" variously interrupts the sermon by calling forth a "scene" from Gabriel's life that contradicts or demonstrates the irony of his sermon. These scenes are taken from the passage in the novel wherein Gabriel gives into his lust for Esther and has sex with her "in the white folks' kitchen." The preacher Gabriel freezes, while an actor playing a younger Gabriel and a female cast member playing Esther, who comes from the congregation, act out the scene downstage left. The sermon and its interruptions by the scene continue, depicting Gabriel's confrontation with Esther when she tells him she is pregnant with Royal, his meeting with Royal on the street, and his confrontation with Deborah about his sending Esther away after discovering that she was pregnant.

The performance concludes with Gabriel's confrontation with Florence near the end of the novel. As the congregation begins to sing "Come to Jesus," God/Florence speaks the following lines:

> Yes…we's all going to be together there. Mama, and you and me, and Deborah – and what was the name of that little girl who died? This girl was a mother, too. Look like she went North all by herself, and had her baby, and died – you ain't forgotten that girl's name, Gabriel! You ain't forgotten her name. You can't tell me that you done forgot her name. Is you going to look on her face, too? Is her name written in the Book of Life? Who is you met, Gabriel, all your Holy life long, you ain't made to drink a cup of sorrow?

The congregation's singing stops abruptly as Gabriel says, "You be careful how you talk to the Lord's anointed," to which God/Florence responds, "Where *is* your life, Gabriel? Where is it?" Gabriel begins to repeat various phrases from his conversation with God/Florence, including "I been doing the work of the Lord," "He speaks," and "He sees the heart." After each line the congregation repeats, "Where's your life, Gabriel? Where is it?" as if a call-and-response to his words. Each repetition of the line gets louder as the actors move upstage toward Gabriel, as if they are going to an altar call or to join a mob scene, while Gabriel begins to back up and eventually kneel as if in prayer. Their movement toward the altar – an act of submission to God – as juxtaposed with their critical view of Gabriel, reflects both their complicity with and resistance to church doctrine. This call-and-response dynamic reaches a crescendo when God/Florence stands and spreads her arms out to end the chant as if directing a choir and says, "If I speak with the tongues of men and of angels, but do not have love, I have become a noisy gong or a clanging cymbal."

As seen in this interpretation, the tenets of chamber theatre, which offer a director/adaptor more freedom to experiment, afforded me an opportunity to draw on Baldwin's dramatic sensibility and use of ritual while still maintaining a space for the audience to have critical distance. This adaptation of *Mountain* not only captures the black church ritual and black theatre ritual embedded in the text – through the music and the sermon – but also allows for an explicit indictment, juxtaposing those rituals with staging and scenes that amplify the hypocrisy of Gabriel and, by extension, that of the institution of the church, which he represents.

Your Blues Ain't Like Mine: *Blues for Mister Charlie*

In many ways, *The Amen Corner* is a traditional play that reflects Baldwin's confinement as a first-time playwright. While his impetus for writing the play was to elaborate more fully on race and religion in a way that he felt he could not in *Mountain*, the indictment of the church is not always fully realized. Adaptations to the stage of his novels, such as the one described above, seem to be more effective in that regard. In his second play, *Blues for Mister Charlie,* however, Baldwin seems to feel freer to experiment with dramatic form – both structurally and thematically – such that the politics of the play are explicit and engage the audience affectively, and not toward identification, but toward critical engagement.

Some critics venerate the play only because of its explicit politics, over-looking the transgressive possibilities it provides. Writing for *The Hudson Review*, theatre critic John Simon published a scathing review of the first stage production of the play on Broadway:

> Since the Negro "Protest Novel" has been around for some time, our the-atre, which nowadays follows fiction at a respectful distance, could have been expected at this point to erupt with the Negro "protest play." Accordingly, we now have on Broadway James Baldwin's *Blues for Mister Charlie.*[25]

I wish to focus on Simon's characterization of Baldwin's work as "protest" theatre, which creates an ironic twist based on Baldwin's stance on "protest" fiction. Indeed, Baldwin's biographer James Campbell writes: "Baldwin felt he could not sit silently by while his play's most politically sensitive lines were snipped out and thrown in the bin.... Anyone who reasoned with Baldwin that the loudest way to speak was not necessarily the best way, was likely to be rebutted with a louder protest still."[26]

Given Baldwin's conviction that "nothing under heaven would prevent [him] from getting this play done," almost as if it were a retribution for Evers's death, it is not surprising that the play resonates with an unrelenting black rage softened only by some of the characters' ambivalence toward whites. Still, the resemblances between *Blues* and *Native Son* persist. In a 1967 review of the play, C. W. E. Bigsby makes an explicit parallel between Baldwin's Richard Henry and Wright's Bigger Thomas:

> Baldwin's essay ["Everybody's Protest Novel"] closes with an attack on the fruitless rage of Wright's *Native Son*.... Yet as we have seen Richard's life is as much "defined by his hatred" as was Bigger Thomas's and if he becomes conscious of a more meaningful existence this awareness is never clearly motivated neither does it destroy the determinism which leads him to his death. So that Baldwin's play matches with disturbing precision his own definition of sterile protest literature.[27]

Ultimately, Bigsby believes that Baldwin's own inner rage about the events of the Civil Rights Movement at the time "betrayed him into the oversimplifications of a sociological literature which he had always consciously avoided."[28]

While Baldwin adamantly opposed the conflation of "sociology and literature," it seems inevitable that a play inspired by specific racist historical events would be "sociological" in nature. Part of the problem is that, given the historical context of the play, it is difficult for the audience to suspend disbelief. The fact that a black man is murdered by a white man and his body discarded at the outset of the play, according to Koritha Mitchell, "troubles the audience members' expectations that they have entered a space of make-believe."[29] Here, Baldwin's political agenda and his aesthetic choices create a tension that he cannot necessarily avoid; in addition, they may speak to the difficulty of rendering a theatrical portrait that would justly indict the institution of racism while also demonstrating the humanity of the very perpetrator of that injustice.

The portrayal of that humanity troubled Baldwin as he penned the white man, or the titular "Mister Charlie" – a title itself that raises question who the play is for. Baldwin writes in the note to *Blues*:

> I absolutely dreaded committing myself to writing a play – there were enough people around already telling me that I couldn't write novels – but I began to see that my fear of the form masked a much deeper fear. That fear was that I would never be able to draw a valid portrait of the murderer. In life, obviously, such people baffle and terrify me and, with one part of my mind at least, I hate them and would be willing to kill them. Yet, with another part of my mind, I am aware that no man is a villain in his own eyes. Something in the man knows – *must* know – that what he is doing is evil.[30]

Perhaps for these reasons, the white characters in the play, and particularly Parnell and Lyle, are not rendered as purely good (as with Parnell) or purely evil (as with Lyle). Yet the same can be said of the black characters, for as much as they become politicized around Richard's death, their deference to whites suggests that they, too, are ambivalent subjects in terms of how they as characters equivocate in their indignation against white racism, as well as how the audience responds to that equivocation. Part of the characters' ambivalence is undergirded by a religious "turn-the-other-cheek" ethos that reflects Baldwin's own Christian idealism.

Just as *The Amen Corner* represents his attempt to call into question the ineffectiveness of the black church against the realities of racism, *Blues* also stages both the impotence and the redemption associated with Christianity. This manifests itself, on the one hand, in Meridian's style of leading, which recalls that of Martin Luther King, Jr. when he states, "Let not our suffering endure forever. Teach us to trust the great gift of life and learn to love one another and dare to walk the earth like men."[31] On the other hand, that attempt is evident in Richard's more radical, militant approach, suggesting that of Malcolm X, as when he exclaims: "You don't own this town, you white mother-fucker.... Don't you raise that hammer. I'll take it and beat your skull to jelly."[32] Neither approach is represented in the play as sufficient, for one leaves the status quo in place, whereas the other leads to death.

This dichotomy is also reflected in the staging and structure of the play itself, which have led some critics to view it as unsuccessful. According to Joe Weixlmann, "the play stages poorly" and thus "[i]t is Baldwin's imperfect sense of stagecraft, not his rhetoric, which makes *Blues for Mister Charlie* a second-rate play."[33] It is not only the staging that prompt critics to doom the play to failure; in addition, Baldwin's use of flashbacks in which the protagonist reappears, despite having been murdered in the opening scene, as well as the long monologues that seem too erudite to come from some of the characters' mouths and the switch to non-realism in Act III, all contribute to this assessment.

Contemporary critics, however, argue that there is something more at work in this play that has escaped earlier critics. They argue that, in fact, Baldwin was challenging the culture of commercial theatre-going at a time when audiences were never asked to think critically about their own complicity in oppression or to experience anything less than collective catharsis. Shonni Enelow, for example, argues that despite its flaws in structure, *Blues* "sparked a searching reflection on the difficulties intrinsic to the performance of racial difference in a theatrical culture that insists on identification."[34] Enelow indexes here Baldwin's disavowal of commercial theatre's pandering to white liberal audiences who were accustomed to "race" plays wherein they could come and witness a downtrodden black person for whom they could feel sorry and then leave the theatre not feeling implicated in the racism the character experienced. On the other hand, Baldwin was also concerned with black audiences who might identify too easily with victimhood without thinking critically about the ways in which black rage is sometimes misdirected or destructive. But in order to push both white and black audiences to understand their complicity in the hegemony of race, while at the same time waging a critique of racism, Baldwin had to move beyond the traditional conventions of commercial theatre such as uncritical identification. He attempts this move through the use of non-realist dramatic structure and staging.

Baldwin's portrayal of the two characters at the center of the play, Richard Henry and Lyle Britten, demonstrate how he interrupts complete identification with or vilification of either. Lyle's murder of Richard and dumping of his body at the opening of the play set up these two characters as the archetypal hero and villain, and do so along racial lines. Typically, such a characterization would solicit identification with the victim of racial violence and disavowal of the perpetrator. Baldwin complicates this identification through the use of flashbacks and seemingly didactic staging. In the process, he reveals more about Richard and Lyle – the former revealed to be a fallible martyr and the latter a pitiable victimizer. Indeed, all of the characters in the play resist identification because none are totally sympathetic. The audience, therefore, cannot be passive in its spectatorship; rather, it must work through the complexity of race, as the characters themselves must do. By disallowing white liberal audiences to take the easy way out by only sympathizing with victimized blacks, and disallowing blacks to only see whites as victimizers, Baldwin, according to Enelow, leaves the audience with "political potentiality: the possibility that new kinds of identification could produce new kinds of alliance."[35] That "alliance" could not be possible without Baldwin's creation of black and white characters who resist total identification and therefore "encourage audience members to do the intellectual work of pushing past social categories."[36]

Moreover, Baldwin also experimented with staging. The staging of BLACKTOWN and WHITETOWN – the two sections of town designated in *Blues for Mister Charlie* – while seemingly reflective of a novice playwright, actually represents a brilliant move to call into question the whole notion of race. The stage directions read accordingly:

> Multiple set, the skeleton of which, in the first two acts is the Negro Church and, in the third act, the courthouse…. The church is divided by an aisle…. This

aisle functions as the division between WHITETOWN and BLACKTOWN. The action among the blacks takes place on one side of the stage, and the action among the whites on the opposite side of the stage – which is to be remembered during the third act, which takes place of course, in a segregated courtroom.[37]

Contrary to Weixlmann and other critics' reading of Baldwin's staging as reflective of poor playwriting, the literal nature of the staging, paradoxically, functions metaphorically. In other words, the staging dichotomy of sacred *rather than* secular and black *rather than* white reinforces visually the tensions between the law of the Heavenly Father (the black church) and the law of Mister Charlie (the courthouse), as well as that between the races. Moreover, BLACKTOWN and WHITETOWN are a part of the larger mythical setting of the play, "Plaguetown, U.S.A." and the plague, according to Baldwin, is race.[38] The nonrealistic staging attempts to call attention both to how race is a construct under which we all suffer, and to how racism is a material consequence that enforces racial segregation and oppression – for instance, BLACKTOWN and WHITETOWN, lynching, Jim Crow, and so forth.

The pivot to non-realism also allowed Baldwin more freedom in staging, allowing him to juxtapose conflicting ideologies, offer ironic commentary, and provoke the audience to engage issues of race differently. The potential of such a method suggests a deeply politically engaged production that can also provide a meta-commentary on events of the past as if they have occurred in the present. As Mitchell argues: "Baldwin designs a play in ways that merge space, place, and time, creating a layered experience that never pretends that the present can be separated from the past or even that spaces can be meaningfully differentiated when they have been shaped by the same history."[39] I am struck, for instance, by how the play is "haunted" by Richard's presence in flashbacks throughout the play, in the same way that the memory of many lynched and unjustly murdered black men haunt us today. Meridian's speech to Parnell in Act I is chilling in that it evokes the sentiments of countless black fathers who have lost their sons to racist violence. Indeed, the conversation between Parnell and Meridian eerily restages the division between those who believed that George Zimmerman was simply "standing his ground" and those who believed that seventeen-year-old Trayvon Martin was killed in cold blood:

> MERIDIAN: He didn't say things *I* longed to say. Maybe it was because he was my son. I didn't care what he felt about white people. I just wanted him to live, to have his own life. There's something you don't understand about being black, Parnell. If you're a black man, with a black son, you have to forget all about white people and concentrate on trying to save your child.

That's why I let him stay up North. I was wrong, I failed, I failed. Lyle walked him up the road and killed him.

PARNELL: We don't *know* Lyle killed him. And Lyle denies it.

MERIDIAN: Of course, he denies it – what do you mean, we don't *know* Lyle killed him?

PARNELL: We *don't* know – all we can say is that it looks that way. And circumstantial evidence is a tricky thing.[40]

A tricky thing indeed, as we know that more often than not the law of Mister Charlie will prevail.

Thus, while Baldwin's politics in the play are overt, implicating him in his own critique of "protest fiction," his break from mainstream theatrical conventions actually provide him a better way to engage the audience – and implicate them – in the social dilemma of race relations – both in the 1960s and today. While the WHITETOWN and BLACKTOWN courthouse quite literally stages the racial divide between black and white, the non-realist effect, resembling a Greek chorus, that the division evokes reminds the audience that the events are both real and fictional – what *really* happened and our *perception* of what happened.

While critics and even Baldwin himself were often dubious about Baldwin's talents as a playwright, the success or failure of his plays cannot be measured by their adherence to conventional aesthetic forms alone. Both plays, and the adaptation of many of his novels, speak to Baldwin's ability to capture in dramatic fashion the complexities of race, religion, and sexuality. If he had to buck traditional conventions – theatrical, literary, or otherwise – so be it. Indeed, there is nothing conventional about the story of race relations, religion, and sexuality in the twenty-first century. Baldwin understood this and refused to be confined by generic aesthetic choices to tell those stories so that he could speak more provocatively about the complex matrix of race, religion, and the human condition – onstage and off.

NOTES

1 See for example, C. W. E. Bigsby, "The Committed Writer: James Baldwin as Dramatist," *Twentieth Century Literature* 13.1 (April 1967), 39–48; John Simon, "Theatre Chronicle," *The Hudson Review* 17.3 (Autumn 1964), 421–30; and Joe Weixlmann, "Staged Segregation: Baldwin's *Blues for Mister Charlie* and O'Neil's *All God's Chillum Got Wings*," *Black American Literature Forum* 11.1 (Spring 1977), 35–6.

2 Baldwin's nontraditional approach to theatre was not unlike that of other black playwrights writing during the 1950s and 1960s, such as Ed Bullins, Adrienne Kennedy, and LeRoi Jones (a.k.a. Amiri Baraka).

3 *The Amen Corner* in particular has been produced quite frequently in the past several years at the following venues: Olivier Theatre in London, (June 4–August

14, 2013); African American Performing Arts Community Theatre in Miami (February 20–March 17, 2013); eta Creative Arts Foundation in Chicago (September 20–October 21, 2012); Penumbra Theatre in Minneapolis (May 5–June 17, 2012); and Hattiloo Theatre in Memphis (April 19–May 6, 2012).

4 James Baldwin, *Go Tell It on the Mountain* (New York: Laurel, 1952), p. 39.

5 James Baldwin, "The Devil Finds Work," in Toni Morrison (ed.), *James Baldwin: Collected Essays* (New York: The Library of America, 1998), pp. 500, 501.

6 Jill Dolan, *Utopia in Performance: Finding Hope at the Theater* (Ann Arbor: University of Michigan Press, 1995), pp. 5–6.

7 James Baldwin, *Blues for Mister Charlie* (originally published 1964), (New York: Vintage Books, 1995), pp. xiii–xiv.

8 James Baldwin, *The Amen Corner* (originally published 1954), (New York: Vintage Books, 1998), p. xvii.

9 Ibid., p. 11.

10 See for example, James Campbell, *Talking at the Gates: A Life of James Baldwin* (Berkeley: University of California Press, 1991), and David Leeming, *James Baldwin: A Biography* (New York: Knopf, 1994).

11 Baldwin, *The Amen Corner*, p. xvi.

12 Victor Turner, *Dramas, Fields, and Metaphors: Symbolic Action in Human Society* (Ithaca: Cornell University Press, 1974), p. 274.

13 Baldwin, *The Amen Corner*, p. xv.

14 Turner, *Dramas, Fields, and Metaphors*, p. 41.

15 Dolan, *Utopia in Performance*, p. 6.

16 Carolyn Wedin Sylvander, *James Baldwin* (New York: Ungar, 1980), p. 96.

17 Barbara K. Olson, "'Come-to-Jesus Stuff' in James Baldwin's *Go Tell It on the Mountain* and *The Amen Corner*," *African American Review* 31.2 (Summer, 1997), 297.

18 Sylvander, *James Baldwin*, p. 91.

19 David Leeming, "Review of *The Amen Corner* by James Baldwin directed by Chuck Smith," *Journal of Religion and Health* 40.3 (Fall, 2001), 391–2.

20 Olson, p. 301.

21 Ibid.

22 Michael Bowman, "'Novelizing' the Stage: Chamber Theatre after Breen and Bakhtin," *Text and Performance Quarterly* 15.1 (January 1995), 1–23.

23 Robert S. Breen, *Chamber Theatre* (Englewood Cliffs, NJ: Prentice, 1978), p. 5.

24 Bowman, "'Novelizing' the Stage," p. 4.

25 John Simon, "Theatre Chronicle," *The Hudson Review* 17.3 (Autumn 1964), 421.

26 James Campbell, *Talking at the Gates: A Life of James Baldwin* (Berkeley: University of California Press, 1991), p. 196.

27 C. W. E. Bigsby, "The Committed Writer: James Baldwin as Dramatist," *Twentieth Century Literature* 13.1 (April 1967), 46.

28 Ibid.

29 Koritha Mitchell, "James Baldwin, Performance Theorist, Sings the *Blues for Mister Charlie*," *American Quarterly* 64.1 (2012), 49.

30 Baldwin, *Blues for Mister Charlie*, p. xiv.

31 Ibid., p. 76.

32 Ibid., p. 80.

33 Joe Weixlmann, "Staged Segregation," p. 35.

34 Shonni Enelow, "The Method and the Means: James Baldwin at the Actors Studio," *Theatre Survey* 53.1 (April 2012), 87.

35 Enelow, p. 102.

36 Mitchell, p. 47.

37 Baldwin, *Blues for Mister Charlie*, p. 1.

38 Ibid., p. xv.

39 Ibid.

40 Ibid., pp. 40–1.

6

DANIELLE C. HEARD

Baldwin's Humor

Baldwin's Double Act

The 2005 DVD release of Horace Ové's film *Baldwin's Nigger* (1969), part of the British Film Institute's Black World initiative, marks a ripe occasion for reflection upon what many of us know, yet rarely discuss outright, as James Baldwin's humor. The short black-and-white film documents Baldwin's visit, along with comedian and Civil Rights activist Dick Gregory, to the West Indian Student Centre in Kensington, London during the tumultuous year 1969. This was one year removed from the assassination of Martin Luther King, Jr.; two from the 12th Street Riot in Detroit; two from the publication of the *Black Power Manifesto* by the Universal Coloured People's Association; six from the publication of *The Fire Next Time*; five from the publication of Gregory's autobiography, *Nigger*; and waist-deep in Lyndon B. Johnson's escalation of the Vietnam War. Urged by recent years' cataclysmal events, Baldwin's reflections on black diasporic identities in relation to cosmopolitanism, black power, and global anti-colonial battles against the "white European Christian industrial drama" not only rivet the audience to their chairs, but also draw nearly as many laughs as Gregory's own characteristic series of darkly exigent, politicized quips. So rich in comic elements is Baldwin's delivery – a combination of satiric analysis, sarcastic wit, and dramatic embodied gestures – that in one instance he prefaces a point of drop-dead seriousness by insisting, "literally – now this is not a figure of speech." Such a disclaimer only heightens the awareness of his audience, and that of the viewer of the film, of precisely the comic mode of engagement that he has established in his address – a comic mode that nonetheless maintains the prophetic sense of urgency for change as expressed in *The Fire Next Time*'s apocalyptic framing of the racial crisis in the United States. Impressed by his friend's speech and its ability to captivate, charm, and arouse regular intervals of laughter, Gregory japes, "You're a very groovy speaker, man, I didn't know that!…'cause you're good at show business, I guess I can go home and write me another book."

The off-camera buildup to this moment tells the story of an evolving activist partnership between Baldwin and Gregory that blurred the boundaries between social criticism and stand-up comedy in the public sphere, particularly at the site of civil rights activism. Gregory's reputation as a cultural and social critic is indebted to his public interactions with Baldwin. Baldwin lacks a reputation for being a humorist – a reputation that I hope will accrue as a result of this essay – yet Baldwin picked up as much from interacting with comedians like Gregory as the comedian honed his social criticism alongside the celebrated author. Baldwin and Gregory originally knew each other in the Greenwich Village scene in the 1950s and 1960s. Both were part of a clique of black artists who socialized, collaborated, and performed for each other at venues like the Village Gate nightclub, where comedians such as Gregory, Bill Cosby, and Richard Pryor got their starts.[1] By the mid-1980s Baldwin felt compelled to defend Gregory's character in his nonfictional *The Evidence of Things Not Seen* (1985) for some of Gregory's infamous actions and more controversial statements in the prior decade.[2]

Despite not being the most intimate of friends (according to *Evidence*), Baldwin and Gregory were represented in the press during the 1960s as something of a double act. Their celebrity profile lent visibility to the 1963 march to register voters in Selma, Alabama, organized by the Student Nonviolent Coordinating Committee.[3] The two were part of a circle of black celebrity activists from the arenas of entertainment and the arts – many having passed through the aforementioned Village scene – who toured together and collectively interposed between the national black freedom struggle for civil rights and the public sphere. This group gave a familiar face to the hotbed "race question" for non-black Americans and observers around the world; they appeared together in mainstream national and international press coverage of benefits for SNCC, the SCLC, and other civil rights organizations, on roundtables on the nightly news, and in televised debates with white celebrities, public intellectuals, and politicians. This circle was also called upon to appear at local events organized by black community and student groups – outside the purview of the mainstream media. Sidney Poitier, Harry Belafonte, Nina Simone, Lorraine Hansberry, Ossie Davis, Ruby Dee, Bill Cosby, Jackie "Moms" Mabley, Lena Horne, and others could often be found on stage, radio, television, and film together with Baldwin and Gregory, fundraising for, participating in, and media-translating local and national actions toward black freedom.

As their visibility in the movement garnered national recognition, Baldwin and Gregory were increasingly acknowledged, both by the media and high-profile politicians, as an activist tag-team who straddled the celebrity world and the Civil Rights Movement. For example, Gregory introduced Baldwin to assistant attorney general for civil rights Robert Kennedy and Burke Marshall, also prompting an unpublicized meeting in which Baldwin and his multiracial entourage of civil rights activists (many of whom were artists) discussed the 1963 crisis in Birmingham with Kennedy.[4] In July of 1963, *Look* magazine featured a story about Gregory and Baldwin, along with Martin Luther King, Jr. and Medgar Evers, and their involvement in Mississippi protests.[5] The following year, they appeared together onstage at the March on Washington for Jobs and Freedom. Literary connections were noted as well: in a review of Gregory's *Nigger*, Gilbert Millstein wrote that the autobiography "is at once as moving, and, in its way, as terrifying as James Baldwin's 'The Fire Next Time' [sic]" published the year before.[6] Indeed, Horace Ové's title for his film references not only the powerful moment when the eloquent orator traces the origin of his name to "Baldwin's nigger," but likely also alludes to Gregory's own book, given its similarly biting autobiographical analysis of race relations and its urgent call for the abolition of race discrimination through a radical ethical shift.

Ové's film juxtaposes Baldwin's address – much longer, and as colorful as it is importunate – with Gregory's briefer one. This juxtaposition, compounded by the comedian's confession that it would be hard to top his friend's act, brings attention to the pair as a recognizable double act where the roles of "funny man" and "straight man" constantly shift. That Baldwin as "funny man" renders so ostensibly in a documentary film highlights the importance of viewing Baldwin's live *and* literary performances through the prism of comedy. These performances from what Caryl Phillips would refer to as the second, public "chapter" of Baldwin's career depend upon the comic dramatization of tropes attached to his author-celebrity persona.[7] Gregory's presence beside his friend at the podium visually invites us to consider the centrality of comic maneuvers to Baldwin's calculable ability to relate to others across seemingly impenetrable cultural barriers.

In the tumultuous 1960s, Baldwin's prophetic oral and written eloquence achieved its trademark apocalyptic urgency. But, as Gregory's quip suggests, Baldwin also deployed a sophisticated sense of humor during this same period. Moreover, beyond the "public chapter" of Baldwin's career, many scholars, biographers, and friends underscore the fact of Baldwin's humor. Usually acknowledged merely as a tangential effect of his persona, in fact, his comic style warrants serious critical attention, especially given recent studies of black humor in literature and performance.[8] In this essay, I make a case for Baldwin's humor not through instances of humor in his fiction, but rather by examining his self-styled public image as represented in memoir, interviews, and televised appearances. What Nicholas Boggs characterizes as Baldwin's "metaphoric masturbation" contributes to a framework for thinking about the legibility of sarcasm and embodied slapstick – particularly though facial expression – in Baldwin's first-person writings.[9] In other words, readers can lift irony, parody, wit, sarcasm, and the sound of laughter from a humorous cadence in Baldwin's writing that might slip under the radar if not for Baldwin's metaphorical references to his own embodied presence. Baldwin's embodied humor indexes a handful of recognizable masturbatory tropes: the *Schadenfreude* of witnessing the encounters of the bumblingly innocent queer child with a terribly shocking and surprising world; a gestural play with the features of what Baldwin would constantly refer to as his ugliness – especially his "big" eyes; a campy channeling of Hollywood divas and the theatre of the black church; and the "funny" sound of the affected black cosmopolitan accent.

Baldwin's Laughter

In Baldwin's essayistic writing and oratory episodes, he often claims that he intends to "dramatize" a particular psychosocial or psychohistorical phenomenon for his readers' or audience's understanding. In his essay "The Creative Process," he explains his vision for the artist:

> The artist is distinguished from all other responsible actors in society – the politicians, legislators, educators, and scientists – by the fact that he is his own test tube, his own laboratory, working according to very rigorous rules, however unstated these may be, and cannot allow any consideration to supersede his responsibility to reveal all that he can possibly discover concerning the mystery of the human being. Society must accept some things as real; but he must always know *that visible reality hides a deeper one, and that all our action and achievement rests on things unseen.* Society must assume that it is stable, *but the artist must know, and he must let us know that there is nothing stable under heaven.*[10]

I find it useful to compare Baldwin's statements about the artist's role of revealing the depth of reality underneath the surface – along with his regular stated mission to "dramatize" – with philosopher Kenneth Burke's "dramatism." Burke theorized that the comic method, culminating in what he termed "dramatism," was a means of analyzing language and thought with the purpose of exposing human foibles and transforming "stupidity" into "maximum consciousness."[11] Dramatism as a method relies upon comic action, rather than explanation, to persuade an audience to come around to the truth of a matter. While Baldwin never cited Burke as an influence, he nonetheless often stated his intent to "dramatize" a problem rather than to explicate it.[12] Baldwin's sense of the term "dramatize" is not unlike Burke's.

To think of Baldwin broadly as a dramatist in the Burkean sense – as we also recall the influence of Dick Gregory upon the artist's public intellectualism – prompts us to recognize a particular angle of Baldwin's humor, one that is central to his self-conception as an artist. Baldwin certainly expresses what Burke calls "the feeling for the negative" inherent in the comic arts:

> The appreciation of surprise, as a formal device, implies a feeling for the negative (since the reader is led to expect one outcome, and a *different* outcome is felt as its *negation*). The feeling for the negative, in this sense, is also implicit in the comic enjoyment of incongruity, as the comic art embodies the thou-shalt-not's of social proprieties by devices that disrupt them. We thus "glimpse the missing link" between man as the rational animal and man as the laughing animal (hyena excepted), since laughter is seen to be one with the "reason" of "conscience" and the sheer nay-saying or no-understanding of verbalization.[13]

The following dramatized episode described by Baldwin in an interview suggests his appreciation of the comic's ability to produce negative feeling, and of the revelation that laughter can produce:

> A cop would come around and chase us off. He was a big cop, a big, beefy man. And I noticed that he never chased the white kids, he always chased me and my brother. At one point I turned round and said: "Why you never chase the white kids, why do you chase us?" And he said: "You stand out better against the daylight." He said that! I started to laugh, and he laughed. And I can't explain it, it was a curious moment. He was about eighteen feet tall, and I was smaller than I am now. And I couldn't stop laughing, and he couldn't stop laughing, and that was the last time he chased us. I'll never forget that…it was my first memory of bewilderment…*something very healthy happened that moment*: he moved himself out of that monolith of white people. The proof being his conduct subsequently, because he did not have to go that far.[14]

Aggressive racial jokes that deal in minstrelesque caricatures of African physiognomy – most notably, exaggerations of the darkness of black skin – circulated in Baldwin's Harlem neighborhood and his country's public consciousness, and bore the power to hurt. Yet both victim and aggressor are unconsciously aware of the absurdity of racial caricature. The child Baldwin's uncontrollably insubordinate laughter at the centuries-old joke rehearsing racial caricature catches the cop off guard so that both can revel in the shared recognition of an absurdity, expressed through the total-body experience of laughter. After that recognition, the cop evolves a bit. In short, the child Baldwin's outburst of laughter at the hackneyed racial joke – intended to hurt rather than entertain the young boy – exposes the whole darkly, hilariously absurd charade of America's obsession with race.

Baldwin narratively dramatizes what Glenda Carpio calls the "power that laughter has in the face of the absurd yet painful distortions produced by racism," which she notes is a prevalent theme in Ralph Ellison's fiction and criticism.[15] Not accidentally, this episode recounted by Baldwin resembles many an Ellisonian moment of dramatized racial revelation surrounded by laughter – as Ralph Ellison's theories of the comic were deeply indebted to Burke's.[16] As Donald Pease notes, "Burke's theory of symbolic action would subsequently become the framework for analyzing the social problems that Ellison would address in his fiction and essays."[17] Furthermore, his theory of the comic is greatly influenced by incongruity theory – in particular Burke's concept of "perspective by incongruity," with a notion of the grotesque akin to those of Charles Baudelaire and Mikhail Bakhtin – such that comedy performs the function of turning the world on its head to gain clarity of vision.[18] Indeed, in *The Fire Next Time* (1963), Baldwin describes himself as similar to the boy Bliss in Ellison's posthumously published novel, *Juneteenth*; he complies with Reverend Hickman's aim to trick his congregation with the performance of a miracle: "Being in the pulpit is like being in a theatre; I was behind the scenes and knew how the illusion was worked."[19]

Burke's notion of dramatism explored in terms of race opens up Ellison's career-long celebration of the potential of comic "masquerade" – both the occasionally benign mode of social engagement in a theatrical climate, and the most logical and effective mode of political action to undo the what he calls the "chaos" of the community. In "Harlem is Nowhere" (1964), he writes,

> Life becomes a masquerade; exotic costumes are worn every day. Those who cannot afford to hire a horse wear riding habits; others who could not afford a hunting trip or who seldom attend sporting events carry shooting sticks. For this is a world in which the major energy of the imagination goes not into creating works of art, but to overcome the frustrations of social discrimination.[20]

And, drawing on W. B. Yeats, he writes in "An Extravagance of Laughter" (1985), "'masking' is more than the adoption of a disguise. Rather it is a playing upon possibility, a strategy through which the individual projects a self-elected identity and makes of himself a 'work of art.' "[21]

I argue that such a critical celebration of the potential of masking provides a primary framework for identifying the dynamics of what can best be described as Baldwin's comic masquerade – one that borders on the forms of masquerade found in queer camp, the theatrics of the black church, and the history of black comic entertainment. I argue that we should take young

Baldwin's cop episode – his effective, albeit unrefined, comic interruption of the dominant discourse on racial difference on the streets of Harlem – as the founding drama that undergirds his first-person writing and speech. This approach allows us to understand that Baldwin's rhetorical strategy hinges upon feeling for the negative, upon masking and a productive strategy, and generally upon trying to make us laugh.[22]

Baldwin's Accent

With an understanding of Baldwin's artistic motive to reveal "things unseen," deep beneath our "visible reality," through the dramatization enabled by comic masquerade, one can observe Baldwin's breakdown of binaries between "real" and "fake," emphasizing instead the salience of performance in social relationships; this also evokes Ellison's celebration of masquerade as "playing upon possibility" to experience freedom from expectation. Statements such as the link between theatre and pulpit in *The Fire Next Time* point to Baldwin's familiarity with what he calls the "hustle" of social relations and the "hoax" of what we are told to believe. In "Alas, Poor Richard," Baldwin unveils the dynamics of intra-racial masquerade, particularly while in exile abroad:

> Negroes know about each other what can here be called family secrets, and this means that one Negro, if he wishes, can "knock" the other's "hustle" – can give his game away. It is still not possible to overstate the price a Negro pays to climb out of obscurity.... Therefore, one "exceptional" Negro watches another "exceptional" Negro in order to find out if he knows how vastly unsuccessful and bitterly funny the hoax has been. Alliances, in the great cocktail party of the white man's world, are formed, almost purely, on this basis, for if both of you can laugh, you have got a lot to laugh about. On the other hand, if only one of you can laugh, one of you, inevitably, is laughing at the other.[23]

While this passage presents a critical take on Wright's "hustle," it nonetheless wryly suggests that Baldwin, too, had a hustle going on in the self-styled performances of the "exceptional Negro" abroad. The passage evokes some of the innovative devices of racial masquerade fashioned by the small set of black cosmopolitan artists of Baldwin's generation who made themselves a "work of art."

Specifically, I am interested in examining the affected accent of Baldwin's speaking voice, with its audible traces of his expatriations in Paris, London, Switzerland, and Istanbul, and its punctuating vocal fry that is more sassy than campy (insofar as it is more brazen than self-deprecatingly parodic, yet nonetheless queerly playful with gender expectations). Indeed, this self-fashioned accessory of Baldwin's comic masquerade is worthy of appreciative analysis. Baldwin's voice sounds something like what Irene Redfield of the novel *Passing* hears in her friend Clare Kendry's performance of racial passing: "Surely she'd heard those husky tones somewhere before…a voice remotely suggesting England."[24] As Joshua Miller explains of this passage, "In the casual conversation the two women pragmatically dissect the techniques of passing, recontextualizing acts of strategic self-masking and voice alteration."[25] This moment of *Passing*, and Miller's analysis of it, helps explore the "dirty secret" of voice alteration as related to Baldwin's dramatic self-fashioning – what might relate more broadly to what Nathaniel Mackey would call "black linguistic and musical practices that accent variance, variability."[26]

One high-profile attempt to expose Baldwin's vernacular as a performance (albeit in an unappreciative spirit) came during a televised debate at Cambridge University in 1965 between Baldwin and William Buckley, the face of the U.S. conservative movement, on the question, "Has the American Dream Been Achieved at the Expense of the American Negro?" After Baldwin's powerful, personal, and prophetic analysis of race in America – far exceeding the scope of the debate's framing question and eliciting a historically unprecedented standing ovation from the Cambridge Union attendance – Buckley faced an uphill battle. Resorting, ignominiously, to character attack, he questioned whether Baldwin was speaking in a different accent than the "British accent he used tonight" when he composed his "threat" against America in *The Fire Next Time*. Meanwhile, the camera caught the intense, brazen look that Baldwin propelled in Buckley's direction. His eyes expressed attitude, popping in Buckley's direction, punctuated by Baldwin's skeptically wrinkled brow and pursed lips, calling out the ridiculousness of the conservative's accusation. Teaching Buckley about the art of black linguistic variance exceeded the limitations of verbal explanation; at that moment only facial theatre would do.

However, by 1979, Baldwin must have thought that an extended lesson about the nuances of black verbal communication was due to white Americans like Buckley. From France, Baldwin wrote to white America via a *New York Times* op-ed titled "If Black English Isn't a Language, Then Tell Me, What Is?" In it, he defends the legitimacy of "black English" as a distinct language that arises, as all language does, from distinct experience. In this meditation on spoken language and its relation to cultural difference, personal identity, and politics, Baldwin implicitly addressed his own self-fashioned cosmopolitan accent, which bore traces of his Harlem origins, Baptist Church rearing, expatriation in Europe and the Middle East, identification with interwar Hollywood divas, and brushes with gay camp. This is the very accent in which he wrote the op-ed while simultaneously claiming black English as his native tongue. Underscoring the implicit commentary on places speech derive from is, among other things, his postmark: "St. Paul-de-Vence, France."

With this, Baldwin performs a simultaneous identification and disidentification with black English, such that his reader hears the dissonance between the author's cadence, diction, and inflection and that of the subject he describes.[27] We hear Baldwin's accent first, of course – while also feeling him cut his eye at us – in the sassy title of his op-ed, "If Black English Isn't a Language, Then Tell Me, What Is?" The dissonance is compounded when the author dips into black vernacular. Baldwin flags this code-switching when he says, "To open your mouth in England is (if I may use black English) to 'put your business in the street'."[28] He then lists black English terms that have been lifted into white English (for instance, "jazz," "sock it to me," "let it all hang out," "right on," "get down") and explains their "funky" origins in hard-knocks experience: "We *were* funky, baby, like *funk* was going out of style."

Baldwin's op-ed aimed to defend not only the legitimacy of black English, at the time not fully recognized as a speech system by most linguists, but also to defend his own tonal inflections from the black cultural nationalist tendency to police black accent.[29] Within the discourse of black cultural nationalism – the movement responsible for attempting to formalize black English within public education – the emphasis on a singular idea of blackness was defined by patriarchal and heteronormative black. This was a masculinity that implicitly and often explicitly excluded women, gays, lesbians, bisexuals, gender queers, and those who too overtly embraced white American or European culture.[30] Thus, when Baldwin wrote that "Language, also, far more dubiously, is meant to define the other – and, in this case, the other is refusing to be defined by a language that has never been able to recognize him," he disidentified with two authenticating logics. Yet, he disidentified while defending black English – both the one seeking formal recognition and his own unique style – as a strategic response to linguistic othering.[31]

In describing the double joke played on different communities of language police, the essay overflows with hilarity, even as it offers serious commentary on how we create language and phonate strategically for our own purposes. In fact, the message about strategic language creation can only be heard through the joke played by the essay itself, via Baldwin's witty, sassy, and subversively camp performance of his invented – albeit no less "real" – speaking voice. He essentially reveals his own strategy, a strategy disguised as an explanation of "black English," when he writes, "People evolve a language in order to describe and thus control their circumstances, or in order not to be submerged by a reality that they cannot articulate. They each have very different realities to articulate, or control." This evolved language "reveals the private identity, and connects one with, or divorces one from, the larger, public, or communal identity."[32] Alongside Muñoz's theory of disidentification, we can detect in these lines a survival strategy.

Baldwin's deft code-switching in this op-ed – voicing his invented accent and also dipping into "black English," while speaking both to white America and the black cultural nationalist agenda – is sustained by a sound resembling what Daphne Brooks describes as "sonic cosmopolitanism" – the purring sass of singer and actress Eartha Kitt.[33] In Kitt's memoir the eccentric songstress comments on her accent, which "someone once described to me as Continental, a British accent with American and French influence. How I could possibly learned this from South Carolina and Harlem is totally a mystery to me, as mysterious as that strange influence I had over my classroom and assembly audiences."[34] In this statement, Kitt plays innocent and then, in a comic reversal almost buried at the end of her sentence, unveils a trickster who not only understands the full mystery of her accent, but also knows, almost wickedly, how to cast a spell on audiences with it. Such an accent can be heard performed by a handful of international black divas, including Baldwin's good friend Nina Simone – and certainly, we could add Larsen's Clare Kendry. Baldwin's speech, too, identifies him with this particular placeless tribe. "Language," he writes, "incontestably, reveals the speaker," and thus Baldwin steps out from behind the mask.

Baldwin's Face

Another "masturbatory" trope of Baldwin's embodied humor involves subversively comical play with the features of what Baldwin would constantly refer to as his "ugly" face – especially his "big" eyes. Scholar Julius Lester wrote that "[he] looks as if he were sculpted in flesh rather than merely being born of it."[35] Nat Hentoff, describing "Baldwin's furtive glancing back at one of a pool of reporters at Downey's on Eighth Ave," wrote, "His eyes intent on his questioner, Baldwin broke into a characteristic smile compounded by irony and challenge."[36] Hollie West wrote: "His eyes, always big, look as if they are about to explode."[37] In a review of Howard Simon's play *James Baldwin: A Soul on Fire* (1999), David Dewitt remarked that Charles Reese was well cast, resembling Baldwin "with large eyes that suggest a singular vision of the human experience."[38]

Such attention to Baldwin's face, especially his eyes, follows Baldwin's own lead. In an interview, he revealed how his stepfather continually attempted to lower Baldwin's self-esteem and belief in his ability to accomplish his dreams: "Because I was black, because I was little, because I was ugly. He made me ugly. I used to put pennies on my eyes to make them go back."[39] In "The Devil Finds Work" (1976), Baldwin unforgettably reflects on his self-described "ugly" visage:

> My father said, during all the years I lived with him, that I was the ugliest boy he had ever seen, and I had absolutely no reason to doubt him. But it was not my father's hatred of *my* frog-eyes which hurt me, this hatred proving, in time, to be rather more resounding than real: I have my mother's eyes. When my father called me ugly, he was not attacking me so much as he was attacking my mother.[40]

Yet later in "The Devil Finds Work," Baldwin remarks that such internalized insults, strangely enough, enabled a kinship between himself and a Hollywood diva, thanks to an outing to the movies with his supportive and racially progressive white teacher, Bill (Osilla) Miller:

> So here, now, was Bette Davis, on that Saturday afternoon, in close-up, over a champagne glass, pop-eyes popping. I was astounded. I had caught my father, not in a lie, but in an infirmity. For, here, before me, after all, was a *movie star: white:* and if she was white and a movie star, she was *rich:* and she was *ugly*...out of the bedroom, out of loyalty to my mother, probably, and also because I sensed something menacing and unhealthy (for me, certainly) in the face on the screen, I gave Davis's skin the dead white greenish cast of something crawling from under a rock, but I was held, just the same, by the tense intelligence of the forehead, the disaster of the lips: and when she moved, she moved just like a nigger.... It was to take a longer time than that before I would cry in anyone's arms, and a long long long long time before I would begin to realize what I myself was doing with my enormous eyes – or vice versa.... I had discovered that my infirmity, or infirmities, might be forged into weapons.

"Mocking or making light of one's own anatomy," notes Mel Watkins in *On the Real Side,* his history of black comedy in the United States, "is not unusual among comedians: Bob Hope's elongated, sloped nose serves as a constant source of one-liners in his stage act, and the late Marty Feldman used his saucer-like eyes as a central element in his comic repertoire. Comedians, after all, are clowns, and for a clown physical abnormalities are just another means of eliciting a laugh."[41] I argue that Baldwin, taught by his father that he and his "frog eyes" were ugly, developed a comic trope around his "physical abnormalities," training those who paid attention to him – his vast, doting, international audience – to associate the embodied or literary deployment of those eyes as a signal of (tragi)comic irony. Not only did Baldwin present characters like John Grimes, or autobiographical passages like the one above; he also frequently referenced his anatomy extemporaneously in public appearances. Responding to British journalist Peregrine

Worsthorne in a televised interview regarding police brutality in Harlem and West Oakland, Baldwin emphasizes, "I'm telling you what I have seen with these own, with my own, big eyes."[42] The eyes in particular provided a convenient anatomical reference point for Baldwin given the historically ambivalent role of eyes in black comic entertainment. They featured, for example, in the performances of celebrated comic performers like Lincoln Perry, Mantan Moreland, and Josephine Baker, and were also fetishized within stereotypical portrayals of black physiognomy.

As such, Baldwin was able to use his face as bait to trap racist looks. In *No Name in the Street* (1972) he recalls,

> London was reacting to its accelerating racial problem and compounding the disaster by denying that it had one. My famous face created a certain kind of hazard – or hazards: for example, I remember a girl sitting next to me in a cinema suddenly seeing me in the light from the match with which she was lighting her cigarette. She stared and shook – I could not tell whether she was about to cry Rape! or ask for an autograph.[43]

In a 1969 interview, Eve Auchincloss and Nancy Lynch asked about a reported incident when Norman Mailer said to his sometime-friend, "You're little, you're ugly, and you're black as the ace of spades." Baldwin explained his comeback: "Oh, I just laughed. After all, it's true…I think it has to do with the fact that like most white liberals – though I am not accusing him of being one exactly – he has always lied to himself about the way he really feels about Negroes."[44] Here, Baldwin reiterates the trope of his "ugliness" that he has helped perpetuate while claiming satisfaction for how it publicly caught Mailer red-handed in racially offensive speech and thought.

And then, of course, Baldwin's face participates in the "quare" act of "throwing shade" upon his verbal competitors, as in his reaction to Buckley's nonsense. E. Patrick Johnson has written about the nonverbal behavior of "throwing shade" as a form of black vernacular signifying (borrowing from Henry Louis Gates, Jr.), and specifically as a "quare vernacular tool" that "attest[s] to the ways in which black gays, lesbians, bisexuals, and transgendered people demonstrate the ways of devising technologies of self-assertion and summoning the agency to resist.[45] Willie Ninja, known as the "godfather of voguing," defined shade as "a nonverbal response to verbal or nonverbal abuse. Shade is about using certain mannerisms in battle. If you said something nasty to me, I would just turn to you, and give you a look like: 'Bitch please, you're not even worth my time, go on.' All with a facial expression and body posture, that's throwing shade."[46] Relating the nonverbal act of shade-throwing to what could be understood as a specifically black tradition of camp, Romi Crawford explains that "the gestural inflection creates a space for words, thoughts, comments too unruly, too black to mention. It brings visibility to, if not a full verbal articulation of such thoughts.... It is at once a question and an ironic response, the shade that follows. The gesture compresses emotional, historical, social information into an image that is at once inquisitive and responsive."[47] Baldwin's facial theatrics thus depend on black camp aesthetics that index the subversive comic irony embedded in queer/quare camp as well as the history of black(face) entertainment.

Baldwin's Child

Shade-throwing Baldwin evolved a long way from the comically pitiable, frog-eyed child, yet Baldwin ensured that readers were aware of the presence of both. Within Baldwin's comic masquerade, there are "Lots of people. Some of them are unmentionable," as Baldwin explains. "There's a man. There's a woman, too. There are lots of people here. Then there's the self-pitying little boy. You know: 'I can't do it, because I'm so ugly.' He's still in there someplace."[48] In discussing Richard Wright's sexual masking (his closeted homosexuality and performance of heterosexuality), critic Robert Reid-Pharr writes about "funniness" – of which Wright himself was a prominent architect – as "one of the major technologies of publicity available to American intellectuals who produced their work in the years defined by World War II and its aftermath."[49] These "funny" "compromises with art, politics, and community would, in fact, be modeled by an entire generation of American intellectuals, a generation whose own lively intellectual practices are themselves structured upon *that childlike funniness suggesting innocence*." To be a funny child – one plagued by, in Wright's case, an "awkward, childlike Black American civility" – is to have not quite matured into the engaged intellectualism that accompanies being "queer." Using Reid-Pharr's formulation, Baldwin stages the dissonance between his funny childhood and his queer, maturely comic adulthood as a trope to expose technologies of publicity that prioritize egoistic image-making over genuine political and intellectual engagement. Part Chaplin's "Little Tramp," part ingénue, and part straight man (so to speak), the child character performs innocence in Baldwin's written and embodied dramatizations of various racial and psychosexual follies so as to expose their laughable absurdities.

In this chapter, we see examples of dramatism in the anecdotes about the cop and the boy behind the pulpit. In "The Devil Finds Work," Baldwin describes his attempts in *One Day When I Was Lost* to "dramatize" the "father-son relationship" between the young, green, "country" Malcolm and Archie, the West-Indian numbers runner whom Baldwin sees Malcolm trying to express (via his amanuensis, Alex Haley) in his autobiography. What is staged in the original scene (though later altered by the producers) is the way street-smart individuals laugh at the naïve in a process of compassionate identification. Archie and his friends joke about the young Malcolm, who "does not know how outrageously young and vulnerable he looks." But, Baldwin explains, "their jokes contain an oblique confession: they see themselves in Malcolm. They have all been Malcolm once. He does not know what is about to happen to him, but they do, because it has already happened to them."[50] It is this dramatization of the comic gap between the elder's wisdom and the child's helpless naiveté that drives much of the humor in Baldwin's self-performance. It is the joke that serves as the "pretext to invite the boy over the table," to initiate the father-son relationship, cajoling as well as initiating through lessons about how the world works. Here, Baldwin plays the role of both father and son. Such a co-presence of wise father and naïve child was captured in a series of photographic portraits of a theatrically posing Baldwin by photographer Mark B. Anstendig.[51] In one image, for example, frog-eyed Baldwin, both innocently wide-eyed and pitiably ugly, with a sailor cap puerilely positioned too far from his hairline, drinks milk. Yet, in this portrait, we also see the adult Baldwin constructing the "funny child" version of himself. In this sense, the portrait crystalizes the performed incongruity behind all of Baldwin's comic gestures.

Baldwin's Humor

Hortense Spillers writes, "The dramatic 'I' of the streets of Harlem, Paris, and the Swiss village, small and isolated enough to render black skin exotic, adopts as *persona* an ancient observer of Western history and politics from which perspective he, Baldwin, announces the *refusal* and the *indictment*."[52] In this essay, I have aimed to cast Baldwin's recognizable persona, the "dramatic 'I,'" as a comic one, and to show how his refusal of the status quo and indictment of human crimes against other human hearts, minds, and bodies occurs via dramatized performances of social, political, and ethical incongruities. I attempted to create a portrait of Baldwin's affinity for the "negative feeling" of the comic mode and for comic masquerade as a strategy for creating it. "Masturbatory" tropes, or self-referential constructions of the different "Baldwins" comprising his theatrical ensemble – such as cosmopolitan Baldwin, "ugly" Baldwin, and young Baldwin – are a primary mechanism by which Baldwin's public comes to know and interpret his humor. Such a framework can provide a starting point for future studies of Baldwin's humor.

NOTES

1 See Nina Simone and Simon Cleary, *I Put a Spell on You: The Autobiography of Nina Simone* (Cambridge, MA: Da Capo Press, 1991); Nadine Cohodas, *Princess Noire: The Tumultuous Reign of Nina Simone: The Tumultuous Reign of Nina Simone* (Durham: University of North Carolina Press, 2012).

2 James Baldwin, *The Evidence of Things Not Seen* (New York: Macmillan, 1985), pp. 85–9.

3 James L. Underwood, *The Constitution of South Carolina, Vol 4. The struggle for political equality* (Columbia: University of South Carolina Press, 1994), p. 203; Prathia Hall, "Bloody Selma," in Faith S. Holsaert (ed.), *Hands on the Freedom Plow: Personal Accounts by Women in SNCC* (Chicago: University of Illinois Press, 2010), pp. 470–2, 471.

4 Nicholas Lemann, *The Promised Land: The Great Black Migration and How It Changed America* (New York: Random House, 2011), pp. 126–7; Edward R. Schmitt, *President of the Other America: Robert Kennedy and the Politics of Poverty* (Amherst: University of Massachusetts Press, 2011), pp. 87–8.

5 *Look*, July 16, 1963.

6 Gilbert Millstein, "First of All a Man," *New York Times* (November 1, 1964), Section 3, 27.

7 See Caryl Phillips, "The Price of the Ticket," *The Guardian* (July 14, 2007); and Robert Reid-Pharr, "Rendevous with Life: Reading Early and Late Baldwin," in Cora Kaplan and Bill Schwartz (eds.), *James Baldwin: America and Beyond* (Ann Arbor: University of Michigan Press, 2011), pp. 126–40. Phillips's piece divides Baldwin's career into three stages: that of the little-known young author; of the Civil Rights Movement public intellectual; and of the reclusive expatriate writer, undistracted by fame. Reid-Pharr argues that Phillips perpetuates the idea that intellectual output has its greatest artistic value when generated in a "cloistered intellectualism," undisturbed by political and social investments (130).

8 See Glenda Carpio, *Laughing Fit to Kill: Black Humor in the Fictions of Slavery* (London and New York: Oxford University Press, 2008); Bambi Haggins, *Laughing Mad: The Black Comic Persona in Post-Soul America* (New Brunswick, New Jersey: Rutgers University Press, 2007); Daphne Brooks, "The End of the Line: Josephine Baker and the Politics of Black Women's Corporeal Comedy," *The Scholar & Feminist Online: The Barnard Center for Research on Women* 6.1–6.2 (Fall 2007–Spring 2008): http://www.barnard.edu/sfonline/; also see Heard's forthcoming *Mavericks of Masquerade: Comic Strategies of Post-Blackness*.

9 Boggs, Nicholas, "Of Mimicry and (Little Man Little) Man: Toward a Queersighted Theory of Black Childhood," in Dwight McBride (ed.), *James Baldwin Now* (New York: New York University Press, 1999), pp. 122–60.

10 James Baldwin, *The Price of the Ticket: Collected Nonfiction, 1948–1985* (New York: St. Martin's Press, 1985), p. 316; author's italics.

11 Kenneth Burke, *Attitudes Toward History* (Berkeley: University of California Press, 1984), pp. 51, 220.

12 Burke did refer to Baldwin's work in *Language as Symbolic Action: Essays on Life, Literature, and Method* (Berkeley: University of California Press, 1968).

13 Ibid., p. 462.

14 James Baldwin and Wolfgang Binder, "James Baldwin, An Interview (1980)," in *Conversations with James Baldwin* (Jackson: University Press of Mississippi, 1989), p. 199; author's italics.

15 Carpio, p. 142.

16 For example, in Ellison's essay "Change the Joke and Slip the Yoke," a "very dark" Southerner and stubborn bargainer remarks to a white businessman, "I know, you thought I was colored, didn't you." In John Callahan (ed.), *The Collected Essays of Ralph Ellison* (New York: Modern Library, 2003), p. 108.

17 "Ralph Ellison and Kenneth Burke: The Nonsymbolizable (Trans)Action," *Boundary* 2 30.2 (2003), 66.

18 Regarding "perspective by incongruity," see Kenneth Burke, *Attitudes Toward History*, pp. 308–14. On the "grotesque," see Mikhail Bakhtin, *Rabelais and His World*, trans. Hélène Iswolsky (Bloomington: Indiana University Press, 1984), and Charles Baudelaire "On the Essence of Laughter" in *The Mirror of Art*, trans. Jonathan Mayne (London: Phaidon Press, 1955), pp. 144–53.

19 James Baldwin, *The Fire Next Time* (New York: Vintage Press, 1991), p. 55.

20 Ralph Ellison, "Harlem is Nowhere," in Callahan (ed.), *Collected Essays*, pp. 320–7, 320.

21 Ralph Ellison, "An Extravagance of Laughter," in Callahan (ed.), *Collected Essays*, pp. 617–62, 633.

22 I elaborate a theory of racial masquerade as a comic strategy, drawing upon Ellison, Burke, W. E. B. Du Bois, and Franz Fanon in my forthcoming *Mavericks of Masquerade: Comic Strategies of Post-Blackness*.

23 Baldwin, *The Price of the Ticket*, p. 282.

24 Nella Larsen, *Passing* (New York: Dover Publications, 2004), p. 9.

25 Joshua Miller, *Accented America: The Cultural Politics of Multilingual Modernism* (New York: Oxford University Press, 2011), p. 23.

26 Nathaniel Mackey, "From Noun to Verb," in Robert O'Meally (ed.), *The Jazz Cadence of American Culture* (New York: Columbia University Press, 1998), pp. 513–34, 514.

27 See José Esteban Muñoz, *Disidentifications: Queers of Color and the Performance of Politics* (Minneapolis: University of Minnesota Press, 1999). According to Muñoz, "disidentification is meant to be descriptive of the survival strategies the minority subject practices in order to negotiate a phobic majoritarian public sphere that continuously elides or punishes the existence of subjects who do not conform to the phantasm of normative citizenship" (4). In this sense, Baldwin refuses to conform to the "normative citizenship" of either white America or black cultural nationalism.

28 James Baldwin, "If Black English Isn't a Language, Then Tell Me, What Is?," *New York Times* (July 29, 1979), Section 4, 19.

29 See Donald Winford, "Ideologies of Language and Socially Realistic Linguistics," in Arnetha Ball, Sinfree Makoni, Geneva Smitherman, and Arthur K. Spears (eds.), *Black Linguistics: Language, Society and Politics in Africa and the Americas* (New York: Routledge, 2003), pp. 21–39. Winford outlines the rise of black linguistics in the 1970s, a response to mainstream linguists' resistance to studying African American Vernacular English (AAVE), also known as Black English Vernacular (BEV).

30 On the relationship between black cultural nationalism and Black English, see Geneva Smitherman, *Talkin that Talk: Language, Culture, and Education in African America* (New York: Routledge, 2000). On the exclusionary discourses of black cultural nationalism, see for example Mark Anthony Neal, *New Black Man* (New York: Routledge, 2006).

31 Baldwin, "If Black English Isn't a Language, Then Tell Me, What Is?"

32 Ibid.

33 See Daphne Brooks, "Planet Earth(a): Sonic Cosmopolitanism and Black Feminist Theory," in Wilfried Raussert, Michelle Habell-Pallán (eds.), *Cornbread and Cuchifritos: Ethnic Identity Politics, Transnationalization, and Transculturation in American Urban Popular Music* (New York: Bilingual Review Press, 2011).

34 Eartha Kitt, *Alone with Me: A New Autobiography* (Washington, DC: H. Regnery Co., 1976), p. 50.

35 Julius Lester, "James Baldwin – Reflections of a Maverick" in *Conversations with James Baldwin*, pp. 222–31, 222.

36 Nat Hentoff, "'It's Terrifying,' James Baldwin: The Price of Fame," in *Conversations with James Baldwin*, pp. 32–37, 33.

37 Hollie West, "James Baldwin: No Gain for Race Relations," in *Conversations with James Baldwin*, pp. 172–85, 172.

38 David DeWitt, "Glimpsing James Baldwin on the Precipice: Review," *New York Times* (April 12, 2000).

39 Eve Auchincloss and Nancy Lynch, "Disturber of the Peace: James Baldwin – An Interview" in *Conversations with James Baldwin*, pp. 82–92, 172.

40 Baldwin, *The Price of the Ticket*, p. 560.

41 Mel Watkins, *On the Real Side: A History of African American Comedy from Slavery to Chris Rock* (Chicago: Chicago Review Press, 1999), p. 113.

42 "A Television Conversation: James Baldwin, Peregrine Worsthorne, Bryan Magee" in *Conversations with James Baldwin*, pp. 113–26, 125.

43 James Baldwin, *No Name in the Street* (New York: Random House, 1972), p. 90.

44 Auchincloss and Lynch, "Disturber of the Peace: James Baldwin – An Interview" in *Conversations with James Baldwin*, pp. 64–82, 64. Baldwin and Mailer regularly discussed pressing social issues on television and radio programs, and also ran in similar social circles. However, Baldwin revealed that a tension around racial issues kept them from getting close.

45 See E. Patrick Johnson, "SNAP! Culture: a Different Kind of 'Reading,'" in Philip Auslander (ed.), *Performance: Media and Technology* (London: Taylor and Francis, 2003), pp. 173–98; "'Quare' Studies, or (Almost) Everything I Learned about Queer Studies I Learned from My Grandmother," in E. Patrick Johnson and Mae G. Henderson (eds.), *Black Queer Studies: A Critical Anthology* (Durham: Duke University Press, 2005), pp. 124–58.

46 Tricia Rose, "A Style Nobody Can Deal With: Politics, Style and the Postindustrial City in Hip Hop," in Andrew Ross and Tricia Rose (eds.), *Microphone Fiends: Youth Music and Youth Culture* (London: Routledge, 1994), pp. 71–177, 174.

47 Romi Crawford presented this theory of shade during "Black/Camp," a panel organized by the author at the 2014 Annual Meeting of the American Studies Association. The panel aimed to identify and theorize "black camp" as an aesthetic space where blackness is not analogical to gay camp; see also, Danielle

Heard, "From Dirty South to Potty Mouth: Cee Lo Green's Black Camp Freedom Project, or, the Profaning of an Utterly Profane Form," *Women & Performance: a Journal of Feminist Theory* 24.1, (2014), 46–60.

48 Auchincloss and Lynch, "Disturber of the Peace," in *Conversations with James Baldwin*, p. 79.

49 Robert Reid-Pharr, *Once You Go Black: Choice, Desire, and the Black American Intellectual* (New York: New York University Press, 2007), pp. 46–7.

50 Baldwin, *The Price of the Ticket*, p. 619.

51 This photographic portrait series is archived at Mark B. Anstendig's Web site. http://www.anstendig.com/Portrait%20Series/Baldwin/baldwin_index.html. The image referenced can be viewed at this URL: http://www.anstendig.com/Portrait%20Series/Baldwin/baldwin8.htm.

52 Hortense Spillers, "Afterword," in Cora Kaplan and Bill Schwartz (eds.), *James Baldwin: America and Beyond* (Ann Arbor: University of Michigan Press, 2011), pp. 241–6, 244.

7

NICHOLAS BOGGS

Baldwin and Yoran Cazac's "Child's Story for Adults"

Perhaps the most critically neglected of all of James Baldwin's literary works is his collaboration with French artist Yoran Cazac on *Little Man Little Man: A Story of Childhood* (1976). Its only full-length review, published in the "Children's Book" section of *The New York Times Book Review* was dismissive in tone. The acclaimed children's book author Julius Lester lamented, "This is a children's book, and not an especially exciting or disappointing one." While he offered lukewarm praise for what he called Baldwin's "effective blend of black English and child's talk," and even admitted that "there are brilliant flashes of the Baldwin many of us love," Lester concluded that the book has "no storyline," "lacks intensity and focus," and fails as a work of children's literature.[1]

Despite the dearth of commercial and critical success garnered by *Little Man Little Man*, and the fact that it went quickly and quietly out of print, the book was profoundly important to Baldwin, who called it a "celebration of the self-esteem of black children."[2] Written in the black vernacular style of the Harlem neighborhood where Baldwin was born, the book features many of the thematic preoccupations engaged in his essays and novels, including poverty, police brutality, crime, intergenerational relations, addiction, racism, loneliness, nonnormative gender expression, and social marginality. What sets this book apart is how it treats these adult themes through the perspective of Baldwin and Cazac's representation of a black child's vision of what it means to grow up in Harlem – a child, it is important to note, who is not innocent.[3]

Throughout his writing, Baldwin was relentless in his insistence that all Americans – including children – should rid themselves of a false belief in American "innocence," as that prevented them from wrestling with the racism of the nation's past, present, and future. As he wrote, "People who shut their eyes to reality simply invite their own destruction, and anyone who insists on remaining in a state of innocence long after that innocence is dead turns himself into a monster."[4] In *Little Man Little Man*, Baldwin and

Cazac take seriously the intellectual and emotional potential of their readers, both children and adults, to eschew this culturally willed innocence and instead open their eyes to the social ills of their time and, in the process, imagine a different future. In doing so, they produce a radically new kind of text at once continuous and discontinuous with the African-American literary tradition – what they, and their publishers, called "a child's story for adults," one that "dances along with a child's rhythm and resilience, making an unforgettable picture of New York as it looks to those who are black, poor, and less than four feet high."[5]

In this essay, I draw on new biographical information about the book's production and fresh critical perspectives to look beyond Lester's view of *Little Man Little Man* as a failed children's book. Instead, I argue that if we highlight the book's status as a "child's story for adults," we can see how this text's interplay of words and images engages the cultural messages that children learn when young – messages that can be particularly damaging for black children. Strategies for change, the book suggests, must be directed at a child's understanding, even if the book is intended for an adult audience. Drawing on the imaginative resources Baldwin associated with the language and experience of black childhood, *Little Man Little Man* provides an important counter-narrative to the dominant representations of black childhood that black children of the time encountered on a day-to-day basis in Harlem and beyond. As we shall see, this counter-narrative articulates alternative models of black masculinity and black kinship that are produced by the child characters themselves and, in the book's remarkable conclusion, disseminated to the adult characters and, by extension, to adult readers. Viewing *Little Man Little Man* in this new light, I offer the following reading in hopes that the book will be recuperated as an exemplary text for future work in Baldwin studies, black queer studies, and African-American literary studies, including but not limited to the study of African-American children's literature.

The canon of twentieth-century African-American children's literature arguably begins with W. E. B. Du Bois's monthly children's magazine, *The Brownie's Book* (1920–21), and extends through Langston Hughes's collaboration with Arna Bontemps, *Popo and Fifina* (1932); Hughes's *The Pasteboard Bandit* (1935); Julius Lester's Newberry Honor book, *To Be a Slave* (1969); Faith Ringgold's *Tar Beach* (1980); and Toni Morrison's *The Big Box* (1999), among others. While many works of African-American children's literature, like children's literature in general, were written with both adult and child audiences in mind,[6] part of what makes *Little Man Little Man* remarkable for its time is its self-conscious presentation as a "child's story for adults" that tackles the mature themes noted above. That *Little Man Little Man* does this through the voice of a black child is especially significant in the context of Baldwin's essay "If Black English Isn't a Language, Then Tell Me, What Is?"

In this essay Baldwin lays bare "the brutal truth...that the bulk of white people in America never had any interest in educating black people, except as could serve white purposes."[7] It is the fate of black children that Baldwin's turns to in order to stake his claim for the necessity of celebrating the beauty of "Black English":

> It is not the black child's language that is despised. It is his experience. A child cannot be taught by anyone who despises him, and a child cannot afford to be fooled. A child cannot be taught by anyone whose demand, essentially, is that child repudiate his experience, and all that gives him sustenance, and enter a limbo in which he will no longer be black, and which he knows he can never become white. Black people have lost too many children that way.
>
> (652)

According to Baldwin, citing Toni Morrison, because Black English is so often tied to the devaluation of black children's experience, it must be recognized for its "sheer intelligence" (651). If language in general, as Baldwin claims, "is a political instrument, means and proof of power...and the most vivid and crucial key to identity" (650), then the black vernacular voice in *Little Man Little Man* engages in a strategic resistance to both standard English and to the cultural messages of that language system in order to imagine a different story of black childhood.

While the celebration of Black English in *Little Man Little Man* aligns it with the cultural mood of black America during the 1970s, as well the "Black Is Beautiful" mantra popular at that moment, the book's literary form and the conditions of its production distinguish it from African-American children's literature of the period. Most African-American children's books of the time were committed to positive representations of the conception of a largely innocent black childhood, and in most cases both authors and illustrators were African-American. By contrast, *Little Man Little Man*, which continually stages the *question* of the representation of black childhood as a pervasive cultural problematic, is the product of an unusual collaboration between an African-American writer and a white European artist initially unschooled in the particularities of the African-American experience. These factors help explain how anomalous *Little Man Little Man* is as a work of African-American children's literature and, indeed, within the African-American literary tradition more generally.

Little Man Little Man has complex interracial origins.[8] In the late 1960s and early 1970s, Baldwin made multiple trips from his home in the south of

France to see his family in New York. During these visits his nephew, Tejan, implored his famous uncle to write a story about him. Around the same time, in 1971, Baldwin renewed his friendship with Yoran Cazac, an artist he had met in Paris back in 1959 through their mutual friend, Beauford Delaney. Delaney, a black gay American painter, had mentored a young Baldwin in New York City and had later served as a champion for Cazac during his early career in Paris. But now Delaney was suffering from the early stages of schizophrenia in a rundown hospital on the outskirts of Paris. Both Baldwin and Cazac were devastated.

Long interested in word-and-image collaborations, in part because of Delaney's influence on him, Baldwin asked Cazac to provide the illustrations for the book he was finally sitting down to write about his nephew – a book he had decided he would dedicate to the ailing Delaney. During their collaboration, Baldwin was romantically interested in Cazac, who returned some of his affection, both emotional and physical, but ultimately remained committed to his wife and children in Italy (*James Baldwin: A Biography*, 330). Thus, *Little Man Little Man* would eventually emerge as a memorial to Baldwin's long friendship and short-lived, intermittent romance with his collaborator, an ode to Baldwin's family back in the States, and his nephew in particular, and a deeply melancholic effort to provide comfort to the man to whom the book was dedicated.

The vision of black childhood Baldwin and Cazac showcase in the pages of *Little Man Little Man* is very much a product of Delaney's influence on both writer and artist. Baldwin famously tells the anecdote of when he was a teenager standing on Broadway and Delaney told him to look down at the gutter. Delaney asked him what he saw and Baldwin replied that he saw a puddle. Delaney said, "Look again," and when Baldwin looked more closely he saw the reflection of the buildings in the "oil moving like mercury in the black water of the gutter," distorted and radiant.[9] "The reality of his seeing caused me to begin to see," Baldwin explained.[10] Baldwin asked Cazac to provide the illustrations in part because he knew his painter friend was also influenced by Delaney's aesthetic philosophy and that together they could enact Delaney's abiding lesson about the art of seeing differently by asking readers to revalue what has been routinely cast aside as marginal, irrelevant, even ugly by dominant culture – namely the lives of urban black children.

In 1972, as Baldwin and Cazac began to collaborate, Baldwin sent drafts of the text of *Little Man Little Man* to Cazac at the painter's home in Tuscany. These drafts are narrated in the third-person voice of an unnamed black child whose free indirect discourse shifts between various perspectives as it tells the story of three children – two black boys, TJ and WT, aged four and seven, respectively, and their friend Blinky, an eight-year-old black girl based on one of Baldwin's nieces, Aisha – as they navigate the pleasures and dangers of their Harlem neighborhood. Cazac had never been to the United States, let alone to Harlem, and he knew little about African-American history, but Baldwin felt that this lack of knowledge was an asset because it would allow Cazac to "see" Harlem with the kind of fresh, defamiliarizing eyes Delaney had taught him to value. Still, he knew that he would have to find a way to educate Cazac about African-American life and his family in Harlem in order to provide a blueprint from which he could craft his imaginative vision in the book.

Baldwin shared various sources with Cazac when he visited him in St. Paul-de-Vence, including a copy of *The Black Book* (1974), a groundbreaking compilation of words and images drawn from African-American history.[11] The book includes everything from seventeenth-century sketches of Africa as it appeared to marauding European traders, nineteenth-century slave auction notices, and disturbing images of lynchings, to patents registered by black inventors throughout the early twentieth century and colorful posters from the "Black Hollywood" films from the 1940s and 1950s. In addition, Baldwin shared photographs of his New York family as models for the characters in the book. These textual and visual sources, along with Baldwin's other writing on Harlem and his vivid conversational descriptions of life in the neighborhood, allowed Cazac to begin work on pencil and watercolor illustrations of a Harlem he had never seen or experienced. He began, as he put it, "to imagine the unimaginable."[12] The final product was a series of illustrations characterized by sketchy lines and bleeding colors, from the faces of neighbors sitting on their stoops to the streetscape of Lennox Avenue itself. It was Harlem and it was not Harlem. Or rather, it was a Harlem distorted and made strangely, unexpectedly beautiful by Cazac, mirroring Baldwin's experience when he heeded Delaney's imperative to "look again" and discovered hidden beauty in the dirty puddle of water so many years earlier.

Throughout the book, the character of Blinky, and her "blinking" eyeglasses in particular, carries the imprint of Delaney's lesson on Baldwin and Cazac's collaborative vision for the book. As the children move through Harlem together, playing ball, skipping rope, and running errands for neighbors, Blinky occupies an increasingly privileged position of sight and knowledge, acting as a surrogate older sister figure looking out for the welfare of WT and especially the younger boy, TJ. At first, however, her eyeglasses are a source of confusion for TJ:

> TJ don't know why she all the time got those glasses on. She say she can't see without them. Maybe that true, if she say so. But TJ put them on one time

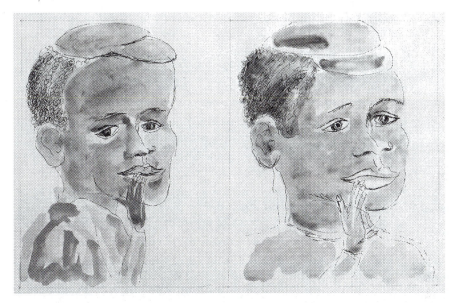

Figure 7.1. Yoran Cazac, Illustration of TJ, watercolor, 1976. Baldwin and Cazac, *Little Man Little Man: A Story of Childhood*, p. 20. Reprinted with permission of Beatrice Cazac.

and he couldn't see nothing with them on. He couldn't see across the street. Everything looked like it was rained on. So TJ ain't too sure about Blinky. It was some white folks at school bought her them glasses. If *he* can't see out them, how *she* going to see out them?

(10)

TJ's initial skepticism is rooted in the fact that he can't see out of the glasses himself, and "that some white folks at school" bought them for her (a possible nod to W. E. B. Du Bois, for whom the notion of double consciousness served as a rationale for what he saw as the need for children's literature tailored specifically for black children).[13] But several pages later TJ is already coming to understand how Blinky's own skin "color changing all the time. She always make TJ think of the color of sunlight when your eyes closed and the sun inside your eyes. When your eyes is open, she the color of real black coffee, early in the morning" (13). TJ's dawning realization of the problem defining the color "black" echoes Baldwin's description of the lesson he learned from Delaney on Broadway: that day he learned that "to stare at a leaf long enough, to try to apprehend the leaf, was to discover many colors in it; and though black had been described to me as the absence of light, it became very clear to me that if this were true, we would never have been able to see the colour; black."[14]

With and beyond the problem inherent in defining the color "black," it is the challenges the boys face in defining and understanding black manhood and black masculinity that constitutes one of the book's major preoccupations. Here too, perhaps unexpectedly, Blinky acts as a guide for the boys. After discussing TJ's confusion over Blinky's eyeglasses, the roving narrative voice approximates TJ's perspective when it says, "And she older than he is. She eight years old. She ought to know better. But she a girl" (10). This apparent devaluation of Blinky's perspective based on her putative gender is complicated as the story continues. A few pages later, the text notes, "One thing TJ understand about Blinky she don't like nothing that wears dresses. She don't hardly never wear a dress herself. She always in blue jeans. But she ain't no boy. Blinky is a girl. But she don't like girls" (33). Here the representation of Blinky exposes the limitations of a reading of *Little Man Little Man* that would focus on black masculinity as necessarily and exclusively linked to boys and men.[15] In fact, throughout the story, "WT do everything Blinky do," from jumping rope to imitating her imitations of black male sports figures Sonny Liston and Hank Aaron. Thus, when TJ imitates WT, he is in fact imitating Blinky as the model for black masculinity in the text. As such, the book does not subscribe to the biological determinism of dominant narratives of what it means to be a man, and a black man in particular. Instead, it "looks again," and with a critical eye, at the problems and possibilities of the cultural construction of black masculinity itself.

A closer look at the book's full title suggests that its story can in fact be read as a rewriting of a key literary text in the cultural definition of black manhood: *Little Man Little Man: A Story of Childhood* reproduces the structure of Richard Wright's novel, *Black Boy* (1945), subtitled *A Record of Childhood and Youth*. Wright's autobiographical narrative of a young black man coming of age in the United States begins when the protagonist is four years old, the same age as TJ. Whereas Wright's text tells the story of a single black boy, the doubling of the title *Little Man Little Man* references the repetitive chain of masculine identification between the three characters: the doubling and redoubling of "little men" in the text that propels the narrative forward as Blinky, slowly but surely, teaches WT and especially TJ what it might mean to be, or rather to become, a "little man" as a culturally constructed and performed identity amid the challenges of a socially and economically distressed Harlem.

These challenges are referenced at an unexpected moment in the text through an allusion to Baldwin's novel *Another Country* (1962) and its central character, Rufus Scott: in one of Cazac's illustrations, the name "Rufus" is scrawled in graffiti on a background wall below the icon of a peace sign. This is a visual and textual memorial to Rufus, who is hounded by the pressures of white racism and conforming to traditional modes of black masculinity. Rufus ultimately jumps off the George Washington Bridge to his

Figure 7.2. Yoran Cazac, Illustration of Blinky, watercolor, 1976. Baldwin and
Cazac, *Little Man Little Man: A Story of Childhood*, p. 11. Reprinted with
permission of Beatrice Cazac.

death, representing a theme of endangered black manhood that is repeated
when TJ looks down his Harlem street and imagines a scene culled from his
experience watching television, film, and the news. In a scene accompanied
by illustrations within boxes representing television screens, TJ pictures a
black man being chased by the police: "The man they come to get he in one
of the houses or he on the fire escape or he on the roof and he see them come
for him" (15). TJ's culturally inherited narrative positions black manhood as
a site of criminality, although the crime is unnamed and the man is unarmed.
The anonymous black man "don't know what to do. He can't go nowhere.
And he sweating" as the "cops keep coming real slow and careful down this
long street with their guns out" (15).

The trope of a black man jumping to his death returns in the narrative
sequence as TJ explains that "if he on one of them roofs don't care which
side of the street he on, he going to have to run like a mother and jump a

roof to get him to another block" (16). In TJ's imagination there are multiple ways the scene could end, all of them deadly:

> Sometime he running down the middle of the street and the guns go *pow!* and *blam!* He fall and maybe he turn over twice before he hiccup and don't move no more. Sometime he come somersaulting down from the fire-escape. Sometime it from the roof, and he scream.
>
> (19)

This text is accompanied by frames of film containing discrete images of these possible endings, and the repetition of *sometime* before each example shows how the image of black men in a criminal stereotype are repeated in the mass media. While this may also reference TJ's own experience witnessing police brutality in his neighborhood, the fact that he articulates the scene in an almost playful manner typified by its onomatopoeia (*pow! blam!*) shows how these stereotypes are normalized for TJ to the point of a childish game.

Little Man Little Man showcases how all three children work together to construct a network of mutual support and understanding that works to provide alternatives to these negative conceptions of black identity. For example, the following scene represents the drug-addicted fate of some of the older boys in the neighborhood, one that both WT and TJ seek to avoid:

> The other boys, when they in the block, sometimes they play stickball in the street. But mostly they sit on the stoop and they play cards and shoot crap and sometimes they get to fighting. They go up to the roof or they go behind the stairs and they shoot that dope in their veins and they come out and sit on the stoop and look like they gone to sleep.
>
> (24)

WT, recognizing that TJ is frightened by the sight of these boys, assumes his role as a surrogate older brother figure: "He say that he look out for TJ, so TJ won't never get to be like that. TJ don't see how he ever going to be like that, but then WT say, just like a real old man, 'They didn't think so neither' " (25). WT's knowledge is borne of the fact that he "got a brother older than him and he sit on the stoop like that a whole lot of times" (26). Here, by hinting at the necessary non-innocence of WT's black childhood, the text suggests that despite – or perhaps because of – the setbacks and social marginality associated with growing up in Harlem, WT is bequeathed an almost preternatural understanding, "like a real old man," of the dangers of childhood in Harlem. Moreover, WT's knowledge allows him to stage an intervention with TJ that may break the cycle of drug abuse by assuring him that the predetermined narratives produced by the mass media – black criminality and drug addiction – can be avoided through the development of precisely

126

the kind of alternative black masculinities and black kinship structures made possible by the network among these three childhood friends.

The necessity of developing these alternative models of black urban life become all the more apparent after a dramatic turn of events that takes place just as the story begins to transition towards its confounding conclusion. Here, in the book's most violent moment, as the children begin to make their journey back to their street after running an errand for a neighbor, Miss Beanpole, TJ whimsically throws WT's ball up in the air, but the three of them are shocked when the ball does not return to earth. Instead, there is a "big explosion, like a bomb falling" (78). TJ, crying, is knocked to the ground, as WT stands in a pool of blood. Not only has he "done lost his ball"; furthermore, "WT got that hole in his sneaker and he done stepped on the ball and his foot be bleeding something awful" (79). The illustrations of bloody footprints and splattered blood that stretch across two pages mark a visceral transition from the playful scene of youthful adventure running an errand for Miss Beanpole into an unexpected scene of trauma that seems particularly ill-suited to a children's book. These bloody illustrations, then, signal that the book's designation as a "child's story for adults" will become particularly important for our understanding of the book's conclusion.

It is this closing scene that brings the narrative of *Little Man Little Man* into direct conversation with a central trope in the "adult" African-American literary tradition, even rewriting it: this is the theme of the underground that is evident in everything from slave narratives through Richard Wright's "The Man Who Lived Underground" (1942) and, perhaps most importantly here, Ralph Ellison's *Invisible Man* (1952). Mirroring the narrative of descent into the underground as a space of escape and potential healing so central to the African-American literary tradition, the children exit the aboveground world to tend WT's injury. With TJ crying and "WT about to vomit" (79), Blinky again takes command. With her eyeglass blinking emphatically, she points at WT's foot and then "she take WT by one hand and TJ hold him by the other and she lead them down to the steps, to the basement, to Mr. Man's house" (82). While *Invisible Man* famously ends with the narrator retreating underground – a complex effort to honor his individuality, but one that risks jeopardizing his commitment to the African-American community – in *Little Man Little Man* the children enter the underground as a space to attempt to heal WT's injury precisely through the resources of their community, both children and adults. That is, unlike the narrator of *Invisible Man*, who seeks hibernation and self-containment, the children attempt to actively engage, and indeed, reconfigure their sense of what an African-American community can be, even if this means contending with its more troubling components.

Nowhere is this tension more apparent than when the children begin to understand that Mr. Man's girlfriend, the alcoholic Miss Lee, was indirectly responsible for WT's injury. In a drunken stupor on the roof, she dropped her liquor bottle and it shattered on the sidewalk below. As a result, "WT foot just keep dripping and dripping blood. It a big cut" (83). Here the text highlights the ways that adults in Harlem do not necessarily protect black children, but can instead put them at risk with their actions and lack of self-knowledge. Nonetheless, the scene does not paint an all-encompassing picture of adults as dangerous figures, as that would only corroborate dominant white representations of the residents of Harlem. Instead, it presents a complex negotiation of the limitations and possibilities of adult figures in their relationship to the children and, significantly, to each other.

The negotiation begins with Mr. Man telling WT, "Don't be scared. It ain't nothing. It just bleeding a lot. We stop that in a minute" (84). He tells Blinky to go upstairs and fetch Miss Lee and some bandages, and he instructs TJ to help by holding WT on a bed as he starts to wash his bleeding foot in a basin. It would be easy enough to read Miss Lee as a wholly problematic figure who has endangered WT and the other children, but the text then repositions her as crucial in the healing process: she comes down into the basement carrying bandages, peroxide, and iodine, and applies them to WT's foot. Then, in the book's first explicit reference to its own title: "'There,' she say, and she look up at WT. 'You a real brave little man'" (87). Yet Miss Lee's words, which seem to subscribe to a conventional model of black masculinity premised on bravery in the face of adversity and pain, fall short: WT is still traumatized and "more scared than he ever been…and he don't know why" (93). It will require a final intervention by Blinky to bring WT out of his state of despondency, and in the process, provide closure for all of the characters, and indeed, for the narrative itself.

Recognizing that the adult efforts to assuage WT's trauma have not fully succeeded and that TJ remains confused and upset, too, Blinky intervenes just as an argument appears about to erupt between Mr. Man and Miss Lee, who starts to cry:

> "Why she crying?" TJ asks Blinky.
> "She been sick," Blinky say. "She real sick."
> WT look at Miss Lee and Mr. Man and he start to shivering again.
> Mr. Man say, real low and evil, between his teeth. "I been telling you about that roof. One of these days I'm going to have to put you away again.
>
> (90–1)

Blinky's understanding that Miss Lee is an alcoholic allows her to explain the situation to TJ in a language she knows he will understand: "She been sick…she real sick." Furthermore, Blinky's privileged vision in the story is reasserted when the text notes that her "glasses just shining like diamonds. Blinky look hard at WT and finally she say, just like she older than time, 'You better start to walking, Little Man'" (93). If Miss Lee's invocation of the titular term, "little man," failed to work, it is this "older-than-time" wisdom of Blinky's black childhood and her "shining-like-diamonds" glasses that finally allow her to push WT toward recognizing that his wound is simply a small cut that can be healed. But it is not by directing WT to meet the expectations of a heroic and stoic black masculinity that Blinky accomplishes this feat. Rather, she makes a crucial turn to the playful resources of childhood, taking advantage of the interconnectedness already established between the three children throughout the text: "Then she start moving, dancing to the music" emanating from Mr. Man's record player. "She putting on a show for WT, really, she want to make him smile" (93).

In the book's final paragraph, the basement finally becomes a space of unification and healing:

> Pretty soon, Blinky do something to the music to make Mr. Man laugh. Then Miss Lee laugh, and Mr. Man put one arm around her shoulder. WT still just lying there, and watching. But then, TJ think *Shucks*, and he start into doing his African strut and WT just crack up.
>
> (95)

In this remarkable conclusion, Blinky has managed to pull off a startling turn of events. First, her movement to the music has brought Mr. Man and Miss Lee back from the brink of fracture, making them laugh and reconnect both physically and emotionally. In a reversal of standard generational expectations, the children have in fact begun to heal the woes of the adult couple rather than the other way around. Second, this same movement has inspired the frightened TJ to dance his playful "African strut" in an effort to cheer up WT. As such, this key moment in the story makes it clear that Blinky's privileged vision and her unexpected maturity – which incorporates rather than disavows the resources of childhood – allow her to expand the network of friendship already established among the children and to set in motion a communal healing for all the characters, both children and adults.

Despite these positive developments, however, the book's concluding line – WT "just crack up" – suggests joyful laughter, but also has the colloquial implication of losing one's mind. The latter interpretation acquires particular relevance given the fact that the book was dedicated to Beauford Delaney, whose schizophrenic condition was deteriorating during the book's production. Indeed, Baldwin felt that Delaney's mental illness was in many ways the result of his years living as a black man in racist America, especially given the trauma of his childhood in the South.[16]

Yet the conclusion's illustrations suggest a reading that revalues the redemptive vision bequeathed to Baldwin and Cazac by Delaney himself. Whereas the earlier illustrations in the underground scene are rendered in black and white, by the end of the book they return to watercolor. Significantly, the earlier scene involving TJ's imagination of a black man being chased by the police is also rendered in black and white, and the racist images in *The Black Book* that Cazac viewed for research are often black-and-white photographs. Thus, as the critic Margo Natalie Crawford has argued, in *Little Man Little Man*

> the blinking is set up, in the words and images, as the new way of seeing what occurs when people try to move past the realism of race in order to find the language and pictures that race does not name....When TJ wears [Blinky's] glasses, "Everything looked like it was rained on." These words "rained on" capture the move from the photography [in *The Black Book*] to watercolor, from the stubborn referent of "what is" to the dreaminess of "what might be."[17]

This final move from black and white to color, then, reenacts on the page what Crawford identifies as Cazac's Delaney-inspired "look-again" transformation, in which *The Black Book's* black-and-white photographs and their stubborn referent of "what is" become the colorful watercolor dreaminess of "what might be." "What might be" at the end of *Little Man Little Man*, in this scene of shared jubilation and relief, is the culturally unimaginable reimagined: an underground scene that neither pathologizes those who are positioned at the bottom of society nor necessitates the kind of isolation from the rest of the world that characterizes the ending of *Invisible Man*. By contrast, this conclusion celebrates the *visibility* and the *vision* of black childhood as it recuperates the complex humanity of these characters as individuals and also as members of a reconstituted community, even a nonbiological family. As such, the conclusion in fact recalls Baldwin's own lifelong effort to construct sustaining, alternative structures of kinship with his expansive network of friends, mentors, and collaborators. Indeed, it is precisely the queer kinship Baldwin forged with Delaney, whom he called his "spiritual father," and with his sometime-lover Cazac, for whose son Baldwin served as godfather, that made possible the conditions for the production of the transformative vision of this interracial, genre-bending work of African-American literature.

The form of alternative black kinship offered by the book's conclusion is recognizable only if readers come to understand what it means to approach this book as it asks to be read: that is, as a "child's story for adults." The book's form encourages readers to see *through* the child's perspective: in watercolor, as if they are wearing Blinky's glasses that make everything look like it was rained on. In the process, readers are placed in the position of being "black, poor, and less than four feet high" as the book teaches them to "look again" and experience the social ills represented in the book – violence, economic disparity, alcoholism and drug abuse, and the distortions of mass media – from a black child's non-innocent perspective. Perhaps, then, it is appropriate that this story ends with WT's ambiguous "crack-up" laughter. For even though the concluding moment in the basement is rendered in watercolor as a redemptive one, personal and social difficulties persist within and beneath this moment of shared joy for the characters in the book.

In retrospect, it is hardly surprising that *Little Man Little Man* has long been consigned to the footnotes of Baldwin's career and to the margins of both the African-American literary tradition and the field of children's literature. There is simply no other book quite like it. Yet contrary to the review in *Book World* that described the book as "an exciting, perhaps an important book, but a book with one fatal flaw: its concept of audience is flawed,"[18] it may be that is has been the book's audience, instead, that has had a skewed view of the book's deceptively complex rendering of the language and experience of black childhood in Harlem. With a proposed new edition of *Little Man Little Man* in the works, hopefully a new generation of students, teachers, Baldwin scholars, and other readers will have an opportunity to make this decision for themselves.

NOTES

1 Julius Lester, "Little Man, Little Man," *New York Times Book Review* (September 4, 1977), 22.
2 David Leeming, *James Baldwin: A Biography* (New York: Henry Holt, 1994), p. 330.
3 My thanks to the anonymous readers of the book proposal coauthored by myself and Jennifer DeVere Brody for a new edition of *Little Man Little Man* at Duke University Press for their comments regarding the "non-innocence" of black childhood in this text. My heartfelt thanks also to Jennifer, to whom I dedicate this article, for her collaborative spirit in thinking and writing about this book. Much of my understanding of the non-innocence of black childhood in this text has been influenced by our work together. I would also like to thank Michele Elam, Alice Underwood, and my colleague in the Department of English at NYU, Sonya Posmentier, for their helpful comments on drafts of this essay. Lastly I would like to thank Beatrice Cazac and the Cazac family for generously granting permission to include images from *Little Man Little Man.*
4 James Baldwin, "Stranger in the Village," in *The Price of the Ticket: Collected Non-Fiction 1948–1985* (New York: St. Martin's/Marek, 1985), p. 89.

5 James Baldwin and Yoran Cazac, *Little Man Little Man: A Story of Childhood* (London: Michael Joseph, Ltd, 1976), jacket description.

6 For example, Michele Elam provides an important reading of how Paul Lawrence Dunbar's poetry for and about children "is clearly meant to be overheard by adults" because it "foregrounds African-American children in ways that counter the late nineteenth-century representations of little black boys and girls as part of the nation's 'Negro Problem.' " See Elam, "Dunbar's Children," *African American Review* 41.2, Paul Lawrence Dunbar (Summer 2007), 259–68.

7 James Baldwin, "If Black English Isn't a Language, Then Tell Me, What Is?" in *The Price of the Ticket*, p. 652.

8 The biographical information in this section draws on the pioneering work of Baldwin's biographer, David Leeming, and new information gathered in my interviews with Yoran Cazac, on May 17, 2003 at the Kiron gallery and May 18, 2003 in Cazac's studio, both in Paris, France.

9 Leeming, *James Baldwin: A Biography*, p. 34.

10 James Baldwin, "Introduction to Exhibition of Beauford Delaney Opening December 4, 1964 at the Gallery Lambert," *Beauford Delaney: A Retrospective* (New York: Studio Museum in Harlem, 1978), unnumbered page.

11 Middleton A. Harris (ed.), *The Black Book* (New York: Random House, 1974).

12 Author interview with Yoran Cazac, May 17, 2003, Kiron Gallery, Paris, France.

13 W. E. B Du Bois, *The Souls of Black Folk* (Chicago: A.C. McClurg & Co.; [Cambridge]: University Press John Wilson and Son, 1903).

14 James Baldwin, "On the Painter Beauford Delaney," in Toni Morrison (ed.), *James Baldwin: Collected Essays* (New York: The Library of America, 1998), p. 720.

15 Indeed, one could argue that Blinky's body, clothed in blue jeans, is a site of performed female masculinity as a preadolescent butch-type who cross-identifies with boys. See Judith Halberstam, *Female Masculinity* (Durham and London: Duke University Press, 1999).

16 David Leeming, *Amazing Grace: A Life of Beauford Delaney* (New York: Oxford University Press, 1998), p. 131.

17 Margo Natalie Crawford, "Adding Watercolors to *The Black Book*: The "Eye-Glasses Blinking' Between James Baldwin and Yoran Cazac," unpublished article. I am grateful to Margo for her thoughtful work on *Little Man Little Man* and for our inspiring conversations about Blinky in particular.

18 Ann S. Haskell, "Baldwin: Harlem on His Mind," *Book World* (September 11, 1997), E6.

PART II

Collaborations and Confluences

8

BRIAN NORMAN

Baldwin's Collaborations

James Baldwin had a penchant for collaboration, especially as his public shadow grew larger and global reach expanded. He teamed up with friends such as portraitist Richard Avedon and editor Sol Stein; with other artists, including young black poet Nikki Giovanni, black feminist icon Audre Lorde, and musician David Linx; with love interests, such as white photographer Theodore Petalowski and French artist Yoran Cazac; and with other important public figures, most notably the anthropologist Margaret Mead. Sometimes Baldwin was forced into collaboration, as when studio executives commissioned a cowriter to finalize his *Malcolm X* film script. What does it mean to think of Baldwin as a collaborator? He is well known as a master essayist, novelist, and dramatist, preeminent civil rights advocate and consummate expatriate writer, as well as, for many, the moral voice of his generation. Yet his collaborations are largely peripheral to our memory of him. Though Baldwin often portrayed himself as a lone prophet, his formidable collaborative record also underscores his relentless engagement across lines of difference, be they racial, generational, creative, or otherwise.

Collaboration, at its core, is two or more people working together to create something new. Often what will be created cannot be anticipated, and so creative collaborations tend toward the unconventional. Wayne Koestenbaum describes collaboration as promiscuous and motley, begetting mongrels and monsters that revel in their difference.[1] Indeed, Baldwin's collaborative products are often surprising: an experimental narrated photo-essay, three staged dialogues, a never-filmed screenplay, an illustrated children's book, and even a jazz record released after his death. Individually, each seems a misfit in Baldwin's oeuvre, an oddity. Taken together, they point to a consistently restless artistry seeking new forms, designs, and possibilities, and engage others in the process.

Beyond literary matters, the collaborative mode asks what it means to be a citizen in communities of difference. Baldwin was always attentive to how much his place in the world depended upon others, a sentiment that fueled his signature drive to cross the chasm between *I* and *you* into the elusive territory of *we*. That is where, for instance, Baldwin ends his flagship civil rights essay *The Fire Next Time* (1962). In a meditation on black anger, white innocence, and American hypocrisy, Baldwin famously concludes with a hopeful image: "If we – and now I mean the relatively conscious whites and the relatively conscious blacks, who must, like lovers, insist on, or create, the consciousness of the others – do not falter in our duty now, we may be able, handful that we are, to end the racial nightmare, and achieve our country, and change the history of the world."[2] It is telling that one of Baldwin's best-known passages is an image of collaboration: individuals purposefully working together to create a country. Though the sentence is conditional, and therefore suggests the possibility of failure, it also affirms Baldwin's faith in collaboration and its possibilities. Such endeavors may be risky and unpredictable, but for Baldwin collaboration could also yield artistic innovation and, perhaps, deliberate communion with another not like oneself. Therein arises collaboration's more nefarious connotation: treason, consorting with the enemy. Baldwin's entire career is based on crossing cemented lines to achieve something new. If we are destined to be strangers or even enemies in this world, Baldwin shows, we shall have to make another country, together.

Nothing Personal and the Difficulty of Knowing One Another

One of Baldwin's earliest collaborations is also his most daring: *Nothing Personal* (1964), an oversized, un-paginated series of Avedon portraits accompanied by a particularly lyrical Baldwin essay. The book is an event: two established artists – writer and photographer, one black and one white – partnering to take on the subject of race in America amid the successes and terrors of the black freedom movement. According to Avedon, the general theme was "despair, dishonesty...things that keep people from knowing each other."[3] The two mediums enact that theme: Avedon's photographs and Baldwin's essay are strangely dissonant. Sometimes the text and images converge; more often they are separate, surrounded by white space. Avedon's subjects include familiar faces of politicians and celebrities; scientists and artists; the wealthy elite and "race men," from Marilyn Monroe and George Wallace to Malcolm X and Linus Pauling; and also more representative figures, such as SNCC activists and Daughters of the American Revolution; an ex-slave and newlyweds; and nameless patients in a mental institution. Baldwin's essay targets the mental acuity needed to make sense of the cacophony of American culture and its ability to house contradictory images while maintaining myths of innocence and equality. In general, collaboration defies the solitary genius model of authorship, which leads many to argue that creative partnership begets mutuality and, when successful, equality,[4] though some scholars also show that collaboration can thrive amid disharmony and difference.[5] In their collaboration, Baldwin and Avedon underscore the difficulty of human connection, and also the desire for it.

In all, *Nothing Personal* is meant to confound. The book is a curiosity: part coffee-table conversation piece, part art object, and part race polemic. It has received relatively little attention in Baldwin studies, as scholars point to its odd nature in what is already a curious form. Joshua Miller describes it as "daring experimentation," a "visual and textual performance of mobility" that "flaunts its very formlessness with rapid shifts of subject…and sudden juxtaposition."[6] Sara Blair suggests that the clashes between text and image affirm a tragic sensibility amid a roiling Civil Rights Movement.[7] The productive dissonance these scholars see in *Nothing Personal* points to Baldwin's overall model of collaboration: it does not demand consensus. Though many scholars define successful collaboration as the achievement of harmony, what Vera John-Steiner calls "the full realization of intimacy and interdependence,"[8] Baldwin and Avedon underscore the failure to achieve a seamless unity. Their collaboration evokes a desire to cross lines of difference, but not to erase them.

Baldwin's essay opens with a meditation on the "irreality" of flipping through television channels. The idealized bodies on display seem without odors, wrinkles, or other imperfections, in contrast to Avedon's close-up portraiture that turns wrinkles into full-page crevices. For Baldwin, the televised bodies generate isolation and despair. "Despair," Baldwin writes, "perhaps it is this despair which we should attempt to examine if we hope to bring water to this desert."[9] While Baldwin delivers an exegesis on the desiccation of American humanity, his essay wends through Avedon's black-and-white portraits, which, like Baldwin's disorienting remote control, marshal strange resonances between contradictory images. One photo spread, for instance, features earnestly saluting members of the American Nazi party, placed opposite a naked, hairy Allen Ginsberg in a similar posture. At times, one image covers two full pages. More often, opposing pages juxtapose images of different sizes, such as when an elderly man born a slave looms large opposite a dwarfed Adlai Stevenson, America's public face to the world. In the essay portion that launches this section, Baldwin writes, "It is, of course, in the very nature of a myth that those who are its victims and, at the same time, its perpetrators, should, by virtue of these two facts, be rendered unable to examine the myth, or even to suspect, much less recognize, that it is a myth which controls and blasts their lives." We must listen to multiple voices and see ourselves in multiple images – the saluting Nazis and smiling poet, the ex-slave and head of state – if we are to see each other beyond television façades.

The event of *Nothing Personal* enacts the coming together that the book cues but does not deliver. The project reunited Avedon and Baldwin, who had been classmates at De Witt Clinton High School in the Bronx, where they worked together on the school newspaper, the *Magpie*. The project began in earnest on June 23, 1963, while Baldwin was in Puerto Rico with his longtime companion and sometime lover, Lucien Hapsberger, just two weeks after President Kennedy's impassioned speech on segregation as a moral issue and the murder of civil rights worker Medgar Evers. Leeming describes the book as "at once a eulogy for Medgar Evers, a love song to Lucien, and a celebration of his love for his family." [10] The experimentally disjointed product reflects the collaborative process, which continued in Paris in an open-ended exploration between two artists seeking new territory. The work was also strained by Baldwin's notoriously hectic schedule and multiple commitments, both artistic and political. In Paris, Avedon practically confined Baldwin to a room for forty-eight hours, after which the writer emerged, exhausted, with five pages in hand. Avedon deemed them a miracle. "One sentence went on for two pages," he recalls. "I thought, 'This is the most beautiful sentence since Proust.'" [11] On the one hand, Blair sees the collaborative process mirrored in how the two "cordoned [their contributions] off in self-contained alternating sections." [12] For Miller, on the other hand, the book produces a coming-together as their identities "blurred," even if the two worked largely independently. [13] Rather than presenting a unified point of view, the product performs the difficult work of joining two visions. And perhaps also the necessity of incompletion. For Baldwin, collaboration is about engaging another, not obliterating oneself into a unified whole.

If the components do not cohere around a singular subject, that is the point: to create unsettled readers, unsure where they fit into the American collage. Baldwin's essay appears in four sections, which roughly coincide with shifts in Avedon's series, though the essay never directly narrates the images. In one of the few instances when text and image occupy the same visual space, the cocked head of a Washington hostess fills the right page, while on the left, Baldwin meditates on alienation:

> Only, sometimes, uptown, along the river, perhaps, I've sometimes watched strangers here, here for a day or a week or a month, or newly transplanted, watched a boy and a girl, or a boy and a boy, or a man and a woman, or a woman and a child; yes, THERE was something recognizable, something to which the soul responded, something to make one smile, even to make one weep with exhaustion.

The face on the opposite page is enigmatic, neither plainly welcoming nor off-putting. Baldwin prompts his readers to look to Avedon's faces in search of humanity, including their own. But it is not clear if it is to be found in that particular portrait, or perhaps whether it is she who seeks connection.

The juxtaposition central to the collaboration lies not only in incongruent text and images, but also in how each pairs the horrifying and mundane, institutionalized and sanctioned, lavish and abject. The most unsettling images go unremarked: an eleven-image sequence of unidentified patients in the East Louisiana State Mental Hospital. The patients writhe in pain and distress, spectacles of vulnerability who could not possibly consent to being displayed. Baldwin's essay has little, if any, direct relation. *Nothing Personal* adorns their silence with yet more silence: the white space of oversized, captionless pages. This section also signals a shift from Avedon's artful portraiture to something more akin to documentary photography. When the patients look at the camera, their visages seem plaintive, terrified, or resigned. Most, however, look away. Some patients look ahead but show no signs of camera awareness, leaving no hope for the mutual connection sought earlier in Baldwin's essay. This produces a sense of nonconsensual engagement. To look is not to reach across a chasm of difference, but rather to risk complicity in violence, not unlike the ethical challenge of regarding the spectacle of lynching photographs.[14] In one image, for example, gaping pajamas reveal the penis of a man whose head does not appear. The reader-viewer is pure voyeur. In another is one striking moment of intimacy: two male patients hold hands. To look seems an intrusion, a violation.

The un-narrated images of mental patients, like the incongruent collaboration overall, do not fit into tidy narratives of the Civil Rights Movement. A counterexample is another photo-text published the same year: *The Movement* (1964), a collaboration between SNCC photographer Danny Lyon and black writer Lorraine Hansberry. That photo-text uses now-familiar images of racist cops, attack dogs, and unarmed SNCC activists to create a sense of moral clarity, whereas *Nothing Personal* resists feelings of certainty. In general, the photo-text genre has proven able to yoke artistic sensibilities to earnest political advocacy. Such endeavors were especially prevalent during the Great Depression, as Jeff Allred explains, with notable examples such as James Agee and Walker Evans' iconic portrait of tenant farming, *Let Us Now Praise Famous Men* (1941), and Richard Wright and Edward Rosskam's *12 Million Black Voices* (1941), which documented black life under Jim Crow. Allred traces how the documentary photo-text can create a sense of collectivity among individual readers.[15] In part, the genre's political utility is due to photography's capacity to generate collective outrage, which can transform racial logic and lead to national mobilization and empowerment of the subjugated, as Leigh Raiford shows in her study of photography in black freedom struggles.[16] The textual component, Miller argues, often functions to convert individual images into representative archetypes in national narratives.[17]

Overall, *Nothing Personal* disrupts feelings of national collectivity at the apex of civil rights struggles to end Jim Crow practices and white supremacy. Baldwin avoids simplistic racial lines and Avedon presents incommensurate figures: born-slave, gleeful white supremacist, stoic activist, and wonky statesman. Reader-viewers must connect the elements, but how to do so is deliberately unclear. The collaboration dances at arm's length with the idea of a national "we." Baldwin's signature pronouns are key:

> But we are unbelievably ignorant concerning what goes on in our country – to say nothing of what goes on in the rest of the world – and appear to have become too timid to question what we are told. Our failure to trust one another deeply enough to be able to talk to one another has become so great that people with these questions in their hearts do not speak them; our opulence is so pervasive that people who are afraid to lose whatever they think they have persuade themselves of the truth of a lie, and help disseminate it.

Many have remarked on the pronoun play in Baldwin's essays. Marianne DeKoven tracks a "slippage in subjectivity" in which "Baldwin uses the first-person plural pronoun...but the reference of this pronoun slips and shifts between a particular African American 'we' and a general, inclusive American 'we.'"[18] The essay in *Nothing Personal*, however, breaks from this tendency such that its collective "we" ranges from condemnatory to elusive throughout the book. And yet this particular passage is one of Baldwin's most moving meditations on trust. To escape American myths requires deliberate engagement with those unlike oneself. This carries great risk, perhaps of one's entire self, because we cannot know one another in advance. Baldwin turns to trust, pairing it with the curiosity about what goes on in others' worlds, be they next door or far away. Collaboration – as both process and product – becomes an alternative to forced kinship or continued alienation.

Collaboration and Public Engagement

Nothing Personal marks the full emergence of Baldwin's collaborative sensibility. It was published at the height of his fame, following the success of an incendiary protest essay, third novel, and foray into New York theatre;[19] a number of radio, print, and television interviews on both literary and political subjects; and a *Time* story on civil rights and racial unrest, for which he graced the magazine cover. The pulls of celebrity, politics, artistry, and personal care proved difficult. Baldwin traveled to Puerto Rico "to become a writer again,"[20] especially following a notorious meeting with Robert F. Kennedy. Baldwin had convened fellow artists and activists in a failed bid to convince the attorney general to approach segregation with moral urgency, not simply political expediency. In one way, *Nothing Personal* reflects that dispiriting meeting: there is no sense of synthesis or even edification, no underlying promise that a black writer and white photographer can come together in America amid all its inconsistencies and fraught history. More important, however, is the attempt itself: Baldwin decides repeatedly to try to create something new with another person. Blair suggests that in *Nothing Personal* Baldwin reconciles the social commitments of civil rights, his status as cultural icon, and his complex literary portrayals of identity.[21] I would go so far as to say that in *Nothing Personal* Baldwin turns to collaboration as a means to overcome despair at American race relations. The collaboration with Avedon was largely panned upon its release, dismissed as what two scholars characterize as "irrelevant, dishonest, hasty overstatement presented in a contorted grammar."[22] Nonetheless, Baldwin retained faith in collaboration as a creative mode. With each venture, Baldwin sought visions and insights unachievable by the individual artist alone.

For Baldwin, collaboration could enact his vision of radical love based in engagement and trust, especially across lines of difference. Next, Baldwin turned to direct exchange in the form of staged dialogues. In August 1970, he met with famed anthropologist Margaret Mead for a taped conversation that would be published as *A Rap on Race*. Each felt called to speak about race as a representative: one a white liberal social scientist, the other a black intellectual writer. Over seven hours, the subjects ranged from Mead's cross-cultural experiences to Baldwin's exile status to America's relationship to God. Leeming reports that the two quickly developed a friendly rapport,[23] though perhaps more interesting are their points of friction, such as over historical inheritance or the limits of universalism when one speaks as citizen of a country. At one point, Mead cries "fiddlesticks" and complains, "Jimmy, you are now going into symbolism that does not get us anywhere. You are just making speeches."[24] In response, Baldwin insists on dialogue among fellow exiles who must trust one another, for "The country doesn't trust you or me. That is the point."[25]

The dialogue format provided a space for trusting engagement between differently marginalized people. Two years after the conversation with Mead, Baldwin participated in another staged dialogue, this time with young black poet Nikki Giovanni. The conversation appeared on the television program *Soul!* and was published as *A Dialogue* by J. B. Lippincott. In that exchange, Baldwin represents the elder statesmen addressing the younger generation. A decade later, another staged conversation about identity and American power paired Baldwin with fellow black writer Audre Lorde for the December 1984 issue of *Essence*. Like Giovanni, Lorde resisted Baldwin's penchant for grand narratives and emphasized her particular exclusions as a woman, as well as a black person, from American promises. "A family quarrel is one thing," Baldwin quips, "a public quarrel is another."[26] The staged dialogue as a collaborative form connects the intimacy of personal engagement with the necessity of public intellectualism. Lorde asserts, "Jimmy, we don't have an argument…. But what we do have is a real disagreement about your responsibility not just to me but to my son and to our boys."[27] As a collaborative format, the staged dialogue is particularly adept at enacting moments of disagreement paired with a crucial element stressed by Lorde: listening.

While the staged dialogue enacts public engagement across social lines, other collaborations entail more intimate engagement. A good example is Baldwin's children's book *Little Man Little Man: A Story of Childhood* (1976), for which he collaborated with French outsider artist Yoran Cazac. Cazac's illustrations are vibrant, coarse watercolors, and Baldwin's tale recounts a day with seven-year-old TJ and his friends WT and Blinky, who are surrounded by a rich, if also troubled and dangerous, Harlem community. WT receives a deep foot wound, and community members nurse and nurture the injured boy. The final image is one of gathering and joy: "WT still just lying there, and watching. But then, TJ thinks *Shucks*, and he start into doing his African strut and WT just crack up."[28] The story connects Baldwin to the next generation and black culture, including through his use of black vernacular – for, as Baldwin asks in a 1979 *New York Times* essay, "If Black English Isn't a Language, Then Tell Me, What Is?" While the setting is Harlem, the book was created in Europe among fellow artist-exiles. Further, Cazac was a love interest, which leads Nicholas Boggs to argue that the book is the couple's queer child, drawing on Koestenbaum's theory of male collaboration as literary procreation.[29]

Whether or not Baldwin himself thought of the book in procreative terms, he certainly turned to collaboration to create what the lone individual could not, and to solidify a connection in the process. At times, the collaborative relationship may have been more important than any product. For instance, in early 1947, Baldwin began a photo-essay on Harlem churches with his first love, Teddy Pelatowski, which they never finished.[30] Baldwin's earliest and longest collaborative relationship was with Sol Stein, a "high school buddy" who became a powerful editor and eventually prompted what became *Notes of a Native Son* (1955), despite Baldwin's objection that "I was too young to publish my memoirs."[31] Their editorial process involved extensive correspondence as friends and fellow admirers, ranging from line edits, to substantive discussions, to what Stein describes as "friendly arguments" about what would make the cut. For instance, Stein ended one letter, "That's all for piddling points. If you don't like what I suggest, change 'em back, some or all, in proof."[32] Likewise, Baldwin once wrote, "After a good deal of fruitless worry, I've decided that the only way to avoid genuine misunderstanding is to be as precise as possible in my text."[33] Like the collaboration with Avedon, the point was not unified agreement, but rather two thinkers attempting "genuine understanding" on the page. The publishing process itself yielded the "Autobiographical Notes" that open the blockbuster book: when Baldwin received the publisher's publicity questionnaire, he simply turned it over and wrote his own narrative.[34] Stein and Baldwin went on to cowrite a short story called "Dark Runner" and the television play *Equal in Paris*, based on Baldwin's essay of the same name; both were unpublished in Baldwin's lifetime. Stein describes himself and Baldwin as "non-collaborators by temperament,"[35] though their relationship and joint ventures belie the claim.

With each collaboration, Baldwin ventured into new territory. The last collaboration that came to fruition is perhaps also most surprising: "A Lover's Question," an experimental jazz album with Belgian-born musician David Linx, released in 1991 by Les Disques Du Crépuscule and expanded in 1999 by Label Bleu. The eight tracks feature Baldwin's spoken word, vocals from Linx and others, and robust musical accompaniment. The lyrics are from "A Lover's Question" and "Inventory/On Being 52," selected from Baldwin's 1986 poetry volume *Jimmy's Blues*. Baldwin also sings a compelling rendition of "Precious Lord." In a 2013 interview, Linx characterizes the collaborative process as "intense." It came about in 1987 over drinks while the young artist was living with Baldwin in Saint-Paul de Vence. "It's amazing how Jimmy trusted me," Linx declares about the mutual selection process. "He left everything to me," he reports, marveling that Baldwin was willing to work with an untested, if enthusiastic, nineteen-year-old.[36] In this final collaboration, Baldwin trusts his legacy to a younger generation and new, experimental forms. Baldwin listened to the final product in 1987 while quite ill. The recording of "Precious Lord" was featured at his funeral at the Cathedral of St. John the Divine and also in the documentary *The Price of the Ticket* – minus the tuba. The producers, Linx reports, thought the tuba "a bit too strange."[37]

Collaboration as Communion

Beyond one-off creative partnerships, Baldwin increasingly pursued collaborative forums to engage the public, such as the open letter, question-and-answer, public debate, and the extemporaneous interview, a format in which the former child preacher particularly excelled. The best example is Baldwin's 1963 televised interview with influential black psychologist and social reformer Kenneth Clark. It followed the infamous meeting with Attorney General Kennedy, which exemplified what Baldwin later described as "that panic-stricken vacuum in which black and white, for the most part, meet in this country."[38] The Kennedy meeting ended in a stalemate; the impassioned interview that immediately followed, however, is a masterpiece. Baldwin engages the fundamental point of *The Fire Next Time*, almost lifting sentences word for word: "The future of the Negro in this country is precisely as bright or as dark as the future of the country," he declares. "It is entirely up to the American people and our representatives, it is entirely up to the American people whether or not they are going to face and deal with and embrace the stranger whom they maligned so long."[39] This is purposeful improvisation: Baldwin applies what is potentially abstract in his essays to the urgency of the moment, entreating his listeners to turn strangers into fellow humans. Extemporaneous public forms such as interviews, conversations, and open debates – most notably with William F. Buckley and Malcolm X – demonstrate civic engagement as mutual exchange, which does not necessarily require knowing the endgame. At his best moments, Baldwin eschewed prescribed talking points and got his interlocutor to do the same. That same spirit informs Baldwin's reputation as a cheerfully combative dinner conversationalist. It also informs other conversational endeavors even when only Baldwin's half is present. For instance, in *Take This Hammer*, a 1963 public-television documentary on race in San Francisco, the famous writer chats extemporaneously while driving around the city, also engaging unscripted conversations with local community members.

Baldwin's desire for public engagement also found a home in the inherently collaborative venue of the theatre. His drama career includes two major plays, *The Amen Corner* (1954) and *Blues for Mister Charlie* (1964), and a novel featuring an actor as its protagonist, *Tell Me How Long the Train's Been Gone* (1968). Baldwin also expanded into film, including a Hollywood venture and a volume of film criticism, and he continued to consult on various productions of his plays throughout his career. "I know that out of the ritual of the church," he opines in notes accompanying *The Amen Corner*, "historically speaking, comes the act of the theater, the *communion* which is theater."[40] The idea of "communion" carries both community and religious valences. Such communion required Baldwin to relinquish some authorial control and trust his fellow artists – a prospect he met with ambivalence, according to some anecdotes about his contentious participation in Actor's Studio workshops for the debut of *Blues for Mister Charlie*,[41] his polemical play based loosely on Emmett Till's lynching. It seems that Baldwin's comfort with creative partnership did not necessarily translate smoothly to theatre's more dispersed collaborative method in which the playwright is but one of many contributors. Nonetheless, Baldwin saw a transformative power in theatre and film, which Koritha Mitchell dubs his performance theory of "flesh-centered imaginative work" in which actual human bodies encounter one another while playing fictional roles.[42] *Blues for Mister Charlie* ends with a rather unsatisfying vision of coalitional politics: after the infamous acquittal of the murderers, the white liberal protagonist asks, "Can I join you on the march, Juanita? Can I walk with you?" The young black woman responds, "Well, we can walk in the same direction."[43] For Baldwin, political solidarity of shared direction is insufficient. Collaboration requires trusting, face-to-face engagement across lines.

That is, not all collaborations equally yield the engagement that Baldwin sought. In the most extreme example, Baldwin encountered an attempt to collaborate that was coerced rather than cooperative when Columbia Pictures commissioned a film script based on *The Autobiography of Malcolm X* (1965). Baldwin transformed the familiar chronological life story into an experimental meditation on identity; in his version, different eras occupy single shots, creating the impression that Malcolm's many names coexist and collide.[44] The studio, however, expected a more conventional – and profitable – script, and eventually included Arnold Perl as cowriter, much to Baldwin's dismay. Baldwin scrapped the project and published his original scenario in 1972 as *One Day When I Was Lost*. As he declares in *No Name in the Street* (1972), "I did not wish to be party to a second assassination."[45] While the original book is a consummate example of willing collaboration between Malcolm X and Alex Haley, Baldwin's forced collaboration with Perl underscores the risk of one vision supplanting or even obliterating another.

Readerly Collaboration and the Welcome Table

In his introduction to *Notes of a Native Son*, Baldwin declares simply, "I want to be an honest man and a good writer."[46] Collaboration provided one key route toward this basic aim. Baldwin never sought the shelter of past successes and prominence, but rather restlessly moved from one project to the next, mastering many genres and formats in the process. So too, each collaboration led him farther into uncharted territory, both creative and political. In 1947, the young Baldwin chastised contemporary novelists for neglecting "the unpredictability and the occasional and amazing splendor of the human being."[47] All of Baldwin's works, but especially his collaborations, welcome that unpredictability and the necessity to reinvent oneself through interaction with others.

For Baldwin, collaboration was more a mode of engagement than an intellectual concept. In fact, he rarely used the term "collaboration" itself. In the final passage of *The Evidence of Things Not Seen* (1985), Baldwin writes, "He who collaborates is doomed, bound forever in the unimaginable and yet very common condition which we weakly suggest as *Hell*."[48] Here Baldwin evokes collaboration's more unpalatable association with consorting with the enemy: in this case the status quo – be it racism, sexual mores, the Western empire, or whatever social arrangements we collectively accept as natural. Yet artistic collaboration provides one pathway out of the status quo and the myths we create. In one of his last political essays, "Notes on the House of Bondage" (1980), Baldwin announces "the breakup – the end – of the so-overextended Western empire." He declares, "This is the charged, the dangerous, moment, when everything must be re-examined, must be made new; when nothing at all can be taken for granted."[49] To make the world anew is a risky venture with unpredictable ends. If the future is an inescapably, frighteningly collaborative project, then the work of remaking the world is already underway. Through his collaborative example, Baldwin invites the reader to participate – or perhaps demands it.

Given Baldwin's record of partnering with other artists and thinkers, it is fitting that after his death many writers and thinkers explicitly extend his legacy by directly emulating him. A good example is Randall Kenan's 2007 essay *The Fire This Time*, which adopts the shape of Baldwin's signature civil rights essay, down to the original cover design. Perhaps most fitting are posthumous productions of *The Welcome Table*, Baldwin's last work. The playscript evokes a dinner conversation with Josephine Baker, a young Henry Louis Gates, Jr., and others living in or stopping by Baldwin's final home at Saint-Paul de Vence one evening in 1973.[50] Other accounts suggest origins in Baldwin's lively days in Istanbul in the 1960s.[51] In either case, the scene itself embodies Baldwin's collaborative ideal: artists, thinkers, neighbors, and friends coming together over a meal and seeing where the conversation leads them, even to areas of discord and pain. Baldwin worked on the play for decades, even enlisting African-American theatre director Walter Dallas to help complete it. Now, the unpublished play presents a peculiar collaborative problem, given that Baldwin is not present to participate in its production. And yet the conceit of the welcome table, and Baldwin's legacy more generally, desires that human-to-human encounter and invites us in.

In the end, Baldwin's readers become his ultimate collaborative partner. As Baldwin asserts in "Notes for a Hypothetical Novel" (1961), "We made the world we're living in and we have to make it over."[52] Baldwin understood that the position of spokesperson involves a two-way contract between the artist and reader, the speaker and spoken-for. Although Baldwin's core audience began to nullify that contract as his status faded in the 1970s, his posthumous renaissance, both popular and scholarly, suggests that the public may be willing once again to sign on as his partner.

It is ironic that the present essay on collaboration itself is not collaborative. Yet in a sense, it is. I began the task in earnest when I lunched with fellow contributors at the American Studies Association in the fall of 2012. The scene reminded me of Baldwin's welcome table. Dining together, we shared knowledge and inklings, not knowing where the venture might lead. It was fitting that we gathered in Puerto Rico, the same place Baldwin sat down with Avedon to begin *Nothing Personal*. There, engaging with Baldwin *was* personal. And it remains so for many of his readers, now and to come.

NOTES

1 Wayne Koestenbaum, *Double Talk: The Erotics of Male Collaboration* (New York: Routledge, 1989), pp. 1–8.
2 James Baldwin, "The Fire Next Time," in Toni Morrison (ed.), *James Baldwin: Collected Essays* (New York: Library of America, 1998), pp. 346–7.
3 Fern Marja Eckman, *The Furious Passage of James Baldwin* (Philadelphia: Lippincott, 1966), p. 200.
4 See, for example, Vera John-Steiner, *Creative Collaboration* (New York: Oxford University Press), esp. pp. 21–5.
5 See, for example, Lorraine York, *Rethinking Women's Collaborative Writing: Power, Difference, Property* (Toronto: University of Toronto Press, 2002), esp. p. 15.
6 Joshua Miller, "'A Striking Addiction to Irreality': *Nothing Personal* and the Legacy of the Photo-Text Genre," in Quentin Miller (ed.), *Re-viewing James Baldwin: Things Not Seen* (Philadelphia: Temple University Press, 2000), pp. 155, 173.
7 Sara Blair, *Harlem Crossroads: Black Writers and the Photograph in the Twentieth Century* (Princeton: Princeton University Press, 2007), pp. 185–6.
8 John-Steiner, *Creative Collaboration*, p. 32.
9 James Baldwin and Richard Avedon, *Nothing Personal* (New York: Atheneum, 1964), unpaginated.
10 Leeming, *James Baldwin*, p. 227.
11 Eckman, *Furious Passage*, p. 212.
12 Blair, *Harlem Crossroads*, p. 183.
13 Joshua Miller, "The Discovery of What It Means to Be a Witness," in Dwight McBride (ed.), *James Baldwin Now* (New York: New York University Press, 1999), p. 344–6.

14 See, for example, Dora Apel and Shawn Michelle Smith, *Lynching Photographs* (Berkeley: University of California Press, 2007).

15 Jeff Allred, *American Modernism and Depression Documentary* (New York: Oxford University Press, 2009), pp. 133–66.

16 See Leigh Raiford, *Imprisoned in a Luminous Glare: Photography and the African American Freedom Struggle* (Chapel Hill: University of North Carolina Press, 2011).

17 Miller, "'Striking Addiction,'" esp. pp. 163–71.

18 Marianne DeKoven, *Utopia Limited: The Sixties and the Emergence of the Postmodern* (Durham: Duke University Press, 2004), 234. See also my *The American Protest Essay and National Belonging* (Albany: SUNY Press, 2007), pp. 101–4.

19 Respectively: *The Fire Next Time* (1963), *Another Country* (1962), and *Blues for Mister Charlie* (1964).

20 Nat Hentoff, "'It's Terrifying,' James Baldwin: The Price of Fame," in Fred L. Standley and Louis H. Pratt (eds.), *Conversations with James Baldwin* (Jackson: University of Mississippi Press, 1989), p. 32.

21 Blair, *Harlem Crossroads*, p. 196.

22 Nancy Burt and Fred Standley, *Introduction to Critical Essays on James Baldwin* (Boston: G. K. Hall, 1988), p. 6.

23 Leeming, *James Baldwin*, p. 310.

24 Baldwin and Margaret Mead, *A Rap on Race* (Philadelphia: Lippincott, 1971), p. 232.

25 Ibid., p. 254.

26 James Baldwin and Audre Lorde, "A Revolutionary Hope," *Essence* (December 1984), 74.

27 Ibid., p. 130.

28 Baldwin and Yoran Cazac, *Little Man Little Man* (New York: Dial, 1976), p. 95.

29 Nicholas Boggs, "Of Mimicry and (*Little Man Little*) Man," in Dwight McBride (ed.), *James Baldwin Now* (New York: New York University Press, 1999), p. 127.

30 See Leeming, *James Baldwin*, p. 54; James Campbell, *Talking at the Gates: A Life of James Baldwin* (New York: Viking, 1991), pp. 36–7.

31 Baldwin, *Collected Essays*, p. 808.

32 James Baldwin and Sol Stein, *Native Sons* (New York: Random House, 2004), p. 43.

33 Ibid., p. 53.

34 Ibid., p. 10.

35 Ibid., p. 16.

36 Douglas Field, "An Interview with David Linx," *African American Review*, forthcoming.

37 Ibid.

38 Baldwin, "Lorraine Hansberry at the Summit," in Randall Kenan (ed.), *The Cross of Redemption: Uncollected Writings* (New York: Pantheon, 2010), p. 110.

39 Fred L. Standley and Louis H. Pratt, *Conversations with James Baldwin* (Jackson: University of Mississippi Press, 1989), p. 45. Originally aired on WGBH-TV on May 24, 1963 and published in *Freedomways*.

40 Baldwin, *The Amen Corner* (New York: Penguin, 1991), p. 14.

41 See Leeming, *James Baldwin*, pp. 230–4.

42 Koritha Mitchell, "James Baldwin, Performance Theorist, Sings the *Blues for Mister Charlie*," *American Quarterly* 64.1 (2012), 55.

43 James Baldwin, *Blues for Mister Charlie* (New York: Dial, 1964), p. 121.

44 See my "Reading a 'Closet Screenplay': Hollywood, James Baldwin's Malcolms, and the Threat of Historical Irrelevance," *African American Review* 39, no. 1–2 (2005), 103–18.

45 Baldwin, *Collected Essays*, p. 358.

46 Ibid., p. 9.

47 Baldwin, *Cross of Redemption*, p. 241.

48 James Baldwin, *The Evidence of Things Not Seen* (New York: Holt, Rinehart, and Winston, 1985) p. 125.

49 Baldwin, *Collected Essays*, p. 806.

50 Henry Louis Gates, Jr., "The Fire Last Time," *New Republic* (June 1, 1992), 37–43.

51 For a history of the production, see Magdalena Zaborowska, *James Baldwin's Turkish Decade: Erotics of Exile* (Durham: Duke University Press, 2009), pp. 249–64.

52 Ibid., p. 230.

9

ERICA R. EDWARDS

Baldwin and Black Leadership

James Baldwin's reputation as a race leader is as fraught as his relationships with black leaders themselves were dissimilar. On the one hand, a May 17, 1963 *Time Magazine* feature claims that Baldwin "is not, by any stretch of the imagination, a Negro leader." "He is," we are told, "a nervous, slight, almost fragile figure, filled with frets and fears. He is effeminate in manner, drinks considerably, smokes cigarettes in chains, and he often loses his audience with overblown arguments."[1] And, of course, the author that *Time* depicts as an effete, not-quite-public intellectual was indeed often positioned as outside of, if not dangerous to, the images of black leadership that circulated in mass culture: Douglas Field points out that "it was common knowledge that he was nicknamed 'Martin Luther Queen,' with the implication that a 'queen' could not participate in the violent and manly battle for civil rights."[2] Baldwin's performance of leadership did not conform to the performative demands of black charismatic leadership that had solidified in U.S. culture by the 1960s. On the other hand, the success wrought by *The Fire Next Time* (1963) launched Baldwin into a veritable career as spokesman for the race. David Leeming writes, "Baldwin became more familiar than ever on television talk shows; soon he was recognized everywhere."[3] And while Negro leaders may have been too nervous about Baldwin's sexuality to invite him into their inner circles, movement activists on the ground, according to Ekwueme Michael Thelwell, "perceived Baldwin as the movement's most eloquent, penetrating and dependably accurate literary voice."[4] That Baldwin is as often referred to a *prophet* as a mere author no doubt captures the admiration with which his contemporary and successive audiences have regarded his truth-telling prose and his damning yet graceful diagnoses of the American condition in the twentieth century.

To speak of Baldwin's performances of leadership as well as his relationship with the very concept of black leadership (or "Negro Leadership," as it would have been called during the height of Baldwin's career) is to be thrown into the trickiest terrains of Baldwin's oeuvre and the scholarship surrounding it. This includes, first, the narrative that blames the decline of his craft on his need for acceptance by black nationalists in the 1960s; second, the story of Baldwin's retrospective self-fashioning as a race representative and civil rights/Black Power activist in the 1970s and the sexual quietism (or outright homophobia) that this self-fashioning demanded; and third, the critical tendency to anxiously attempt to connect Baldwin's literary aesthetics, his relationship to an American literary *tradition*, and his bluntly rendered articulation of a radical politics of black survival.[5] To turn to Baldwin's own depictions of religious and political leadership, then, offers the reader a unique opportunity to analyze how Baldwin's work responds to the ideological and performative parameters of black leadership after World War II.

As I argue elsewhere, the 1950s and 1960s saw the mass reproduction of a leadership *scenario* that had solidified in black U.S. culture at the end of the nineteenth century. It was during these decades that television sets became ubiquitous and the black freedom struggle "went live" on the evening news.[6] In this context, the *charismatic scenario* – a portable sketch for black social and political movements that links the performance of *charisma* to political and narrative authority – provided the visual, aural, and narrative language for mainstream accounts and public perceptions of civil rights (and later, Black Power) leaders and organizers. That Baldwin's work spans this era explains the twists it effects to at turns celebrate, mourn, and defend the leaders whose visages and quotables have defined that era in public memory. These include King and Malcolm X, of course, but also Eldridge Cleaver, Stokely Carmichael, Bobby Seale, Huey Newton, and others. Furthermore, Baldwin mobilized the autobiographical essay form to draw readers into intimate scenes of loss, anguish, and shame, feelings that accompany his texts' encounters with quieter forces like Angela Davis, Dorothy Counts, and the fictional fallen prophet, Gabriel Grimes, who inspires terror in two of Baldwin's early protagonists.

If Baldwin's own rise as a political celebrity in the 1960s accompanied the sense of political alienation and rage he articulates in his work by the publication of *Blues for Mister Charlie* in 1964, the relationship between his body of work and the public ideals of late-twentieth century black leadership cannot be understated. And Baldwin's relationship to charisma – as I understand it, black U.S. culture's complex of ideological, bodily, narrative, political, and psychosocial responses to the containments and terrors of Western modernity – is, throughout his work, articulated in the language of debilitating loss and arresting despair. In this essay, I read Baldwin's figurations of the prophet, loss, and profit across three texts in Baldwin's oeuvre: the short story "The Death of the Prophet" (1950), the autobiographical essay *No Name in the Street* (1972), and *One Day When I Was Lost* (1972), the screenplay adaptation of *The Autobiography of Malcolm X*. Through these texts, I argue that the leader, often fallen or lost, or pictured at a distance, figures in Baldwin's work as a contact point, or pivot, between two scales of the political (the intimate and the public), two registers of political sentiment (hope and shame), and two sites of political production (the political event and the cultural artifact sent to the marketplace). Both the lost prophet and the lost profit, in this case, tell the story of Baldwin's politics of leadership.

Lost Prophets

Throughout Baldwin's work, the figure of the lost prophet – the gifted mouthpiece for the Lord lost to himself or lost to the world, or both – surfaces to register the alienation of modern black life in the United States as well as to point to the labor of survival that marks the scene of blackness in the New World. The exacting prophet-father in *Go Tell It on the Mountain*, the dying prophet-father in "The Death of the Prophet," a young Malcolm X gone too soon in *One Day When I Was Lost*, and at least ten martyrs (*"Oh, pioneers!"*) of the Civil Rights and Black Power Movements in *No Name in the Street* populate the world of Baldwin's prose as testaments to both the devastating power of white supremacy and the value, or profit, of black mourning.[7] Black mourning might be understood in this context as Baldwin's orientation to the work of art itself, an orientation defined by the writer's abiding attention to the fragility of black life threatened by black death. Mourning encapsulates multiple related impulses in Baldwin's work: the impulse to lament black vulnerability to premature death; to grieve the loss of his intimates; and to reimagine the possibilities of black living in the face of black life. In what Fred Moten calls "black mo'nin,' " we witness "the augmentation of mourning by the sound of moaning, by a religious and political formulation of morning." Black mo'nin, for Moten, "holds an affirmation not of, but *out of*, death."[8] In the modes of *mo'nin'* in his work of the 1950s and 1960s, Baldwin cries out for the dead as he also cries out to the *living*: to Angela Davis and Dorothy Counts, Tony Maynard, Jr., and Huey Newton. In both kinds of lament, and even in the lamentations' circulation as the foundational conceit in Baldwin's oeuvre – whether the epigraphs from the Book of Job or Revelations, the moans of the saints, or the refrains from the spirituals and hymns that provide so many entries into his work – the cry is the joint that binds black death to art and to life. These characters in Baldwin's work, then, can be said to function as targets of the cry and spindles of grief in Baldwin's work; that is, they are pivots – central joints that allow a given narrative to turn or shift registers – between intimate shame and a weighty public fame, repeated loss and burdensome personal gain, sure defeat and surer survival.

"The Death of the Prophet," Baldwin's first short story, published in 1950 in *Commentary*, introduces the lost prophet into Baldwin's body of work. It tells the story of John Grimes's journey home to visit his father, Gabriel Grimes, who lies comatose in a hospital. Like the John Grimes of Baldwin's first novel, *Go Tell It on the Mountain* (1952), the John of "Prophet" suffers an existential crisis that issues from his rejection of his father's god and his reaching out for intimacy across the impasse that separates father and son. As John walks down the city street on the way to the train that will take him to the hospital where his father lies dying, the story reveals the crisis of faith occasioned by John's coming of age:

> His faith was nothing but panic and his thoughts were all confusion. Then he hated his father. He fought to be free of his father and his father's God, now so crushingly shapeless and omnipotent, Who had come out of Eden and Jerusalem and Africa to sweeten the cotton-field and make endurable the lash, and Who now hovered, like the promise of mercy, above the brutal Northern streets.[9]

Here, Gabriel's need to be free of both earthly father and Heavenly Father occasions existential panic. More importantly, this existential panic revolves around the elimination of the distinction between pleasure and debasement that the patriarch, the F/father who sweetens the cotton field and makes endurable the lash, effects. John's impotent god who hovers recalls the story's image of the impotent father, unable to provide for his children, who punishes. When John as a younger child, hungry and alone, curses his father Gabriel's god, Gabriel "stripped him naked and beat him until he lay on the splintery floor, in feverish sobbing and in terror of death" (257). John's journey through the city to visit his father's deathbed is a walking meditation on both intimate-level and population-level abjection, the "history of humiliating defeat" that issues from both his father's and God the Father's hand.[10] The kind of vexed masculinity that Darieck Scott reads as a privileged mode in black cultural production for the expression of abject blackness, then, is the thematic context for the story's hurried walk through city street, over subway platform, and down long white-white corridor to the prophet's deathbed. For Scott, abjection "is a way of describing an experience, and inherited (psychically introjected) historical legacy, and a social condition defined and underlined by defeat."[11] Figurations of "vexed masculinity" in African-American literature, in this case, reveal how injury and defeat can be tools for historical transformation. The story's plot, then, which follows

John's journey through the city toward the hospital, tracks not the protagonist's effort to overcome the shame that structures his relationship with
his father, but rather the possibilities of transformation *within* defeat and
humiliation.

The hospital where John goes to visit his father appears as a purely eschatological structure: here, souls depart to their eternal destinations. Passing
through a neatly manicured white neighborhood on his way to the hospital
and "imagin[ing] his father lying helpless on white sheets, among strangers," John "passed through the gates, for suddenly he had to look at this
father's face again" (258). Afterward, John enters the white hospital, passing through a long corridor that again points the hospital's significance as a
gateway between the present and eternity:

> The floor was white, of some material like marble, slippery and veined with
> gray. They opened a door and mounted a flight of steps, marble like the floor
> and whiter. At the top of the staircase was a series of doors, secret, dark-brown,
> against the pressing white. The thin fall sun crept in through opaque windows;
> it was like an old house in mourning.

(259)

The multiple passageways that Gabriel passes through – the gates, the long
corridor, the door, the flight of steps, and then the final door to his father's
room – symbolize the story's eschatological interests in the destination of
souls. In these in-between spaces, the story reveals the core of John's quest
and Baldwin's theology: the urgency to liberate oneself from the oppressive
F/father *and* the refusal to relinquish the promise of redemption and sal-
vation first uttered by the F/father. Having earlier left home and "forsaken
the righteous to make his home in the populous Sodom and entered into
an alliance with his father's enemies and the enemies of the Lord," John
revisits the relationship with the F/father with fear and trembling, and with
heaven and hell on his mind (258). The prophet thus becomes a figure for
Baldwin's meditations on humiliation on two scales: the intimate/bodily and
the social/historical.

If Gabriel mediates between John's embodied now and his eternity, then
he, too, joins the story's depictions of loss and damnation to its images
of life and endurance. John discovers that his father is in a coma, having
suffered tuberculosis, and the doctor tells him that his father was hospitalized because he and John had quarreled, John had left home, and Gabriel
became paranoid and anorexic, fearing that his family would poison him.
John's bodily sensations during the hospital visit point to his experience
of what Scott calls "racial vertigo": the "existential vertigo that provides
psychic material for the production of racial identity."[12] And, in fact, this

disorientation marks the encounter with the father as both a loss and a launching. When John meets the doctor whose gray-green eyes "looked at him sharply," he looks at the doctor's "smouldering cigar" and the "string of his loins threatened to snap" (259). When the doctor rises from his desk, he crushes the cigar; at the same time John "rose too, bracing his shaking legs" (259).

If the meeting with the doctor raises the specter of castration in this Oedipal quest, the encounter with Gabriel is no less charged with anxieties of emasculation and fantasies of domination. For example, in Gabriel's hospital room, John looks down on his father:

> He saw the white bedposts, he was aware of a body's outline on the bed; then, with a wrench, as though some strong hand had grasped the back of his head and turned it roughly, as though his father were forcing him to look down on the evidence of some misdemeanor, he forced himself to look down on the bed. There lay his father, black against the white sheets.
> And his gorge rose.
>
> (260)

John's encounter with the dying prophet is a contest of power, imagined here as a clash of phalluses and wills. As John looks upon his father's body, now naked and frail (the "thigh was no thicker than the forearm"), he is placed in a position of power (260). He knows that "no longer would this violent man possess him" and "Now he was the man, the conqueror, alone on the tilting earth" (260). John feels his power to dominate but chooses instead to occupy the position of abjection. John, "like a two-year-old," lays himself "on his face and belly and burning knees, into an unfamiliar room, screaming with that unutterably astounded, apocalyptic terror of a child" (260). The posture of abjection is the prone position of the moaning, screaming mourner. And the cry is that of the son who feels his freedom from the F/ father as a loss that terrifies and terrorizes. As John "moved nearer to the bed and murmured *Daddy,*" Gabriel stops breathing. "Now communication, forgiveness, deliverance, never, the hope was gone" (260).

If Gabriel serves as the passageway between John's present and his eternity, the prophet's death seals John's existential condition as an outsider, as a stranger in a cold universe. As he screams for his father, "he knew ... that it was himself who cried and himself who listened, that his cry would never be heard; it would bang forever against the walls of heaven and he would live with his recurring cry" (260). Still, the loss launches John's new quest, now through a dark, sinister world. Now "the gray-veined, marble floor opened up and dropped him a long way down" (261). John's fall at the end of the story situates loss – the prophet "gone to meet the Lord" – not as the event that seals John's power as a sovereign subject but rather as the occasion for the solidification of what Scott, after Merleau-Ponty, calls "anonymous existence." This is the space of the body in abjection; it is "a space of irrepressible existence even in the absence of ego-protection, at the point of defeat" (90). For Scott, this is a space of black *power*. John's fall, the fall of the lost son of the lost prophet, throws him into the very kind of existence that wrings life from terror. It is an existence borne, in this instance, out of the pained cry of the mourner.

In "The Death of the Prophet," there is no hint of Gabriel's charismatic power – one wonders, how did this preacher inspire the saints of God? How did he win souls for the kingdom of heaven? Instead, the power of the prophet's ministry is made legible only through the intimate, psychic process of John's mourning: we are told that though young Johnnie "feared his father and was frightened and troubled at church, he did not doubt that the gospel his father preached ... was the truth" (257). In *No Name in the Street* (1972), quite to the contrary, the lost prophet is a figure who surfaces to tie the intimate experience of loss to the public denouncement of white supremacy and the individual's experience of abjection to the black public's hunger for justice, as I discuss below.

In the nearly two decades between "Prophet" and *No Name*, black culture bore witness to the heights of antiracist, decolonial hopes and dreams occasioned by black resistance on the local, national, and international scales, as well as to the disillusionment unleashed by unrelenting assassinations and state-sanctioned violence against black activists in the name of law and order. *No Name* can so be read as an autobiography of mourning and a testament to Baldwin's political and creative fatigue, a personal essay that is marked by epitaphs for fallen soldiers of the black freedom struggle. *No Name* is the essay in which Baldwin calls Malcolm X "a genuine revolutionary, a virile impulse" (98), and in which he nearly defends Eldridge Cleaver's homophobic assault against him in *Soul on Ice* by explaining, "I was focused in his mind with the unutterable debasement of the male – with all those faggots, punks, and sissies, the sight and sound of whom, in prison, must have made him vomit more than once" (172). Field argues that throughout *No Name* Baldwin uses the "borrowed rhetoric of black radical writers" to depict himself "as a radical *picaro*" and to, in effect, adopt the voice of a race leader.[13] But focusing on *No Name*'s apologies for the masculinist leadership practices of Black Power could forestall an opportunity for critics to wrestle with what Baldwin's own mourning in *No Name* makes available to analyses of Baldwin's relationship to his own writerly enterprise, and how this relationship was affected by the premature black death that surrounded him. As Baldwin's work turns from the fictional account of the lost prophet in "Death of the Prophet" toward the autobiographical stories of Baldwin's own encounters with fallen leaders in *No Name in the Street*, it continues to situate the lost prophet as a figure who mediates between two scales of defeat and possibility: again, the intimate/bodily and the social/historical.

Indeed, as an autobiographical series of essays that recounts Baldwin's work as a race leader during the 1960s, *No Name in the Street* represents the figure of the lost prophet as one who mediates between public bravado and the despair and alienation suffered because of his celebrity. Opening *No Name* with a meditation on his troubled relationship with his father, now dead, Baldwin states the book's central preoccupation with loss and leadership: "Since Martin [Luther King, Jr.]'s death, in Memphis, and that tremendous day in Atlanta, something has altered in me, something has gone away."[14] Baldwin's reunion with his junior high school best friend brings into relief how King's death inflects his self-understanding as a writer and literary celebrity. Baldwin explains that he goes to dinner at his former friend's home because, after having divulged in an interview that he would never again wear the suit he wore to King's funeral, he agrees to give his suit to his friend: "Martin was dead, but *he* was living, he needed a suit, and – I was just his size" (15). Throughout the account of the dinner, Baldwin highlights the distance between two old friends caused by fame and social position: "[What] in the world was I by now but an aging, lonely, sexually dubious, politically outrageous, unspeakably erratic freak? And what was *he* now? he worked for the post office and was building a house next door to his mother, in, I think, Long Island" (18). The suit, then – a perfect fit in the end – symbolizes the longing for connection, and the frustration of longing, that marks the encounter. "For that suit," Baldwin writes, "was *their suit*, after all, it had been bought *for* them, it had even been bought *by* them: *they* had created Martin, he had not created them" (21). The dark suit, the funereal costume weighted down by Baldwin's sorrow, is the object that *No Name* manipulates to attempt to bring Baldwin the writer/celebrity/ leader in closer communion to Baldwin the friend, Baldwin the man. The attempt fails: "There went the friendly fried chicken dinner. There went the loving past" (20).

Baldwin's account of the 1963 March on Washington, like the several meditations on the meaning of King's death and funeral in *No Name*, serves to center the lost prophet in this story of the 1950s and 1960s. Here Baldwin turns from his recollection of an appearance with King in Los Angeles in which he remembers that by the late 1960s, "Martin's speeches had become simpler and more concrete," to the scene of mass protest at the National Mall (138). Recalling how he watched the "I Have a Dream" speech on television with a group of actors and activists who were away taping a show for Voice of America, Baldwin remembers, "All of us were very silent in that room, listening to Martin, feeling the passion of the people flowing up to him and transforming him, transforming us. ... That day, for a moment, it almost seemed that we stood on a height, and could see our inheritance" (140). Writing from a decidedly less hopeful perspective in a text whose very materiality bears the temporal protraction of grief – "This book has been much delayed by trials, assassinations, funerals, and despair" (196) – Baldwin visits King's death to revisit his own role, and his own faith, in the post–World War II black freedom movement.

No Name's account of the King's assassination articulates the unseverable link between loss and leadership in Baldwin's work. When Baldwin learns of King's death, he is, ironically, in California working on the screenplay adaptation of Alex Haley's *The Autobiography of Malcolm X*. While spending a day at his rental home in Palm Springs with Billy Dee Williams (whom he wants to cast as Malcolm) and a reporter who is interviewing him about the film, Baldwin receives the call from David Moses about the assassination.

> It took awhile before the sound of his voice – I don't mean the *sound* of his voice, something *in* his voice – got through to me.
> He said, "Jimmy –? Martin's just been shot," and I don't think I said anything, or felt anything. I'm not sure I knew who *Martin* was. Yet, though I know – or I think – the record player was still playing, silence fell. David said, "He's not dead yet" – *then* I knew who Martin was – "but it's a head wound – so –"
>
> (152)

The broken speech in the telephone conversation – "– so –" – captures Baldwin's sense that "something has gone away" inside of him since King's death, and depicts him in a singular state of grief, all alone, surrounded by nothing and no one. He writes, "I hardly remember the rest of that evening at all. ... We must have turned on the television set, if we had one, I don't remember. ... I remember weeping, briefly, more in helpless rage than in sorrow, and Billy trying to comfort me. But I really don't remember that evening at all" (152). If the image of Baldwin as the inconsolable mourner who, as John Grimes, alone sounds the cry of loss – *it was himself who cried and himself who listened* – Baldwin again figures black abjection as the site where one experiences the self as an indeterminate range of possibilities, the site where anguish becomes a resource for more intimate self-knowledge even as the self effects a posture of abjection and alienation. The text further creates the image of outsiderness in its structure. Baldwin abruptly ends the recollection of the telephone call on April 4, 1968 with a dark line on the page and then, swiftly, turns to another recollection, this time an account of

his last encounter with Medgar Evers. In this way, lost prophet ("– so –; "---
------"; "Medgar. Gone.") is a figure of intimate struggle with both historical,
racial trauma – white supremacy – and the struggle to bring loss itself into
the vocabulary of black literature.

No Name in the Street, as one of the unfinished projects of Baldwin's
later years and one of the texts in Baldwin's oeuvre that explicitly addresses
leadership, suggests the intimate relationship between loss and political
leadership for its author. Baldwin writes in the epilogue, "This book is not
finished – can never be finished, by me" (196). Writing of the 1971 Attica
uprising, Baldwin gestures to the unfinished project of black liberation, situ-
ating his book squarely within that larger undertaking still under way. With
a final note of mourning, Baldwin laments the lost prophets of the era:

> Angela Davis is still in danger. George Jackson has joined his beloved baby
> brother, Jon, in the royal fellowship of death. And one may say that Mrs.
> Georgia Jackson and the alleged mother of God have, at last, found something
> in common. Now, it is the Virgin, the alabaster Mary, who must embrace the
> despised black mother whose children are also the issue of the Holy Ghost.
>
> (197)

With this incantation, Baldwin offers the reader the lost prophet as the
redemptive figure of a despairing era. George and Jon Jackson surface in
No Name's epilogue to announce the end of racial injustice even as they
stand as the martyrs who, like Mary's Jesus, have died too soon. "There will
be bloody holding actions all over the world, for years to come," Baldwin
writes, "but the Western party is over, and the white man's sun has set.
Period" (197). In these final lines of *No Name in the Street*, Baldwin juxtaposes the righteous prophecy of freedom – writing, "An old world is dying,
and a new one ... announces that it is ready to be born" (196) – and the
expression of anguish and sympathy for Mrs. Jackson and her fallen sons.
In this way, to return to Moten, the cry of the mourner – indeed, the wailing
of the weeping prophet – is the utterance that links the intimate work of
assimilating loss to the black public's hunger for black freedom. The figuration of the lost prophet, in this way, unites the unfinished labor of fighting
for freedom.

Lost Profits

Baldwin's writing during the late 1960s and early 1970s was indelibly
marked by the author's relationship to civil rights and Black Power leaders; these were relationships structured by loss and defeat, and they were
relationships that profoundly shaped Baldwin's body of work. Baldwin

referred to the time he spent in Hollywood during these years, working on a screenplay adaptation of Haley's *Autobiography of Malcolm X*, as a dangerous misadventure. "I think that I would rather be horsewhipped, or incarcerated in the forthright bedlam of Bellevue," he writes, "than repeat the adventure." He concludes, "It was a gamble which I knew I might lose, and which I lost, a very bad day at the races: but I learned something" (99). In this unfinished project, attempted during the very years that Baldwin was writing *No Name in the Street* – the years of dark suits, prison waiting rooms, funerals and more funerals – Baldwin unites the depiction of the lost prophet to his relinquishing of profit, or, his refusal to sell his craft to serve the interests of the mainstream film industry. In this way, *One Day When I Was Lost: A Scenario*, the version of the screenplay published by the Dial Press in 1972, can be read as both a mourning project and a work of sheer writerly expenditure. In the scenario and in his meditations on the screenplay project, Baldwin situates the charismatic leader's appearance in visual culture as both a moment of potential political foreclosure and as an open invitation to more radical political and artistic engagement; here, again, the leader is a pivot between scales of activist intervention (the intimate and the public), between registers of political sentiment (hope and shame), and between sites of political expression (the political event and the cultural artifact sent to the marketplace).

The source of conflict during what Baldwin calls his "Hollywood sentence" was the incompatibility between Baldwin's fidelity to a multifarious, multilayered vision of Malcolm's life and the production company's desire for the sensationalist story of charismatic leadership and intraracial betrayal: Baldwin was instructed that "the tragedy of Malcolm's life was that he had been mistreated, early on, by some whites, and betrayed (later) by *many* blacks."[15] I have described this conflict as a clash between the demands of realism and Baldwin's kaleidoscopic depiction of Malcolm's life. Baldwin mobilizes the flashback and the placement of mirrors throughout the script to produce a narrative that attempts to render Malcolm out of linear representation, disrupting the reader's – or viewer's – expectations for political leadership and cinematic closure.[16] More important, though, is how this tendency toward refraction and abstraction in *One Day When I Was Lost* allows the screenplay to reveal the self-shattering story of loss and defeat, the story that each appearance of the charismatic leader in Baldwin's oeuvre attempts to tell.

In the screenplay, Malcolm's assassination is prefigured by an account of a lynching. When Malcolm's spiritual mentor, Luther, recalls his brother's death at the hands of a lynch mob, Baldwin depicts the scene in "Late afternoon, remembered time. A Georgia landscape" (149). The flashback places the viewer in a relatively vulnerable position with respect to the camera angle. As Luther tells Malcolm that his brother "had a fight with a white man about his wages," Baldwin pictures the scene "from the child Luther's point of view: the feet of many men" (149). There is, here, an impressionistic arrangement of sounds and sights that not only reflects the hazy nature of recall in general and the fractured nature of traumatic recall in particular, but also disorients the viewer so as to make tangible the sense debasement and shame: the viewer hears "male and female voices, jubilant, loud," "labored, agonized breathing," and "one lone, human, despairing scream" (149). The cry of terror gives way to a succession of close-ups – "naked black feet, being dragged," "the black man's sweating face," "the sun: very bright," "hands gathering firewood," – and then "Traveling shots: swift, blurred, distorted, of some of the faces of the people as the mob hurry their victim to the tree" (149). When Luther's voice says, "the people weren't people anymore," Baldwin shows "a wolf leap[ing] on his invisible prey, tearing it" (150). Here the images – body parts dislocated from the whole, the blurred mob, and the fantastic image of the wolf and its invisible victim – only cohere momentarily in the recollection of black pain.

Baldwin's reflections on black activists and leaders allows us to see how the lost prophet functions as a central figuration in Baldwin's work, one that grounds his meditations on the value of black life. In addition, they redraw the visual life of black loss and black pain. In *No Name*, for example, Baldwin recounts two arresting encounters with the visual culture of white supremacy. Writing of his participation in the first International Conference of Black Writers and Artists in Paris in 1956, he describes an afternoon during which he and a group of other conference attendees were halted in their stroll to lunch:

> Facing us, on every newspaper kiosk on that wide, tree-shaded boulevard, were photographs of fifteen-year-old Dorothy Counts being reviled and spat upon by the mob as she was making her way to school in Charlotte, North Carolina. There was unutterable pride, tension, and anguish in that girl's face as she approached the halls of learning, with history, jeering, at her back.
>
> It made me furious, it filled me with both hatred and pity, and it made me ashamed. Some one of us should have been there with her! I dawdled in Europe for nearly yet another year, held by my private life and my attempt to finish a novel, but it was on that bright afternoon that I knew I was leaving France. I could, simply, no longer sit around in Paris discussing the black American problem.

If the photograph of white supremacist violence draws Baldwin close to the domestic context of racial terror, calling him home, then the visual culture object supersedes both Baldwin's "private life" and his writing project as the true impetus of his work as an artist and activist in the late 1950s. Later, Baldwin relates that "the photograph of Angela Davis has replaced the photograph of Dorothy Counts," disabusing his "so innocent and criminal countrymen" of the notion that vicious white supremacy evaporated with the landmark civil rights legislation of 1964 and 1965 (52). The photograph, for Baldwin, makes legible the American scene of racial violence. Conversely *One Day When I Was Lost* makes available the alternative photography of black life and black death in its impressionistic scenes of lynching and in its attempt to render Malcolm X in all of his complexity and nuance. In this way, it sets the film at odds with Western visual culture's representations of black activists.

Baldwin published *No Name in the Street* and *One Day When I Was Lost* at a historical moment when what could be called "black politics," broadly conceived, was on its way to being funneled into state narratives of ascent and success. These accounts dispersed failure and *descent* (the death of activists, the decline of the black underclass) as handy tropes in narratives of state abdication, beneficence, and multiracial democracy through the Reagan era and beyond. If Baldwin's leadership and his relationship to leadership attest to the sheer power of loss to orient a writer's whole body of work, they also ask us to grapple with loss as a problem of present political and cultural life.

Throughout his career, James Baldwin rendered the leader as a figure of political possibility and profound loss. The lost prophet surfaces throughout Baldwin's oeuvre, then, to express the personal and collective losses of the 1950s and 1960s, even as that figure becomes a site for radically reimagining the histories and futures of black art and black sociality. From "The Death of the Prophet" to *One Day When I Was Lost*, Baldwin's work across genres is driven by the intimate relationships between the lost prophet and the lost self, and between fallen leaders and Baldwin's own writerly enterprise.

NOTES

1 "Root of the Negro Problem," *Time* 80.20 (1963), 26.
2 Douglas Field, "Looking for Jimmy Baldwin: Sex, Piracy and Black Nationalist Fervor," *Callaloo* 27.2 (2004), 461.
3 David Adams Leeming, *James Baldwin: A Biography* (New York: Knopf, 1994), p. 219.
4 Ekwueme Michael Thelwell, "A Prophet Is Not without Honor," *Transition* 58 (1992), 93. Gates argues that "When Baldwin wrote *The Fire Next Time* in 1963, he was exalted as *the* voice of black America .... Perhaps not since Booker T. Washington had one man been taken to embody the voice of 'the Negro.' By the early '60s his authority seemed nearly unchallengeable." See Henry Louis Gates, "The Fire Last Time," *The New Republic* 206.22 (1992), 38.

5 On Baldwin's wrong turn toward black nationalism, see James Campbell, *Talking at the Gates: A Life of James Baldwin* (New York: Viking, 1991), p. 181. For useful refutations of the declension narrative, see Bill Lyne, "Gods Black Revolutionary Mouth: James Baldwin's Black Radicalism," *Science & Society* 74.1 (2010); Brian Norman, "James Baldwin's Confrontation with U.S. Imperialism in 'If Beale Street Could Talk'," *MELUS* 32.1 (2007). On how Baldwin embraced black nationalist vocabularies of homophobia and masculinism, see Dwight A. McBride, "Can the Queen Speak? Racial Essentialism, Sexuality and the Problem of Authority," *Callaloo* 21.2 (1998); Field, "Looking." On the importance of Baldwin's early radical associations and his own unwillingness to embrace them, see Douglas Field, "James Baldwin's Life on the Left: A Portrait of the Artist as a Young New York Intellectual," *ELH* 78.4 (2011).

6 See Erica R. Edwards, *Charisma and the Fictions of Black Leadership, Difference Incorporated* (Minneapolis: University of Minnesota Press, 2012); Sasha Torres, *Black, White, and in Color: Television and Black Civil Rights* (Princeton: Princeton University Press, 2003).

7 Baldwin's repetition of the phrase "Oh, pioneers!" throughout *No Name in the Street* refers to civil rights martyrs such as Martin Luther King, Jr., Malcolm X, Jonathan Jackson, Emmett Till, George Jackson, and Medgar Evers. On black mourning, see Fred Moten, "Black Mo'nin'," in David L. Eng and David Kazanjian (eds.), *Loss: The Politics of Mourning* (Berkeley: University of California Press, 2004).

8 Ibid., pp. 63, 72.

9 James Baldwin, "The Death of the Prophet," *Commentary* 10 (1950), 258.

10 Darieck Scott, *Extravagant Abjection: Blackness, Power, and Sexuality in the African American Literary Imagination, Sexual Cultures* (New York: New York University Press, 2010) p. 4.

11 Ibid., p. 17.

12 Ibid., p. 126.

13 Field, "Looking," p. 469.

14 James Baldwin, *No Name in the Street* (New York: Vintage Books, 2007), p. 9.

15 James Baldwin, *The Devil Finds Work: an Essay* (London: Corgi Books, 1976), p. 100.

16 See Erica Edwards, "Through the Other Looking Glass: Kaleidoscope Aesthetics and the Optics of Black Leadership," *African Identities* 11.2 (2013). On *One Day When I Was Lost*, see also Brian Norman, "Reading a 'Closet Screenplay': Hollywood, James Baldwin's Malcolms and the Threat of Historical Irrelevance," *African American Review* 39 (2005); Patsy Brewington, "James Baldwin: A Critical Evaluation" in Therman O'Daniel (ed.), *James Baldwin: A Critical Evaluation* (Washington, DC: Howard University Press, 1977).

10

ALIYYAH I. ABDUR-RAHMAN

"As Though a Metaphor Were Tangible": Baldwin's Identities

"One's identity cannot possibly be summed up by the phrase or any
of its derivatives – Negro queer, colored sissy, nigger faggot."
– Robert Reid-Pharr

"Metaphors sustain us."
– Hilton Als

The opening essay of Hilton Als's *White Girls*, titled "Tristes Tropiques,"
is a love story that ends, possibly predictably, in the anguished loss of a
beloved, who is presented over the course of the chapter as a love object,
a best friend, a never-lover, a twin, a proto-self. I hint at the predictability
of love lost because it is anticipated by the query that concludes the very
first paragraph of the chapter: "How can I be a we without him?"[1] Though
proffered initially as an existential or psychoanalytic quandary about the
sovereignty of the subject constituted in and through relationality, the question carries the lament: Who am I without her/him? The narrator's query
is central to the investigation of identity. Individuals are born into social
worlds that precede them. Systems of meaning and communication are
inherited. The trajectories of individual lives are determined in part by personal, familial, communal, and even national histories. If one's identity is
preconditioned always by social relations, sedimented material histories,
and structures of both perception and habit, then how is any I an I without
a we? This question was one pursued relentlessly by James Baldwin – black,
queer, author, civil rights spokesperson, public intellectual, man – throughout the four-decade expanse of his writing career, and the primary inquiry
of this essay.[2]

Returning briefly to Als, it is notable that the beloved in his opening essay
is a straight black man who varies his gender expression and inhabits race
improperly; he is called, affectionately and euphemistically, "Sir or Lady,"
or SL, to indicate his slippage between the identity categories that shape his

existence. As a person and as a beloved, SL is both elusive and illusory. "We are not lovers," writes the narrator –

> It's almost as if I dreamed him – my lovely twin, the same as me, only differ-
> ent.... Like most people, I respond to stories that tell me something about
> who I am or wish to be, but as reflected in another character's eyes. With it all,
> though, I know that I will lose sight of SL eventually. I have before. To movies
> and movie kissing. To his love of women.[3]

The narrator's desire for SL is depicted paradoxically as a quest for self-recognition and a form of self-abnegation. SL is a filmmaker who recites and reenacts movie scripts, specifically heterosexual love scripts in which resistant beloveds, mainly white women, are seduced into rituals of romance by ardent and determined male movie heroes. The narrator is never the object of SL's romantic pursuit, and ninety pages later the two no longer know each other. The narrator's loss of SL undoes him piecemeal over the course of the essay, yet it is this undoing that produces the narrator, enabling him to become a subject in the first place. That is, the loss of the beloved SL simultaneously shatters *and* shapes the black gay man who narrates the piece.

I open with this brief synopsis of "Tristes Tropiques" to introduce the themes and terms around which my investigation of identity will cohere in this essay: desire, subjectivity, race, sexuality, autonomy, belonging. Identity is understood in this essay as it is depicted and theorized above: as rela-tional, contextual, processual, and contingent. Furthermore, in Baldwin's works, individual identity is defined with and against others who are neither fully knowable nor available to the subject in the first place. The social constitution of identity, thus, is linked to formative loss and renders self-making a perpetual and fragile affair. Identity emerges, moreover, at the nexus of intersecting and overlapping categories of race, sexuality, class, gender, and nation that shape both societal structures and people's lives. As identities assume classificatory functions and political utility within social and geopolitical realms, acts of identification accrue psychic and material consequences, with specified risks and rewards for different persons and populations.[4]

Theorizing identity in James Baldwin's fiction, this essay analyzes Baldwin's second novel, *Giovanni's Room* (1956) – which links sexuality, subjectivity, and nationality – alongside the short story "Going to Meet the Man" (1965), which addresses sexual desire, racial violence, and civic par-ticipation. By reading these two texts together, I attend to Baldwin's medi-tation on identity as it informed both his imaginative work and his political commitments. Combining a critical race and queer analytical framework,

I pursue two motives: the first is to examine Baldwin's work as it anticipates and exemplifies poststructuralist deconstructions of identity, which dismantle the figure of the rational, a priori, autonomous humanist subject. Noting the centrality of the humanist subject to the discourses of rights and representation, I show how Baldwin manages to politicize identity – without stabilizing it as internally coherent. My second, related objective is to theorize race and sexuality as mutually imbricated categories of identity and social organization that (1) define the contours of being, becoming, and belonging in Western modernity, and (2) that structure the economic, juridical, and sociopolitical disparities in the United States that Baldwin consistently decried and that he narrativized in fiction as the imaginative site of social repair.[5]

On Sexual Identity

In this section, I analyze Baldwin's critical linkage of identity and social belonging, sexuality, and nation in *Giovanni's Room*. Considering Judith Butler's work on queer abjection, I explore the interrelation of race and sexuality in the United States as it is invoked in the Parisian setting of this novel. I contend ultimately that in *Giovanni's Room* Baldwin locates the solidification of sexual identity and sexual alterity within social disparities of race and class, even as he depicts the basic human struggle toward self-discovery and communal acceptance. Like Als's "Tristes Tropiques," *Giovanni's Room* tells the story of a fated, failed romance between men. The novel opens on the eve of its protagonist's return to Paris, the city in which David has forsaken love in order to "find himself" – the stakes of which journey have been inordinately high for both his male and female lovers, Giovanni and Hella. The novel unfolds over a single night and is told through a series of flashbacks in which David arranges and rearranges his memories trying to make sense of and come to terms with his identity as a queer, white American man.[6] Many of David's memories, occurring in a seamless chronology of narrative divergences, center on finding, falling in love with, and ultimately leaving his Italian male lover, Giovanni. As he plumbs the depths and meanings of his recollections, David seeks absolution and acceptance, as it is revealed over time to him and to the reader that David's identity – his whiteness, his masculinity, his homosexuality, his nationality – was secured at the expense of the love and the life of Giovanni. The events that lead to the night of this novel are the same events that land Giovanni on the guillotine. David's tortured self-discovery, thus, corresponds with his tortured acceptance of the death of his lover as the cost of his own investment in normative identity. David muses:

Now, from this night, this coming morning, no matter how many beds I find myself in between now and my final bed, I shall never be able to have any more of those boyish, zestful affairs – which are, really, when one thinks of it, a kind of higher, or, anyway, more pretentious masturbation. People are too various to be treated so lightly. I am too various to be trusted. If this were not so, I would not be alone in this house tonight. Hella would not be on the high seas. And Giovanni would not be about to perish, sometime between this night and this morning, on the guillotine.[7]

In *Giovanni's Room*, identity is rooted in desire, social positioning, and the convergence of the two. Although the novel thematizes the pleasures and catastrophes of romance, placing these at the center of individual becoming, it nonetheless exposes the enduring impact of ideologies of difference on social relations. Identity categories shape what is possible in the realm of the social and predefine who people understand themselves to be while navigating society's matrices. David's deep desire for Giovanni is undone, ultimately, by disparities of class, national difference, and by David's internalized homophobia. In other words, Giovanni's desperate poverty leads to his downfall, while David's relative privilege as a middle-class American grants him an irresponsible escape. For Baldwin, not even the compulsions of felt desire or its (un)fulfillment exceed the logics and the structures that comprise the social arena. As Baldwin biographer David Leeming writes, "[Baldwin] merges the question of racism with the question of self-identity, which had always been his concern and which had been most fully treated in the context of homosexuality in *Giovanni's Room*."[8] For Baldwin, individual identity is neither overdetermined by nor fully divisible from the various systems of meaning, habit, and social organization that make up society. Thus, despite the French setting and the narrative preoccupation with romance, *Giovanni's Room* is concerned deeply with racial, gendered, and sexual hierarchies within the capitalist economy of a stratified social sphere.

In a 1979 interview with Kalamu ya Salaam, Baldwin declared famously, "The people who call themselves white have really invented something that is not true.... White people invented black people to protect themselves against something which frightened them."[9] When asked what that "something" was, Baldwin replied, "Life, I guess."[10] Baldwin's quip is key to understanding the construction and preservation of normative identity through a dialectal process of constructing and repudiating both racial and sexual otherness. Not only do racist (and homophobic) logics support the inequitable distribution of rights and resources and determine who can qualify as human and citizen; further, these logics mitigate the ordinary vagaries, dangers, delights, sufferings, and risks characteristic of human experience.

In Baldwin's estimation, racial blackness operates as a figment or a fiction of the white imagination and serves as a repository for the longings and fears of white Americans. Defined always in the negative, blackness signals the deviance against which white identity is defined and legitimated. As Robert Reid-Pharr asserts, "The Black has been conceptualized as the inchoate, irrational non-subject."[11] Blackness is the exiled, negated, outside of the black/white binary that brings whiteness into being, delineates its contours, and secures its psychic, civic, and material advantages.

The dialectic of race and the contingency of racial definitions is depicted in the opening scene of *Giovanni's Room*, which exposes blackness as the frame and backdrop for the emergence of white identity. David stands at the window, glaring at his own reflection, and declares:

> I watch my reflection in the darkening gleam of the window pane. My reflection is tall, perhaps rather like an arrow, my blond hair gleams. My face is like a face you have seen many times. My ancestors conquered a continent, pushing across death-laden plains, until they came to an ocean which faced away from Europe's darker past.[12]

David's invocation of the "darker past" of Europe indicates his dawning, subtle identification with color and, thereby, begins Baldwin's work in *Giovanni's Room* of undoing whiteness. David's acknowledgement that his identity as a white American man is borne of European imperialism and domination establishes a crucial link between Europe and the United States that constitutes Europe as a suitable setting for Baldwin's interrogation of U.S. ethos and social inequities. It is important to note that Baldwin valorizes racialization as the experience of shared suffering and sacrifice and presents it as key to U.S. national redemption.[13] As Baldwin insists, "To be white is a moral choice. It's obviously a very deliberate challenge to people who think they're white to re-examine all their values, to put themselves in our [black people's] place, share in our danger.... They must get back in touch with reality. They can't avoid it, if they want to live."[14] As David studies his reflection in the "darkening gleam of the window pane," his initial declaration of whiteness is undermined by the perceptual darkness framing his visage, his view of himself. Even as David claims whiteness at the beginning of a narrative that is simultaneously the endpoint of its plot, he has endured the grittiness of life and lust that, once repressed and repudiated, becomes the material of blackness. As David constantly violates heteronormative codes and as sexual variance is perceived as the terrain of the socially ousted black (or dark) figure, David undergoes a progressive racialization throughout *Giovanni's Room* that throws his avowed whiteness into question and makes possible his own redemption.

As a novel, *Giovanni's Room* anticipates by nearly forty years the deconstructive approach to analyzing identity, which posits that, rather than being rooted in an essential, a priori, core self, identity depends on difference. In other words, it relies on the construction of an Other who is derogated, marginalized, exploited, and rendered socially expendable. In *Bodies that Matter*, Judith Butler, one of the primary American architects of deconstruction, dissects the regulatory practices of identification in the arena of sexuality.[15] Emphasizing, as in her earlier work *Gender Trouble*, the performativity of identity – which is not to imply its theatricality but the process by which it is made intelligible through continually reiterated behavioral (conceptual, linguistic, and gestural) norms[16] – Butler enters the territory of sexuality to critique heteronormativity as the reigning social and sexual paradigm. She describes heteronormativity as the "exclusionary matrix by which subjects are formed [that] requires a simultaneous production of a domain of abject beings, those who are not yet 'subjects' but who form the constitutive outside to the domain of the subject."[17] Speaking of the homosexual person in culture as "the abject," she explains further, "[t]he abject designates here precisely those 'unlivable' and 'uninhabitable' zones of social life which are nevertheless densely populated by those who do not enjoy the status of the subject, but whose living under the sign of the 'unlivable' is required to circumscribe the domain of the subject."[18] As those who are abject are relegated to the social and symbolic periphery of being, they do not register as legitimate subjects and citizens. Despite the lived reality of masses of people as queers, the social location of queerness in culture and its conceptual location in the symbolic order provide the "defining limits"[19] of heterosexuality, its enabling boundaries. I want to emphasize Butler's designation of the queer as always already "inside the [straight] subject as its own founding repudiation"[20] because this demonstrates not only the utility of the invention of queerness, but also its status as fixed, an orientation – an identity, as it were. In other words, the notion of deviant sexuality sets the stage for both the conception of a coherent, centralized, seemingly autonomous heterosexual identity and for the regulatory practices of identification by which it is preserved. The undoing of normative categories of identity depends on accepting their dialectical composition – the extent to which they project disavowed, though fundamental, elements of human experience onto exiled others.

When David flees from the United States, becomes engaged to Hella, and abandons Giovanni, he is seeking to preserve his identity as a straight, white American man. Notably, even before his sojourn in Paris, David's first homoerotic experience threatens to divest him of his whiteness and his masculinity, and this terrifies him. David recalls the morning after making love with his best friend, a "brown" boy named Joey:

> We were both naked and the sheet that we had used as a cover was tangled around our feet. Joey's body was brown, was sweaty, the most beautiful creation I had seen until then. I would have touched him to wake him but something stopped me. I was suddenly afraid.... My own body suddenly seemed gross and crushing and the desire which was rising in me suddenly seemed monstrous. But, above all, I was afraid.[21]

The monstrous desire budding in David is both homoerotic and cross-racial. David's experience of panic is a result, then, of his participation in two outlawed sexual behaviors that threaten his claim to uncontaminated whiteness. Nevertheless, in the hierarchy of debased sexualities, interracial love is, during the 1950s, the more socially deplored and thus, the more threatening to David's white identity. This is evident in David's registering Joey's racial difference before noticing their anatomical male sameness. That the heterosexual basis of David's masculine identity has come undone occurs to him only after he has begun to confront the meaning of his interracial desire. He finally realizes that Joey is "a boy." David narrates:

> I saw suddenly the power in his thighs, in his arms, in his loosely curled fists. The power and the promise of that body made me suddenly afraid. That body suddenly seemed the black opening of a cavern in which I would be tortured till madness came, in which I would lose my manhood.... The very bed, in its sweet disorder testified to its vileness.... A cavern opened in my mind, black, full of rumor, suggestion, of half-heard, half-forgotten, half-understood stories, full of dirty words. I thought I saw my future in that cavern. I was afraid...for not understanding how this could have happened to me, how this could have happened *in* me.[22]

David describes his desire for the male body as being drawn into a dark cavern. Even though Joey is beautiful to David, Joey's body represents the very opening of the cavern. A metaphor for homosexuality, racial blackness, and failed masculinity, the cavern sucks him in only to castrate and then to define him.[23] A number of words that David uses to describe same-sex desire signify simultaneously racial blackness: half-forgotten, madness, half-understood, black, dirty. Joey's brownness – his being raced – is both pollutant and contagion to David; to his mind, desiring Joey defiles David. Both David's proximity to and desire for Joey's brown body undermine his claims to heteronormativity, to masculinity, and to whiteness; David's descent into queerness is a literal descent into a black body. It is important to note that David attempts to recover his white masculinity by comparing the smallness of Joey's body to the largeness of his own and by conceiving the fulfillment of his desire as a form of dominance. In other words, in his imaginative reconstruction, David disregards Joey's consent to their sexual exchange and refigures it as an act of racial aggression, the broader history of which helped to establish normative white masculinity in the United States. The day after their lovemaking David quickly and unceremoniously discards Joey. Thus, even before Giovanni enters the action of the novel, it is clear that, for his investment in whiteness and dominant masculinity, David will abandon his dark Italian lover – who operates in the novel as both the figure of the black and the figure of the homosexual.

Much of the action of *Giovanni's Room* takes place within spatial enclosures: bars, hotel rooms, trains, bedrooms, prison cells. Evoking both the homosexual closet and the psychic space of interiority, the various enclosures depicted in *Giovanni's Room* are sites of human suffering, human relating, and human becoming. From David's childhood home – which is haunted by his dead mother and deserted daily by his philandering father – to the executioner's cell where Giovanni takes his last breath, the novel roots subjective development in concrete sites where characters interact in ways that are messy, loving, alienated, stifled, frightening, temporary. These sites are transient spaces of containment and development, and the most significant of them is Giovanni's room.

Guillaume's bar is the first significant site of queer self-becoming and belonging that David encounters in Paris. On the night he meets the beautiful Italian-born bartender Giovanni, David experiences a familiar hunger for love and sex with men. Despite spending time with two older, wealthy gay men, Jacques and Guillaume, David attempts before this evening to pass himself off as straight. In fact, he often expresses his disgust for Jacques and Guillaume, who, in their desperation for touch and for significance, purchase sexual favors from emaciated, foreign boys. David is, likewise, revolted by the young, queer, femme boys:

> les folles, always dressed in the most improbable combinations, screaming like parrots the details of their latest affairs…I always found it difficult to believe that they ever went to bed with anybody, for a man who wanted a woman would certainly have rather had a real one and a man who wanted a man would certainly not want one of *them*.[24]

David associates male homosexuality with assailed masculinity and with the perversion of acceptable desire. Like the abject figures of Butler's theorization, queerness for David signals failure, excess, and eventual social exclusion. Within Giovanni's room David's internal struggle with his queerness is staged, even as it is dramatized in his tortured affair with Giovanni. David, guilt-ridden and contemptuous, leaves Giovanni for the brief domestic solace of the hetero-patriarchal white home.

After his aborted engagement with Hella, David eventually accepts his own same-gender desires. Though not fully redeemed by novel's end, the despondent David has matured into viable, ethical personhood according to Baldwin's conception of subjective development. David accepts his culpability in Giovanni's execution, which entails releasing his own commitments to normative identity. Imaginatively reconstructing Giovanni's final moments, David dwells with him psychically, in terror and in love. By bearing with Giovanni the inexorable end of life, David acquires a beautiful, if weathered, and meaningful sense of self. As Emmanuel Nelson describes:

> Reaching a genuine sense of self and forging an identity depend largely on self-knowledge and self-awareness which, according to Baldwin, come only through suffering. In other words, suffering, if endured creatively, leads to self-knowledge, which, in return, can offer the possibility of achieving a genuine sense of self.... But self-discovery is never an entirely private battle; it can be achieved only in spiritual communion with others."[25]

On Racial Identity

The existential linkage of life and death is central to the construction of identity in James Baldwin's writing. Life and death are not arbitrary states but manufactured social conditions wherein specific populations are marked for living while others are marked for dying. Baldwin writes in *No Name in the Street* (1972), "[W]hite men have killed black men for sport, or out of terror or out of the intolerable excess of terror called hatred, or out of the necessity of affirming their identity as white men."[26] In this sprawling personal essay, published as Baldwin's fourth book of nonfiction, Baldwin grapples with the recent assassinations of Martin Luther King, Jr. and Malcolm X, tying these murders to the midcentury Southern practice of lynching black people in communal spectacles meant to terrorize and to thwart the socio-economic and political advancement of black people. Baldwin recognizes the appallingly low value placed on black life, likening black murder to sport. He suggests here that the mass lynching of black people between the post-emancipation period and the height of the civil rights era was animated by fear and hatred, two emotional resonances ironically displaced onto the victims of lynching. Notably, the predominant justification for lynching was the putative defense of white womanhood. Lynch mobs purportedly acted in spontaneous, panicked outrage to avenge and protect the sexual safety and sanctity of white women, thus casting black men as sexual terrorists and not victims of racial terrorism. Baldwin asserts that white identity emerged in the United States in concert with racial blackness – through ideologies and acts of violent disavowal. White identity was secured, that is, through the (customary and legal) sociopolitical exclusion of black people, and, for much of the twentieth century, through repetitive public stagings of black bodily demise.

For Baldwin, black identity structures, through resistance to the symbolic and social practices of negation, determines the contours of personhood and rights-bearing citizenship in the United States. Racial difference is not the exclusive province of the racialized figure; blackness emerges, rather, as the method and measure of an embedded and asymmetric sociopolitical dynamic. The short story "Going to Meet the Man" is a harrowing tale of lynching, narrated in flashbacks over the course of one evening of failed lovemaking between the protagonist, a white deputy sheriff Jesse, and his wife, Grace. Published in the fall of 1965, the story emerged in the wake of Malcolm X's February 1965 assassination and the three civil rights marches from Selma to Montgomery, in which hundreds of protestors for voting rights were brutalized by state and local police.[27] The story – like the later, longer *No Name in the Street* – strikes a tone of weary anguish and sardonic disbelief that the nation had not yet extended ordinary rights of citizenship and protections of the state to black Americans. Beyond its setting in the couple's bed, the story marks the general upheaval of the time, foregrounding the weariness, desperation, and frustrated longing of the white male protagonist. Jesse lies beside his slumbering wife, wanting to make love, or at least wanting "to let whatever was in him come out; but it wouldn't come out."[28]

This night, Jesse is haunted and horrified by memories of protestors who repeatedly showed up at voting sites in nonviolent protest and in song. Despite the beatings, the jailing, the raping and the lynchings, the young black protesters refuse to relinquish the fight for their basic rights of enfranchisement; they continue to protest, and they continue to insist on their right as American citizens to vote. Jesse is aware, moreover, that some black men have entered the U.S. army and become soldiers; some have guns and might eventually use them. At the thought of this, Jesse finds himself – his whiteness, his masculinity – imperiled:

> He turned again, toward Grace again, and moved close to her warm body. He felt something he had never felt before. He felt that he would like to hold her, hold her, hold her, and be buried in her like a child and never have to get up in the morning again and go downtown to face those faces, good Christ, they were ugly! and never have to enter that jail house again and smell that smell and hear that singing; never again feel that filthy, kinky, greasy hair under his hand, never again watch those black breasts leap against the leaping cattle prod, never hear those moans again, or watch that blood run down or the fat lips split or the sealed eyes struggle open.[29]

Jesse's inability to feel aroused by his wife is due, in part, to his refiguring her body as a maternal site of comfort, concealment, and care: "This was his wife. He could not ask her to do just a little thing for him, just to help him out, just for a little while, the way he could ask a nigger girl to do it."³⁰ Jesse's memories of black girls whom he arrests under the false charge of prostitution in order to sexually assault them initiate an arousal that his wife's warm body cannot sustain. The sensual, pictorial (re)collection of black body parts that come quite literally apart – blood falling, lips splitting, eyes struggling open – under the brutality of police assault both exhausts and disgusts him, impeding further his arousal. In the face of persistent black resistance, Jesse is rendered impotent. Baldwin here depicts the mutual constitution of race and sexuality, of identity and desire. In order to reinvigorate and reclaim the white male citizen-subject who has become undone in the face of strident black political mobilization, Jesse remembers a lynching that his parents brought him to as a boy. The lynching is a formative experience for Jesse, as his racial, gendered, and sexual identity are stabilized in a moment of terrified spectatorship, or terroristic viewing. As a child, that is, he participates in the lynching simply by being present and watching. Reminiscent of the oft-cited exclamation in Fanon's *Black Skin, White Masks* – "'Look a Negro!'…'Look, a Negro!'…'Mama, see the Negro! I'm frightened!'"³¹ – Baldwin adapts the Lacanian mirror stage to suggest that it is witnessing antiblack racism within the context of nuclear normativity that establishes both white American identity and African-American degradation. As Fanon shows in his depiction of an exchange between a white child and its mother or primary caregiver, the acknowledgement, disavowal, and (mental/material) subjugation of the black are procedural steps in the development of white subjectivity.

First published in 1952, *Black Skin, White Masks* is Fanon's effort to explain the psychological and cultural assaults of racism and colonial subjection on black people. He uses psychoanalytic methods and theory to approximate the experiences of people of color under racist regimes. Although his study is concerned primarily with colonialism in Martinique, it is applicable to other race-based, oppressive regimes, including slavery and U.S.-styled democracy. Moreover, Fanon expands psychoanalysis beyond the study of the nuclear family to consider the wide-ranging effects of racism and colonialism on individuals within oppressed communities. His study is, finally, concerned less with the formation of the (white) subject – that is, how blackness services whiteness – than with the impact of abjection on the psychological and social development of black individuals. This is a critical distinction between Fanon's work in *Black Skins, White Masks* and Baldwin's in "Going to Meet the Man," in which Baldwin presents a harrowing tale of white masculine becoming. Fanon inhabits the derided position of the black – felt and described primarily in terms of corporeal demarcation: "[c]onsciousness of the body is solely a negating activity"[32] – in terms of trauma, fragmentation, and the constant threat of dissolution/ demise. He states:

> I was responsible at the same time for my body, for my race, for my ancestors. I subjected myself to an objective examination, I discovered my blackness, my ethnic characteristics; and I was battered down by tom-toms, cannibalism, intellectual deficiency, fetichism (sic), racial defects, slave ships, and above all else, above all: "sho' good eatin'."
>
> On that day, completely dislocated, unable to be abroad with the other, the white man, who unmercifully imprisoned me, I took myself far off from my own presence, far indeed and made myself an object. What else could it be for me but an amputation, an excision, a hemorrhage that spattered my whole body with black blood?"[33]

Although Fanon does not relinquish entirely his claim to a (semi-)autonomous subjectivity that can think and act on its own behalf – that is, he *subjects himself* to objective examination, *takes himself* from his own presence, and *makes of himself* an object – the activities he undertakes reveal the fragmenting effects of race and racism on his self-conception.

In "Going to Meet the Man," Baldwin locates the spectacle of black psychic and bodily disintegration at the heart of white self-making. In Jesse's memory, ritual lynching was a festive occasion. He recalls the drive on the way to the lynching site, his head cradled in his mother's lap, his father jovial. Jesse's father teases his mother for the pretty ribbon in her hair: "When that nigger looks at you, he's going to swear he throwed his life away for nothing. Wouldn't be surprised if he didn't come back to haunt you."[34] Jesse's father's compliment invokes the predominant discourse of lynching: black men's insatiable, criminal desire for white women. His jokey delivery mocks such discourse, calling attention to its fallacy. Jesse notes that as white families dress up and joyously gather at the lynching site, all the town's black residents disappear. In Baldwin's potent (re)telling, lynching instantiates black removal in two distinct ways: first, in the form of the black body that materially falls away as it is hung, burned, castrated, and mutilated into tiny pocket-sized bits, and second, in the form of generalized disappearance, in which an entire black community, grasping the meaning of lynching, absents itself from ordinary, everyday sites and practices of civic engagement (purchasing goods, boarding a bus, attending school or prayer services, buying postal stamps, visiting friends, and so forth).

The power to disappear a body or an entire population is presented by Baldwin as one feature of white entitlement. Once the body of the victim has been burned into something that is "both sweet and rotten," Jesse looks to his parents and the other white townspeople.[35] His mother's "eyes were very bright, her mouth was open; she was more beautiful than he had ever seen her, and more strange. He began to feel a joy he had never felt before."[36] In the afterglow of satiation, Jesse's mother is even more beautiful and beloved by him. As he observes a man castrating the burning, hanging man, Jesse, at eight, wishes that it were he doing the cutting. Later, Jesse's father, also in the peaceful aftereffect of psychosexual release, refers to the lynching as a memorable picnic. Jesse understands his presence at the lynching as a rite of passage: "At this moment Jesse loved his father more than he had ever loved him. He felt that his father had carried him through a mighty test, had revealed to him a great secret which would be the key to his life forever."[37] White male identity is secured not simply through the propertied entitlements of citizenship but also through communally sanctioned rights/rites of black negation, which are passed on as white male inheritance. His consciousness returning to the present night, Jesse experiences renewed vigor and initiates furious lovemaking with his wife, invoking repeatedly, and ironically, the now neutralized prowess of "the [dead] nigger."[38]

"Going to Meet the Man" thus ends, like *Giovanni's Room*, with the sobering reminder that identities take shape in and through constitutive loss. For Baldwin, the index of a just society is determined simply by how evenly such losses are distributed across different persons and populations. Through his writing, Baldwin perpetually found ways of naming and opposing structural processes of marginalization that disproportionately impact the poor, the queer, the black – without essentializing group difference. Considering race, class, sexuality, gender, and nation, and preventing social injustice in its many individual and systemic iterations, requires a reckoning with power as it manifests in social conditions rather than in discrete identity categories. Famously uttering, "No label, no slogan, no party, no skin color, and indeed, no religion is more important than the human being,"[39] Baldwin insisted on the innate value of every human being regardless of the accident of their birth, which determines the various social groups in which s/he might find herself. He insisted, moreover, that the necessary, existential work of personhood is the willful untethering of one's identity from the categories bequeathed at birth, a practice of ongoing negotiation among self, society, and circumstance. "Identity," he wrote in "The Devil Finds Work" (1976),

> would seem to be the garment with which one covers the nakedness of the self: in which case, it is best that the garment be loose, a little like the robes of the desert, through which robes one's nakedness can always be felt, and, sometimes, discerned. This trust in one's nakedness is all that gives one the power to change one's robes.[40]

Regardless of social positionality, belief in one's complicated humanity is at the heart of self-discovery, and what is most needed to navigate and to repair our complex and stratified social world.

NOTES

1 Hilton Als. *White Girls* (San Francisco: McSweeney's, 2013), p. 1.

2 It is noteworthy that Baldwin did not use the term "queer" to refer to his sexuality. In fact, he eschewed sexual labels altogether. I use the term "queer" in reference to Baldwin to recognize, first, Baldwin's avowed practice of same-gender love, and, two, his central place as both historical figure and author in the development of contemporary LGTBQ activism and queer theory. My thinking here follows that of Dwight McBride, who notes that the publication of *Giovanni's Room* was Baldwin's "'public' outing of himself," which was significant in "the development of this particularized tradition of queer African American fiction." In "Straight Black Studies: On African American Studies, James Baldwin, and Black Queer Studies," in E. Patrick Johnson and Mae G. Henderson (eds.), *Black Queer Studies: A Critical Anthology* (Durham: Duke University Press, 2005), p. 72.

3 Als, *White Girls*, p. 10.

4 This essay utilizes a queer-of-color critique, which places gender and sexuality in critical conversation with race, class, and nation as intersecting and overlapping categories of analysis, and as contingent factors that shape both societal structures and people's lives.

5 Writing on Baldwin's use of literature to redress the social harms that U.S. law can and does not, Shireen K. Patell writes, "Literature accommodates the unsettled and unsettling nature of language, affords ambiguities free range, indulges the complex and nonclosural, and thus testifies to that which the law cannot admit into evidence, that which cannot be responded to within the stark framework of 'yes' or 'no' but that relentlessly demands subtle accounting, an other accounting, a would-be narration of the unnarratable, nonetheless" (357). In "'We the People,' Who?: James Baldwin and the Traumatic Constitution of These United States." *Comparative Literature Studies* 48.3 (2011).

6 My use of "queer" to describe David's sexuality is not synonymous with gay or homosexual. I use queer as it is commonly used in both academic and common discourses to sexual proclivities and practices that fall outside of a strict heterosexual paradigm. For a fuller account of the term's expansive meaning, see Aliyyah I. Abdur-Rahman, Introduction in *Against the Closet: Black Political Longing and the Erotics of Race* (Durham: Duke University Press, 2012).

7 James Baldwin, *Giovanni's Room* (originally published 1956) (New York: Dell Publishing, 1988), p. 5.

8 David A. Leeming, *James Baldwin: A Biography* (New York: Knopf, 1994), p. 117.

9 Kalamu ya Salaam, "James Baldwin: Looking toward the Eighties," in Fred R. Standley and Louis H. Pratt (eds.), *Conversations with James Baldwin* (Jackson: University of Mississippi Press, 1989), pp. 179–80.

10 Ibid., p. 180.

11 Robert Reid-Pharr, "Tearing the Goat's Flesh: Homosexuality, Abjection and the Production of a Late Twentieth-Century Black Masculinity," *Studies in the Novel* 28.3 (1996), 373.

12 Baldwin, *Giovanni's Room*, p. 3.

13 For Baldwin, national redemption and sustainable collective futurity will be produced only through an interracial national polis in which black men and women are regarded as equals in sociopolitical, juridical, economic, and humanistic terms. As Chandan Reddy astutely puts it, "It is precisely [the] loss of national identity through black racialization, an uprooting from the national landscape, that dialectically opens up a new set of possibilities" (73). My use of racialization thus refers to an identification with aspects of black experience and the various concepts that are believed to constitute blackness. See Reddy, *Freedom with Violence: Race, Sexuality, and the U.S. State* (Durham: Duke University Press, 2011).

14 Mel Watkins, "James Baldwin Writing and Talking." *The New York Times* (September 23, 1979), 36.

15 Deconstruction refers to a method of analysis prevalent in contemporary literary and cultural analysis. With roots in continental philosophy and linguistics, deconstruction interrogates the notion of absolute, intrinsic value and meaning and argues that within systems of signs, meaning is derived from the pairing of oppositions that are accorded differential values. Judith Butler deploys deconstruction to theorize gender and sexuality as concepts and modes of being in western society.

16 Judith Butler, *Gender Trouble: Feminism and the Subversion of Identity* (New York: Routledge, 1990).

17 Judith Butler, *Bodies that Matter: On the Discursive Limits of Sex* (New York: Routledge 1993), p. 3.

18 Ibid.

19 Ibid.

20 Ibid.

21 Baldwin, *Giovanni's Room*, p. 9.

22 Ibid., p. 10.

23 For analysis of the castration complex in psychoanalysis and feminist theory, see Jacques Lacan, "The Agency of the Letter in the Unconscious," in *Écrits* (originally published 1966), (New York: W. W. Norton & Co., 2006) and *The Seminar of Jacques Lacan* (New York: W. W. Norton, 1988); Luce Irigaray, *This Sex Which Is Not One* (Ithaca: Cornell University Press, 1985); and Jacques Derrida, *Dissemination* (Chicago: Chicago University Press, 1981).

24 Baldwin, *Giovanni's Room*, p. 29.

25 Emmanuel S. Nelson, "James Baldwin's Vision of Otherness and Community," *MELUS* 10.2 (1983), 27–28.

26 James Baldwin, *No Name in the Street*, in *The Price of the Ticket: Collected Nonfiction, 1948–1985* (New York: St. Martin's, 1985), p. 550.

27 For a thorough account of pressing historical conditions out of which "Going to Meet the Man" was produced, see James Campbell, *Talking at the Gates: A Life of James Baldwin* (New York: Viking, 1991).

28 James Baldwin, "Going to Meet the Man," in *Going to Meet the Man* (New York: Dial Press, 1965), p. 230.

29 Ibid., pp. 230–1.
30 Ibid., p. 229.
31 Frantz Fanon, *Black Skin, White Masks*, trans. Charles Markmann (New York: Grove Press, 1967), p. 112.
32 Ibid., p. 110.
33 Ibid., p. 112.
34 Baldwin, "Going to Meet the Man," in *Going to Meet the Man*, p. 244.
35 Ibid., p. 247.
36 Ibid.
37 Ibid., p. 248.
38 Ibid., p. 249.
39 James Baldwin in Karen Thorsen, et al. *James Baldwin: The Price of the Ticket* (San Francisco: California Newsreel, 1989).
40 Baldwin, "The Devil Finds Work," in *The Price of the Ticket: Collected Nonfiction, 1948–1985* (New York: St. Martin's, 1985), p. 537.

11

CHRISTOPHER FREEBURG

Baldwin and the Occasion of Love

> To be loved, baby, hard, at once, and forever, to strengthen
> you against the loveless world.
> – James Baldwin, "A Letter to My Nephew," 1962

Love's Currency

When reading James Baldwin's seminal prose, readers cannot escape the concept of love. Not only is love central to Baldwin's writing; it is central to his thinking about social change. Notably, in the proliferation of criticism on sexuality and gender, love plays little if any role in the evaluation of Baldwin's prose.[1] This is not to say that critics never mention love. Critics casually refer to love, since it is undeniable in Baldwin's corpus, yet the silence around love's central connection to Baldwin's racial and sexual politics is both conspicuous and surprising. Baldwin is everywhere talking about love, yet critics set the topic aside. In prose masterpieces like *The Fire Next Time* (1968), short fiction such as *Going to Meet the Man* (1965), and novels like *Go Tell It on the Mountain* (1953), *Another Country* (1962), and *If Beale Street Could Talk* (1974), love remains central. Baldwin invokes love or its explicit absence in many varieties. Baldwin repeatedly comes back to a singular emphasis: if one faces up to the most challenging truths that shape their lives, instead of keeping up a façade, one can maintain deep personal and political connections that define the basis for love. Love surfaces in a variety of guises throughout Baldwin's rich discussion of racial and sexual conflict in the United States.

Baldwin writes in *Another Country* (1962), "How do you live if you can't love? And how can you live if you do?"[2] Baldwin answers this question throughout his work by cultivating different sites for love – such as the family, the sexual life of married couples, or the bond between two male friends. These sites enhance Baldwin's critiques of homophobia, racial myopia, Northern white liberals, and Southern racism. In this vein, love allows Baldwin to deepen his readers' sense of the personal, political, and historical aspects of characters' lives. Critics can read Baldwin without noting the symbolic force of love, yet by keeping love in focus, critics can continue to enrich ongoing discussions of race and sexuality.

One reason that critics tend to avoid the subject of love is that so often, its representation reinforces the idea that professing love for an individual is good enough as a commitment to social change and that declaration is equivalent to the hard work of telling the truth about oneself – which, as Baldwin demonstrates in the texts this essay studies, can be terror-inducing and chaotic. Baldwin's writing shows how popular art can enable American audiences to wrap themselves in a "protective sentimentality" that represses feelings of instability and inner "chaos."[3] He makes a distinction between deep love and sentimental love by suggesting that the sentimentality found in popular novels and films like *The Postman Always Rings Twice* (1946) and *The Best Years of Our Lives* (1946) discourages audiences from facing the most challenging aspects of American racism. Facing these dilemmas like racism courageously, he suggests, may upend the way people think about the world, thereby exposing them to feelings of inner "chaos." From this perspective, when characters find and profess love, it becomes an escape from difficult social conflicts and reinforces fantastical abstractions, normative social categories, and social inequality. Baldwin's interest in love, and his battle to wrench it from the popular films and novels Americans consume, is based on the question of whether people can define their own terms, face who they are or have become, and consider how they treat others. Thus Baldwin deploys situations that involve love to disclose the difficulties that prevent individuals and groups from creating new social relationships without – or at least with less – racism, sexism, and homophobia.

Love's currency in Baldwin's prose hinges on its ability to signify interpersonal instability, moments in life when subjects are rocked by emotion, physical intimacy, and vulnerability – moments that, in his work, are crucial to identity-making. This essay confronts love in Baldwin's work by addressing how both his disdain for sentimentality and his critiques of U.S. racism are defined by his portrayals of moral and spiritual courage. The role of love also indicates Baldwin's unassailable belief in the importance of one's ability to deepen and transform oneself, both morally and spiritually, to effect necessary social change. By analyzing selections from Baldwin's fiction, as well as from his essays, interviews, and speeches, this essay probes Baldwin's critiques of racist and sexist conditions in order to suggest how Baldwin showcases the radical dimensions of love.

Feeling the Cost

Despite being a fierce critic of sentimental fictions, Baldwin was labeled sentimental himself by an icon of the intellectual left, Irving Howe. Referring to *Giovanni's Room* (1954) and *Another Country* (1962), Howe discerns a "disconcerting kind of sentimentalism, a quavering and sophisticated submission to the ideology of love."[4] Beyond this statement, Howe does not elaborate on love's "ideology." What Howe misses about Baldwin is fundamental. Across most of his writings, love presents opportunities for characters to grapple with issues that prevent them from addressing personal and social problems. In my view, because love is so mired in the mass-market sentimentality that Baldwin rails against, critics like Howe miss opportunities to see the transformative possibilities and social change in Baldwin's vision of love.

Howe's misdiagnosis of love in Baldwin calls attention to recent criticism's tendency to treat this theme with insufficient seriousness. Critics have yet to reconcile Baldwin's forceful commitment to social and political change with his commitment to concepts such as love. Baldwin unapologetically invokes the importance, even the necessity, of love in everyone's life. In *The Fire Next Time*, Baldwin proclaims:

> Love takes off the masks that we fear we cannot live without and know we cannot live within. I use the word "love" here not merely in the personal sense but as a state of being, or a state of grace – not in the infantile American sense of being made happy but in the tough and universal sense of quest and daring and growth.[5]

Love is crucial for growth and capturing the "universal sense of quest," which Baldwin identifies, requires us to "dare everything."[6] This is a tall order for serious self-transformation, requiring one to sacrifice things one may cling to in order to insulate oneself from troubling social, psychological, and political disruptions.

Baldwin often critiqued popular U.S. films and novels that centered around love, yet the texts he targeted display the opposite of what Baldwin considered love to require. In addition to criticizing films like *The Best Years of Our Lives* and novels like *The Postman Always Rings Twice*, Baldwin was not shy about criticizing the much-hyped black film, *Carmen Jones* (1954). *Carmen Jones* is an all-black operatic film remake of Georges Bizet's opera *Carmen* (1875). Donald Bogle characterizes the film release as a major event: "*Carmen Jones*, released in 1954, was the 1950s' most lavish, most publicized, and most successful all-black spectacle."[7] Bogle also depicts "pop creations" and "stock situations" which Baldwin no doubt found problematic.[8] *Carmen Jones* – in which eroticism, violence, and a melodramatic finale are central – can be viewed in a similar vein as other films Baldwin labeled superficial and lifeless. Discussing *Carmen Jones*, Baldwin submits: "One is not watching either tenderness or love and one is certainly not watching the complex and consuming passion which leads to life or death – one is watching a timorous and vulgar representation of these things."[9]

Americans celebrate the films that Baldwin criticizes. Baldwin, by exploring what Americans like so much about them, can get closer to what he imagines as the "interior life of Americans."[10] Baldwin's broader sense is that the very fact that *Carmen Jones* was created shows the disturbed state of America. Baldwin writes that the film assumes stereotypical ideas about what the American public thinks about blacks and sex[11] – he explains that what is most distressing is "the conjecture this movies leaves one with as to what Americans take sex to be."[12] Yet Baldwin, in writing his critique of the film, sees his writing as enhancing America's readiness to think seriously about the mass media's representations of blacks. For Baldwin, bad films encourage hiding and avoidance in ways that are dangerous and threaten an individual's beliefs and way of life. Americans need to turn inward, as Baldwin imagines, in order to confront the only way to deal with the racist conditions and social exclusions that led to the creation of a movie like *Carmen Jones*.

In "Stranger in the Village," Baldwin explains that racist lynch laws, segregation, and other racist practices reveal the way whites found a "way to live with the Negro in order to live with himself."[13] According to Baldwin, for whites to accept blacks as "one of themselves" means jeopardizing their own superior status as whites.[14] Thus, segregation, racial violence against blacks, and other racist practices point to whites' efforts to feel disconnected from blacks even when they may share local, familial, religious, or other connections. Baldwin takes this idea further in the culminating moment of his speech to the West Indian Student Centre in London. In the speech, he argued that whites must be ready to face their own truths about their relationships and connectedness to blacks. Many whites need to admit that:

> brother has murdered brother knowing it was his brother; white men have lynched negroes knowing them to be their sons; white women have had negroes burned knowing them to be their lovers. It is not a racial problem of whether or not you are willing to look at your life and be responsible for it and be willing to change it.... American people are unable to face the fact that I am flesh of their flesh...they cannot face that...and that is why the city of Detroit went up in flames.[15]

Baldwin emphasizes that people who get lynched or burned may be actually related to or in love with one of the whites in the lynch mob. Whites, he suggests, especially in moments of crisis, neither acknowledge nor defend their brothers. Although he does not mention love specifically, the father/son, brother/brother, and lover/lover relations that he mentions connote an ideal of closeness, affection, and loyalty. For Baldwin, whites' denial of their connection to blacks and family members or lovers is not simply a racial problem. Baldwin exclaims, "It is not a racial problem of whether or not you are willing to look at your life and be responsible for it and be willing to change it."[16] In the midst of talking about racial disavowal, Baldwin says that, at its core, the "problem is not racial." By this remark, he does not mean that it does not involve race (it obviously does), but rather he indicates that whites' unwillingness to tell the truth about who they are connected to animates racial conflict. Baldwin asks the question: Are you willing to look at your life, be truthful about what you see and take "responsibility for it"? Baldwin presents the absence of love, truth, and responsibility between family members, or broader still, between the citizenry of the United States, as moral violation, as something his audience should be outraged against enough to prompt a moral and political reform that would lead to social acceptance between the races.

Baldwin's truth-telling about the blood ties between the races recognizes that this can be a world-shattering event. One must risk "falling to pieces," with no guarantee of the potential to be put back together again. Baldwin claims, "This may take away one's dreams, but it delivers one to one's self."[17] To bring one to one's self is a personal inward journey, the specifics of which Baldwin brings to life in his fiction. For Baldwin, the bonds of love reflect social mores and political realities of racial difference. While Baldwin understandably had his own doubts in desperate times, throughout his career he remained committed to the notion that if one cannot risk the destruction of his or her ideas and way of life, then "longed-for love" will not be possible.[18]

Violent Longing

In his fiction, Baldwin turns to the marriage bed to draw out how whites' avoidance of the history of racial violence actually prevents them from keeping separate any part of their lives. The title story in the short story collection *Going to Meet the Man* (1965) concerns a local town sheriff named Jesse as he deals with blacks in the South at a historical moment of racial unrest. Baldwin begins the story with Jesse's inability to perform sexually with his wife. In an attempt to overcome his impotence, Jesse thinks about an "image of a black girl" to excite him, but the thought actually makes it impossible for him to have sex with his wife.[19] Baldwin invites the reader to closely observe the physicality of the sex act. The closeness is not simply about aesthetic detail but rather involves the disclosure of a scene in which the naive reader may not expect racial difference to make such an impact. Jesse's ability to perform sexually is linked to race. His predilection for "a black girl" is not merely about racial exoticism but is also linked to family history and racial violence in his community and in the South generally. At the end of the story, Jesse is sexually aroused after recalling how his parents took him to see a lynching; only through that memory can he be sexually aroused. The narrator describes how "[h]e grabbed himself and stroked himself" after thinking of the lynching (950). Jesse could experience neither the fullness of love with his wife Grace during sex nor the feeling of grace while the image of "a nigger" possessed him. In Baldwin's world of love, Jesse cannot even enjoy socially and legally consecrated intimacy with his spouse because he cannot confront his own role in the history of racial violence, and injustice haunts his community's daily life.

In "Going to Meet the Man," then, racial unrest, social relations, and intimacy are intertwined. Hence, the lynching is also significant because Jesse's memory of whites' destruction of the black man quiets Jesse's anxiety over current black protests – social unrest that, in the time of the story, he cannot control. Yet what he believes insulates him from danger in fact represents the loss of his identity. While it appears that the lynching made him capable of sex, the sex act harnesses Jesse with feelings of further constraint. He says to Grace, "Love me like you'd love a nigger," and only by using the word "nigger" is he able to make love to his wife (950). The body of the "nigger," not of his wife, energizes his titillation. Jesse cannot reciprocate such intensity with the woman he loves while the "nigger" is there, and he can neither live nor love while he refuses to confront the reason behind this. Furthermore, the lynch mob, whose consciousness Jesse inherits, "never dreamed that their privacy could contain any element of terror...that their past so stubbornly refused to be remembered" (941). It is significant that Jesse never confronts or tries to answer the questions he asked when he was child on the way to lynchings – questions about Otis, the black servant of his childhood, or other blacks he was friendly with.

Love Acts

While "Going to Meet the Man" exemplifies an environment in which love cannot thrive, Baldwin's *Another Country* (1962) wrestles with the relationship between one's sexual acts, the love one professes, and truths one is willing to face with courage. In *Another Country*, the death of Rufus, a jazz performer, sets in motion new opportunities for his peers and friends to think about their connections to him, to one another, and to themselves. As in "Going to Meet the Man," the role of sex in *Another Country* is crucial.

But sex in the bohemian Greenwich Village is not inherently good, pleasurable, or devoid of consequences. As Baldwin writes, the people in his neighborhood had plenty of great sex "and still chopped each other up with razors on Saturday nights."[20] In the novel, Rufus and his friend Vivaldo use sex as a weapon to destroy, humiliate, and use people, as well as to hide their own anxieties, pain around their past, and uncertainty about the future – things they are unwilling to face or accept. Rufus's sexual encounters are not "acts of love" (53); Rufus beat and humiliated his white girlfriend Leona; he destroyed her. He used Leona in whatever "way would humiliate her the most" (53). Cass, one of Rufus's friends, describes Vivaldo similarly. She says, "you get involved with impossible women – whores, nymphomaniacs, drunks – and I think you do it in order to protect yourself from anything serious" (96). Sex is the sine qua non of identity, but the novel shows how in facing one's dark inner fears and pain, sex can be transformed from a scene of objectification to one of meaningful intimacy and love. One can say that the discourse of sexuality and power in the novel is mediated by the central question that nags Vivaldo after Rufus's death: "How does one live without love? And how can you live if you do?" (340).

Rufus faces similar questions during his own life. "'Do you love me?'...this was the question Rufus heard" as he listens to the performances by musicians he watches with Vivaldo (8). What Rufus hears in the music foreshadows Vivaldo's failure to comfort Rufus on a night when the latter needs to be held and loved. This moment also marks the culmination of an ongoing silence between Vivaldo and Rufus, one that continues despite their friendship. They both justify their individual sexual exploits and exploitations of others, even as they look beyond their own limitations and see the abuses perpetrated by each other. They do not address why they use and abuse others, and they fail to discuss the problem of racial tensions with other friends. These discussions are "minefields they dare not cross" (320). Baldwin makes affective personal bonds appear to be a cold and impersonal space. On the night Rufus desires comfort, Vivaldo confesses, "I had the weirdest feeling that he wanted me to take him in my arms...I had the feeling he wanted someone to hold him" (342). But Vivaldo is afraid – afraid that Rufus would not understand that it was only love. "Only love." Fear arrests Vivaldo, and, perhaps more importantly, a scared Vivaldo does not face what frightens him enough to forego his instinct to try to embrace Rufus.

Perhaps most important of all, Vivaldo's act of love with Rufus's former lover Eric has transformed Vivaldo. Eric's warmth and openness inspire Vivaldo to break the silence that has constrained his relationship with Rufus. Vivaldo's revelation of his truth leads to a closer connection with Eric, which leads them to express their love and have sex. Vivaldo caresses and makes love to Eric. Eric loves him as well. The physical intimacy unlocks Vivaldo further (386–7). Baldwin uses the connection between facing fear, telling the truth, and experiencing bodily sensations to produce the discourse of love. For Vivaldo, loving Eric "[is] a great revelation" making "for an unprecedented steadiness and freedom" (387). In these scenes, Baldwin emphasizes the power of love and the present-ness of the characters' actions.

After Vivaldo's act of love with Eric, he faces his lover Ida – also Rufus's sister – with renewed honesty and courage, despite the fact they have both had sex with other people. Baldwin presents their secret sex acts as transformational for them individually, because both were prompted by sincere moments of expression. That is, both Ida and Vivaldo expose themselves to what they were most afraid of: the process of connecting with people they care about. Their willingness to discover and accept themselves in new ways allows Ida and Vivaldo to confront the variety of tensions between them – racial and otherwise – on new grounds of understanding, instead of based on the antagonism that characterizes their earlier interactions. Baldwin does not show Ida and Vivaldo discussing their racial difference but does depict how they both admit to having had sexual affairs with others for different reasons. In their last interaction with one another, Ida asks Vivaldo not to be kind or to understand. Vivaldo promises he won't, and then says, "You seem to forget that I love you" (431). The novel moves through Ida and Vivaldo's intense and honest dialogues, but the novel's central point is their acceptance of another person's shortcomings, even without understanding, in a way that shows compassion and demonstrates love.

In other words, *Another Country* comments on love by displaying what must be sacrificed to experience it, while "Going to Meet the Man" shows how racism suppresses love's possibilities. In "Going," the castrated black man shapes Jesse's own mode of expression, and a strangling sense of oppression remains for everyone involved in the lynching; in *Another Country*, sex is liberating only when it accompanies a character's ability to face horrific experiences of truth. Jesse and Grace, as well as Vivaldo and his lovers, then, point to a link between sexuality and racialized identity. More importantly, *Another Country* and "Going" point to deeper divisions Baldwin expresses through various social relations. The physicality of sex, as used in Baldwin's prose, constitutes how his characters relate to themselves, others, and the institutions around them. More specifically, in "Going," the marriage bed demonstrates the larger traps related to white supremacy.

Generally, whites who deny their connection to blacks lose the truth of their own identity; legal and social structures within the United States, according to Baldwin, reflect the white desire to maintain a fantasy of distance from blacks even though blacks and whites are actually connected. In

"Stranger in a Village," Baldwin says this in another way: "lynch law and law, segregation and legal acceptance, terrorization and concession – is the way whites found a way to live with the negro in order to live with himself."[21] Similarly, one telling image in *Another Country* emphasizes a collective future that requires social cooperation in the present: "Many white people and many black people, chained together in time and in space, and by history, and all of them in a hurry. In a hurry to get away from each other" (86). In contrast, acts of love are transformative events for individuals, as they expose the motives that shape individual moral choices and beliefs. Baldwin sees such acts as key to imagining social transformation. In *The Fire Next Time*, Baldwin insists that "[t]he price of liberation of whites is the liberation of blacks" (375). Love, Baldwin writes, is a vehicle and state of being through which this "daring growth" can be made manifest (375); that is, one cannot get liberation for whites or blacks without the "universal sense of quest" love captures (375). Thus, to reimagine the promise of love, as Baldwin does, is not an evasion of history, but instead a crucial method for confronting it – its history and ideologies, as well as the reasons that individuals cling to structures they have created, as if they believe that if these structures fail, they will be lost in chaos and darkness. Love constitutes Baldwin's site of critiquing the American fantasy of "the good life," a fantasy sustained by the denial of a world of violence and reinforced by the social hierarchy that it creates.

Intimacy and Truth

By presenting personal encounters between loved ones, Baldwin asks readers to face their vulnerability to other people, events, and forces that shape social life. Baldwin encourages his readers to think beyond the limits of history, into a spiritual affirmation of individual existence and an acceptance of whatever consequences reality may bring. In other words, the dream vision and spiritual threshold that Baldwin depicts in *Another Country* – or *Go Tell It on the Mountain* (1953), for that matter – can be seen as stripping away the knowable conventions of history. When Vivaldo dreams of Rufus after the latter's death – a dream that precipitates the confessions of love and intimacy between Rufus and Eric – the moment is violent and unruly. Enduring his emotions, Vivaldo dreams of Rufus as he holds Eric. The fury and chaos within the dream are linked by Vivaldo's attention to the flesh and his expressions in facing that which he formerly avoided based on his sense of shame.

But what must be emphasized here is that the physical and the psychological push against all discernible boundaries. Time becomes long and imprecise instead of immediate: "How old was this rite, this act of love, how deep?" (386). As demonstrated with these words, Vivaldo feels that he has stepped off a precipice into thin air – and that from here, he can see down, "into the bottom of his heart" (386). That physical threshold saturates every level of Vivaldo's consciousness. At this moment, Eric is sobbing and praying, and it takes everything – in body, mind, and spirit – to sustain Vivaldo. He feels that he has risked everything. Here, Baldwin's apocalyptic imagery portrays the intensity of pain, as complemented by loud drums, trumpets, and the blues, that fill the earth with a sound so "dreadful [Vivaldo] could not bear it" (382).[22] What Baldwin means is that Vivaldo cannot bear these feelings alone. At the threshold of pain and terror, Vivaldo realizes that it is "Eric to whom he clung" (383). Vivaldo needs to be able to love, having been shaken to the foundations of his life, even to every recognizable object around him. Vivaldo feels that Eric loves him, and "with a groan and sigh" Vivaldo comes fully awake and pulls Eric even closer (383).

While thus far I have discussed Baldwin's use of physical intimacy, sex, and sexuality as acts of love, in *Go Tell It on the Mountain* Baldwin unites love, sensuality, and tenderness without explicitly depicting the protagonist involved in the sex act. *Go Tell It* is one of the novels in which Baldwin writes directly about how love and sexual desire reveal how characters define their religious experience and identity. This novel is the story of the family of John Grimes, who struggles throughout the book for spiritual self-definition. Familial love plays a central role in this struggle. John's father Gabriel, a leader in the church, makes his son John feel profoundly alienated because of his abuses. John, who comes to be "saved by the church," ultimately rediscovers his relationship with himself, the community, and God – but on his own terms, not his father's. It is key that he undergoes this change by means of self-affirmation, as aided by the encouragement of the church community, the voices of ancestors, and his dear friend Elisha.

John's spiritual experience is one of the most significant in African-American letters, yet it is a spiritual flight that is defined by sexuality, intimacy, and touch. When the novel begins, John wonders if he is a sinner or a saint after touching himself until he reaches orgasm.[23] He is also thrilled during a heated wrestling match with his friend Elisha, which takes place while they are cleaning at the church. Initially, John's only view of himself is through his condemnation of his father, who had constituted John's understanding of himself, family, and God. The major problem with this configuration is that Gabriel's authority and self-righteousness had been based on his keeping the truth of his own past a secret. John's father's hypocritical religious life lead him to damn his own sexual impulses, even when he previously acted on them.

The church service creates space for John to reclaim himself by realizing that his father's God, as well as his overall worldview, do not have to be his; in this process, time and space converge through the elation and prayer that characterize the spirited church service. The singing, praying, and testifying create John's moment of ultimate undoing, when he must face his own despair, intense loneliness, and even the prospect of death. Led by prayers of the saints, he ultimately proclaims to himself, "I am saved...and I know I'm saved" (210). The service is rich with sound and indescribable bouts of anguish, which together push John to his limits. Yet in this case, John is able to say yes to life differently. Throughout the novel, John has developed a friendship with and attraction to a young man, though slightly older than himself, named Elisha. Elisha, who at one point had been publically chastised by the church, accepts John unconditionally and becomes a pivotal part of John's voyage to define himself. If it were not for his friendship with Elisha, none of the changes he undergoes would have been possible. Elisha's unconditional love and acceptance of John spiritualizes the social bond between the two, and this sensation fortifies John's final statement: "I'm ready...I'm on my way" (226).

Interestingly enough, Vivaldo's dream and John's threshing-floor experience, which is key to his religious transformation, share apocalyptic imagery. Both scenes are intensely physical and related to Baldwin's antiracist perspective, yet the scenes are centrally spiritual. Baldwin opens up the concept of history in time and space, heaven and hell, but only as it is realized in the body. He suggests a high bar for what a person must be willing to risk to effect change in his or her own life: "If it cost me my life" are John's words as he chooses to pursue new relationships with his family, community, and the broader social world (222).

A similar story of risk and self-discovery, *If Beale Street Could Talk* (1974) is a novel about a black man falsely accused of rape by a Puerto Rican woman and a police conspiracy aiming to convict him. Baldwin highlights how the family of the accused endures these traumatic circumstances. Although it is the character Fonny who is falsely accused of rape, Baldwin chooses to tell the story from the perspective of Tish, Fonny's fiancée. Baldwin portrays Tish as spiritually resilient. Overall, *Beale Street* is another novel about family love; lovemaking between Fonny and Tish is also central. What is also clear is that family members do everything possible (including traveling to Puerto Rico) to help vindicate their beloved son. There is no giving up. At the same time, the characters demonstrate an acceptance of what they cannot control, especially on behalf of Tish and Fonny. This acceptance is key, as the district attorney's coercion of witnesses and other orchestrations and intimidation are used to keep Fonny in jail.

In one of the novel's significant final moments, Fonny feels especially defeated by the resources the state has brought against him. He worries; he panics – but Tish both pleads and advises, saying about his fears, "there's no point in thinking about it like that." Tish directs Fonny's attention to her and to them as a couple: she says with a soothing voice, "Did you miss me?"[24] Fonny, despite the odds, affirms his attitude about the future: "I'll be better when I come out, than when I came in" (184). He believes that he will be vindicated eventually, however unlikely that may be. When it is Fonny's time to go back to his cell, Tish's words are: "A silence falls and we look at each other.... Something travels from him to me, it is love and courage. Yes. Yes. We are going to make it, somehow. Somehow. I stand, and smile, and raise my fist. He turns into the inferno. I walk toward the Sahara" (184). The paired images of the Sahara and the inferno harbor the concepts of loneliness, suffering, and death. What is key is that the lovemaking between Fonny and Tish, as well as the actions and presence of the family around them, helps them face the sensations of hell and loneliness that they cannot control. Love is what they create and renew by facing their own shifting levels of power and powerlessness.

Love after History

Crucial in Baldwin's works is that love is seen as an infinite category of human possibility. In other words, while Baldwin's numerous lectures, speeches, and essays demonstrate his desire to solve immediate social problems and promote new ways of thinking about political and economic reform, he does not promise that people will cease to be plagued by the need to lie to themselves or objectify others to sustain their own realities. Hence, it is not only because of various forms of oppression that people continue to lie. Baldwin's beliefs about people are fundamentally moral and existential. Love represents one way of exploring Baldwin's engagement with humanity's ongoing spiritual conflict and encompasses how this is expressed historically as well as personally.

The philosopher Soren Kierkegaard shares much with Baldwin with respect to his views on love and spirituality. He writes, "Love's hidden life is in the innermost being, unfathomable, and then in turn is in an unfathomable connectedness with all existence."[25] Baldwin fashions a similar vision through a relentless commitment to the individual's materiality – through nakedness, sex, and a mysterious vulnerability. Baldwin's version of "all existence" is materialized as the texture of history, but Baldwin wants readers to think of existence as exceeding history – transcending material life – which encourages people to want mastery over their lives precisely in moments when they may have little or no control. Baldwin's characters Vivaldo and John Grimes surrender and accept their limitations, and, in Baldwin's world, this acceptance means that they are free to thrive in love in new ways – ways that may not be perfect but are certainly new. One cannot accept that mode of freedom without paying the price, without taking risks, or at least without seriously contemplating the horrifying costs of such a freedom.

Another key problem that makes the subject of love as treated by Baldwin less prescriptive and more challenging is the elusiveness of that very subject. In all of Baldwin's novels, the protagonists who do change for the better do not actively seek their problem. Rather, events pounce on them: the circumstances of their own history find and strip them, accost them, troubling all their pursuits – especially those of love and substantive social connections.

Significantly, Baldwin places his characters in situations wherein they have the opportunity to unveil truths they badly want to keep hidden. He places them at a crossroads, allowing them to choose between freedom and innocence, love and hate, life and death. These distinctions are the universal terms of Baldwin's writings. Those critics seeking to see love or sex as enigmas solely defined by political solutions – or even something more robust, such as a politics of everyday life – are left wondering from the start. Baldwin's work calls for social and communal engagement, which may be ultimately beneficial politically – yet he does require that the moral dilemmas he presents include direct answers to pressing civic problems. The varied means by which Baldwin reveals the desire for, absence of, or manifestation of love are transformed into artifacts of history; they are produced by an individual self and within a social community. Baldwin's depictions of social relationships query how the fabric of love is woven.

NOTES

1 Roderick Ferguson, "The Parvenu Baldwin and the Other Side of Redemption: Modernity, Race, Sexuality, and the Cold War," in Dwight McBride (ed.), *James Baldwin Now* (New York: New York University Press, 1999), pp. 233–61; Marlon B. Ross, "White Fantasies of Desire: Baldwin and the Racial Identities of Sexuality," in *James Baldwin Now*, pp. 13–55; Susan Feldman, "Another Look at *Another Country*: Reconciling Baldwin's Racial and Sexual Politics," in D. Quentin Miller (ed.), *Re-Viewing James Baldwin: Things Not Seen* (Philadelphia: Temple University Press, 2000), pp. 88–104.

2 James Baldwin, *Another Country* (originally published 1962), (New York: Vintage Press, 1993), p. 340. Subsequent references appear parenthetically.

3 James Baldwin, "Many Thousands Gone," in *The Price of the Ticket: Collected Nonfiction 1948–1985* (New York: St. Martin's Press, 1985), p. 65. All of Baldwin's essays, unless otherwise noted, come from this volume.

4 Irving Howe, "Black Boys and Native Sons," *Dissent* (Autumn 1963), 353–68. While he does not mention "love" specifically, Henry Louis Gates Jr. also criticizes

Baldwin for reproducing melodrama and aspects of sentimentality in his later fiction. See Gates, "Introduction," in Henry Louis Gates Jr. and Hollis Robbins (eds.), *The Annotated Uncle Tom's Cabin* (New York: Norton, 2007), p. xxxvii.

5 Baldwin, *The Fire Next Time*, in *The Price of the Ticket: Collected Nonfiction 1948–1985* (New York: St. Martin's Press, 1985), p. 375.

6 Ibid., p. 379.

7 Donald Bogle, *Toms, Coons, Mulattoes, Mammies, and Bucks: An Interpretive History of Blacks in American Films* (New York: Continuum, 1973; 2012), p. 169.

8 Ibid.

9 James Baldwin, "Carmen Jones: The Dark is Light Enough," p. 111.

10 Ibid., p. 112.

11 Ibid.

12 Ibid.

13 "Stranger in the Village," p. 88.

14 Ibid.

15 Horace Ové (dir.), *Baldwin's Nigger* (London, United Kingdom, 1969). Film.

16 Ibid.

17 James Baldwin, "The New Lost Generation," p. 312.

18 Ibid.

19 James Baldwin, "Going to Meet the Man," in *Going to Meet the Man; Early Novels and Short Stories* (New York: Library of America, 1998), p. 933. Subsequent references appear parenthetically.

20 Baldwin, "The New Lost Generation," p. 309.

21 Baldwin, "Stranger in a Village," p. 88.

22 Joseph Brown S.J., "I John, Saw the Holy Number: Apocalyptic Vision in *Go Tell it on the Mountain* and *Native Son*," in *Religion and Literature* 27.1 (Spring 1995), 53–74.

23 Baldwin, *Go Tell It on the Mountain* (New York: Dial Press, 1981), p. 15.

24 Baldwin, *If Beale Street Could Talk* (New York: Vintage, 2006), p. 183. All subsequent references appear parenthetically.

25 Søren Kierkegaard, *Works of Love* (Princeton: Princeton University Press, 1998), p. 9.

12

DOUGLAS FIELD

Baldwin's FBI Files as Political Biography

In his essay, "The Discovery of What It Means to Be an American" (1959), James Baldwin observes that "Every society is really governed by hidden laws, by unspoken but profound assumptions on the part of the people, and ours is no exception," and adds that "it is up to the American writer to find out what those laws and assumptions are."[1] As Quentin Miller argues in *A Criminal Power: James Baldwin and the Law* (2012), the law is a defining narrative in the writer's life and work, to the point that "virtually all of Baldwin's novels and plays have at their core a narrative of imprisonment, or police brutality, or police intimidation, or a rigged trial."[2] Baldwin's non-fiction, too, frequently decries the injustices of a legal system – or "criminal power," as he termed it – that upheld the racial inequities of the civil rights era.[3] "We have a civil rights bill now," Baldwin wrote in his essay "The American Dream and the American Negro" (1965), continuing, "We had the 15th Amendment nearly 100 years ago. If it was not honored then, I have no reason to believe that the civil rights bill will be honored now."[4] In Baldwin's work – as scholars including Miller, Lovalerie King, and Lawrie Balfour have argued – the writer exposes the moral bankruptcy of the American legal system alongside the more sinister "hidden laws" that govern U.S. assumptions about class, race, and sexuality.[5]

Baldwin undoubtedly took on his own challenge, directed to American writers in general, "to find out what those laws and assumptions are," yet it is unlikely that he would have known the price of that particular ticket in 1959. By 1960, the Federal Bureau of Investigation had started collecting a file on Baldwin that would amount to 1,884 pages by its closure in 1974. As late as 1972, the FBI justified keeping Baldwin under surveillance, concluding: "It is believed that the subject, *due to his position as an author*, is likely to furnish aid or other assistance to revolutionary elements because of his sympathy and/or ideology" (my emphasis).[6] The Bureau's focus on Baldwin's role as a writer, with the corollary that an author is, by default, radical, says much about the FBI's concerns that writers, and African-American writers in particular, posed a threat to the social order. As Bill Maxwell documents, J. Edgar Hoover "fostered an intimate relationship between state surveillance and African-American literary experimentation from the birth of the Harlem Renaissance in 1919 to the height of the Black Arts Movement in 1972, the year Hoover died."[7] The size of Baldwin's FBI file, however, which is five times larger than that of Richard Wright – also one of the most influential African-American authors of the twentieth century, who at one stage identified as communist – raises important questions, both about Baldwin's political activity and the reasons that the Bureau continued to monitor a writer who, though a self-confessed "disturber of the peace," hardly constituted a national security risk.[8]

By analyzing Baldwin's files, I contend that several crucial pictures emerge. First, the files call attention to the extent of Baldwin's political activity. While biographers have previously noted the author's involvement with civil rights organizations, the files add considerable detail to these accounts, shedding light on the extent of Baldwin's energy and commitment to a wide range of political agendas and organizations, particularly as the FBI files were declassified after the publication of David Leeming and James Campbell's biographies.[9] Although there are many errors in the files, the numerous newspaper clippings and letters of support to publications such as *Freedomways*, a prominent civil rights journal, ultimately constitute the closest thing we have to a political biography of the writer. As Gary Holcomb observes about the FBI report of renowned Jamaican American poet and novelist, Claude McKay (whom the FBI was convinced was a communist sympathizer): "even bearing in mind its sometimes laughable manifestation of the banality of evil," it is nonetheless "in some ways a more reliable representation of his life during the 1920s than his own 1930s autobiography."[10] In the case of Baldwin, who claimed allegiance to no organization but supported many, the files produce a significantly fuller picture of the writer's political contributions. Furthermore, a close reading of Baldwin's files has the secondary, but also important function of shedding light on why the Bureau gathered so much information on African-American writers during the 1960s and 1970s. Finally, since Hoover believed that the files would never be declassified, the handwritten notes he and others added to the files also tell us much about the FBI's attitudes toward "un-American" behavior, particularly considering that Baldwin was not only a high-profile African American but a homosexual one, too.

Baldwin's files are presented in approximately chronological order and offer an eclectic mix of media; they include memoranda, letters, and news clippings in what resembles a biographer's chaotic attempt to map out his or her subject. According to James Lesar, a tireless crusader for the Freedom of Information Act, Baldwin's files "were not compiled for law enforcement purposes"; instead, they represented "a compendium of every piece of gossip that the FBI picked up through wiretaps and other sources that relate to Baldwin, but none of it relates to illegal activity."[11] The files make it clear that Baldwin's phone was tapped on numerous occasions. He was also followed in his travels to France, Italy, and Great Britain by agents or informants posing as publishers or car salesmen (FBI, 891).

Although Baldwin endured relentless surveillance, the Bureau's findings are remarkable for their basic mistakes, which raise important questions about the competency of the FBI's intelligence gathering at a time of international and domestic unrest. For example, Baldwin is incorrectly labeled as "communist" (FBI, 1052); his date of birth is frequently wrong; and one report even notes that they cannot find a record of his birth, perhaps because the Bureau had not established that the author was born James Jones.[12] Baldwin the "Boston-novelist" (FBI, 1010) is listed as the author of *Go Tell It to the Mountain* (FBI, 51) and *Another World* (FBI, 1505), and another file reports on how he spoke about his "boyhood in the South" – which is unlikely given that he was born and raised in Harlem (FBI, 60).[13] In 1968, when Baldwin was at the height of his fame, reports abound claiming that the author's sister, Paula, was his wife (FBI, 698). As James Campbell points out, "The entire edifice manifesting the FBI's interest in Baldwin was based on a falsehood."[14] That this incompetency seemed particularly acute when it came to issues of race was highlighted by Baldwin when he asked "why the FBI can find a junkie but cannot find a man who bombs the homes of Negro leaders in the Deep South."[15]

Despite the Bureau's careful monitoring of individual subjects, Baldwin's files illustrate how the FBI often overlooked specific details of those under investigation, resorting instead to generalizations about how a homosexual, communist, or African American was expected to behave. In Baldwin's case, it was enough for the Bureau to conclude that he was linked to the Communist Party through association. In 1961, along with many other people, Baldwin had sponsored a news release from the Carl Braden Clemency Appeal Committee.[16] While it is unlikely that Baldwin knew that Braden, a journalist and social justice activist, was marked as communist by the FBI, the writer was now guilty by association, and the Bureau remained convinced that Baldwin was a "fellow traveler." The Bureau kept detailed records of Baldwin's political activities, including newspaper articles, interviews, signatures on petitions or letters, and fund-raising events he attended or at which he spoke. Given the scrutiny of his activities, however, it is surprising that there is no mention of his self-confessed Trotskyite past, nor any suspicion that his early publications in leftist magazines might have indicated an active left-wing mind.[17]

Baldwin and Surveillance

Although there is no corresponding record in his files, in The Devil Finds Work (1976) Baldwin recollects being accosted by two agents in 1945. Noting that his color had already made him "conspicuous," Baldwin concludes that the FBI "frightened me and they humiliated me – it was like being spat on, or pissed on, or gang-raped."[18] Baldwin's recollection of the Bureau's violation connects his sexual "perversion" (a word used by the FBI about the writer and his fiction) and his racial identity to the specific ways in which he was scrutinized. This surveillance was orchestrated by, as Baldwin described him, "J. Edgar Hoover, history's most highly paid (and most utterly useless) *voyeur*," a term that reduces the Bureau's monitoring of its subjects to little more than a prurient gaze, evoking an era of surveillance famously captured by Alfred Hitchcock in his 1954 classic *Rear Window*. Unlike the voyeuristic protagonist of Hitchcock's movie, who watches his neighbors and uncovers a murder, Baldwin suggests that Hoover's surveillance serves no purpose other than to expose his subjects' racial or sexual identities for sinister reasons.[19]

While Baldwin may indeed have been watched by Hoover's agents in the 1940s and 1950s, his first FBI file was opened after he supported the Fair Play for Cuba Committee (FPCC), an organization set up by Vincent T. Lee in 1960 to petition for the end of the United States' economic boycott of Cuba. Baldwin's association with the organization was brief: Richard Gibson, an organizer of the FPCC who was acquainted with Baldwin in Paris, recalled that he "tried to get him more deeply involved," though Baldwin "always avoided aligning himself politically."[20] By signing an advertisement that stated the FPCC's aims in the *New York Times* (April 1960), however, Baldwin unwittingly alerted the Bureau to his revolutionary potential, opening up an unusually large sequence of files that was twice the length of Allen Ginsberg's FBI file and four times as long as Norman Mailer's.[21]

Baldwin, in fact, makes an earlier appearance in Richard Wright's FBI file. The 1955 report discusses Wright's American Fellowship Group in Paris, ostensibly a forum to sponsor young writers. The informant concluded that the organization was "'Leftist' in the nature of its discussions" and noted Baldwin's detachment from Wright and his group:

> According to the informant, Wright and his group were the target of attacks from one James Baldwin, a young Negro writer who was a student in Paris. Baldwin attacked the hatred themes of the [sic] Wright's writings and the

attempt of the Franco-American Fellowship Group to Perpetuate "Uncle Tom Literature Methods."[22]

Baldwin, who had been living in Paris since 1948, was not a student; this basic mistake, along with the garbled account of the former's strained relationship with Wright, is typical of the many basic errors found in the files. The informant here has clearly muddled details from Baldwin's 1949 essay "Everybody's Protest Novel," in which he famously dismisses the political and aesthetic impact of the protest novel in a devastating critique of Wright's best-selling 1940 novel, *Native Son*. The informant conflates the protagonist of Wright's novel, Bigger Thomas, with Uncle Tom, the eponymous character in Harriet Beecher Stowe's 1852 best-seller. Furthermore, the misapprehension of "Uncle Tom Literature Methods" – suggesting a new school of Uncle Tom literature – highlights the Bureau's lack of attention to, or interest in, literary analysis, as well as underscores its lack of awareness about intra-racial literary debates.

Despite the numerous factual errors, the entries in Baldwin's FBI files nonetheless offer a useful overview of his political activities, not least because they highlight the writer's commitment to the Civil Rights Movement, particularly during the early to mid-1960s as he became a well-known author and celebrity. Specifically, surveillance on the writer was heightened following his meeting with Robert Kennedy on May 24, 1963. At a meeting at the attorney general's New York City apartment, Baldwin took along friends, including performer and activist Harry Belafonte, psychologist Kenneth Clark, playwright Lorraine Hansberry, and Jerome Smith, a young African American from the South who had been beaten during the Freedom Rides of 1961.[23] The meeting, as Clark himself admitted in an article in the *New York Post* – an article duly clipped to Baldwin's file – was not a success. Communication broke down as Kennedy expressed shock at Smith's admission that he could not conceive of fighting for his country, and the meeting, in Clark's words, changed from "a dialogue into a diatribe" (FBI, 47). Matters got worse when Baldwin reproached Kennedy after the latter alluded to his family's history of oppression as Irish immigrants. The article also notes how the African Americans present "raised questions about the dubious role of the FBI in civil rights cases," a topic that would no doubt have infuriated the Bureau's director. A later report records Baldwin's statement in the *New York Times* of September 19, 1963: "I blame J. Edgar Hoover in part for events in Alabama. Negroes have no cause to have faith in the FBI" (FBI, 106). After several articles appeared in the press about Baldwin's contentious altercation with Kennedy, Hoover sent Kennedy (who referred to Baldwin as "a nut") dossiers on all those who attended the meeting.[24]

The ill-fated meeting with Kennedy illustrates Baldwin's willingness to get involved in civil rights issues not just as a writer, but as a participant, or, to use his preferred term, "witness."[25] Baldwin's activities of the 1960s, as recorded in his FBI files, show the extent to which he offered his services to civil rights organizations, whether donating money, giving speeches, granting interviews, writing articles, or appearing on television. Baldwin had, in fact, been actively involved in civil rights work since his first visit to the South in 1957, an experience he wrote about in "A Fly in the Buttermilk" (1958) and "A Letter from the South: Nobody Knows My Name" (1959). Baldwin returned to the South at the height of the sit-ins in 1960 and forged close links with the Student Non-Violent Coordinating Committee (SNCC) and the Congress of Racial Equality (CORE), also publishing two further essays: "They Can't Turn Back" (*Mademoiselle*, 1960) and "The Dangerous Road Before Martin Luther King" (*Harpers*, 1961). By the summer of 1961, following the publication of *Nobody Knows My Name*, Baldwin emerged as a spokesperson for the Civil Rights Movement, lending his charisma and support to numerous organizations. Baldwin published interviews, letters, and speeches in periodicals ranging from *Muhammad Speaks* to the journal *Freedomways: A Quarterly Review of the Negro Freedom Movement*. With the 1963 publication of *The Fire Next Time*, his best-selling book that first appeared in two parts in *The New Yorker*, Baldwin became the most prolific African-American writer of the civil rights era.

Baldwin's emerging role in the early 1960s as a high-profile commentator on the Civil Rights Movement no doubt precipitated the volume of FBI files on the writer. A 1964 file, for example, listed as a reason for keeping Baldwin on the Security Index his "personal involvement in the current civil rights struggle"; here, the implicit acknowledgement is that any involvement is tantamount to civil disobedience. Paradoxically, the report notes that "Baldwin is against all forms of violence and shedding of blood" but elsewhere talks of the author's "dangerousness" (FBI, 308). His observers were perhaps picking up on the shift in the writer's register, which became increasingly embittered as the Civil Rights Movement became bloodier. Baldwin, who had urged his nephew in *The Fire Next Time* to accept white people "and accept them with love," now announced that "many people, even members of my own family...would think nothing of picking up arms tomorrow."[26]

In a revealing file, an agent notes "the inflammatory nature of his writings" and reaches the conclusion that any attempts to interview the writer would cause embarrassment to the Bureau, presumably because of what they describe as Baldwin's "gift for publicity," with the implicit acknowledgement that he would use such opportunities to his advantage (FBI, 393).[27] On the one hand it's hard to see how Baldwin's position as articulate celebrity activist is commensurate with his place on the Security Index as "a dangerous individual who could be expected to commit acts inimical to the national defense and public safety of the United States in time of an emergency" (FBI, 230). And yet the FBI's acknowledgement of Baldwin's "gift for publicity" underscores ways in which writers posed a threat to the Bureau; that writers could control public representation and perception of the FBI, as well as, in the case of Baldwin, challenging the Cold War distinctions between "American" and "un-American" behavior that Hoover sought to police and control.

Just as Baldwin's files reveal much about the Bureau's attitudes toward the Civil Rights Movement, they also reveal the extent of the author's political commitment. There is a record of Baldwin speaking in October 1963 at the National Lawyers Guild (FBI, 132-2), an organization the FBI claimed was "a communist front" (FBI, 145). More seriously, Baldwin is listed as a sponsor of "a rally to abolish the House un-American Activities Commission" in 1961 (FBI, 195). Although there are frequent memos that cite Baldwin's connection with "Communist Influence in Racial Matters" – part of a wider investigation into the communist presence in African-American politics and culture – there are no firm reports on Baldwin's "red" credentials. A 1963 report, for example, acknowledges that "Confidential sources familiar with various phases of CP in the New York area were unable to furnish any additional information concerning the subject" (FBI, 209). Yet it was enough for the FBI to justify surveillance of Baldwin because he was frequently guilty of associating with communist or suspected communist individuals or publications. He supported the Committee to Aid the Monroe Defendants, a group that that the FBI claimed was formed by the Socialist Workers Party,[28] and was composed of black and white activists who supported North Carolina NAACP leader Robert Williams's call for citizens to arm themselves against the Ku Klux Klan.[29] Furthermore, according to the FBI, *Freedomways*, which Baldwin supported and wrote for, was "in [the] hands of a mixed group of Marxists and non-Marxists" (FBI, 219). Though the report is vague, the implicit suggestion is that Baldwin was again fraternizing with leftist subversives.

Baldwin's Critique of the FBI

The FBI's interest in Baldwin during the 1960s was fueled by the fact that he was an increasingly high-profile figure. Though he did not change his behavior, Baldwin was intensely aware of the Bureau's presence in his life; he complained that he was being bugged and reported that several agents came to his apartment several days after his meeting with Robert Kennedy.[30] Furthermore, during the 1960s in particular, Baldwin frequently questioned the integrity and neutrality of the FBI – and especially that of the Bureau's director, J. Edgar Hoover. Indeed, Baldwin criticized Hoover through every available media, and the Bureau dutifully recorded these transgressions. A memo from December 1963 records that Baldwin "said that J. Edgar Hoover had warned the Negroes against allowing Communists to get into the civil rights movement" (FBI, 253–4); a later file on the same talk records Baldwin's comment that he was "not interested in Hoover's statement that the Negro in his quest for equality should not fight established institutions" (FBI, 333).

Interest in Baldwin's attacks on the Bureau grew by June 1963, when a "decoded copy" of a teletype revealed a conversation between two of Martin Luther King, Jr.'s advisors, Stanley Levison and Clarence Jones, about Baldwin's plans to embarrass the FBI by exposing the Bureau's incompetence. Jones, a trusted aide and lawyer of King, is reported to have told Levison that "I have seen some statements on the FBI, but I have never seen one like this. He is going to nail them to the wall" (FBI, 1021–2). The reason, Jones states, is "the harassment of himself"; he adds that "[t]his is going to be like an atomic bomb when it is dropped...it really will because he is a name in the news" (FBI, 1022). Jones's acknowledgement of Baldwin's presence in the media illustrates not only the writer's fame (he appeared on the cover of *Time* magazine that year), but also Baldwin's ability to galvanize the media, whether radio, newspapers, or interviews. A *Washington Post* article from June 1964 clipped to Baldwin's files discusses the author's proposed books at Dial Press: first, *Talking at the Gates* – "about a Southern Plantation the day that news arrived that slavery had ended," and second, a book about the FBI in the South (FBI, 1249). Mention of Baldwin's book about the FBI also appeared in the *New York Herald Tribune* (July 14, 1964); this time claiming it would be serialized, like *The Fire Next Time*, in the *New Yorker* (FBI, 1255). By July 17, there was a memorandum summarizing Baldwin's proposed exposure of the FBI, citing the *Playbill* interview in which he discussed beginning "a long article about the manner in which Negroes are treated by the FBI" (FBI, 1256). The memo about the proposed book includes a note that "discreet checks" would be made in the publishing industry, with the hope of getting hold of the galleys (FBI, 1256). The book, reputedly called *Blood Counters*, never appeared, and there is no evidence to suggest that Baldwin even started the book.

Reading the FBI, the FBI Reading Baldwin

The rumors about *Blood Counters* provide fascinating insight into how the FBI expended considerable energy and resources investigating a book Baldwin never wrote, while missing the actual stories he published. According to Natalie Robins, "The FBI was as interested in Baldwin's writing as it was in his life," but in fact there are surprisingly few mentions of the writer's work, and there are notable omissions.[31] There is no discussion of *Giovanni's Room* (1956), for example, despite its theme of homosexuality, even though "deviant sexuality" was directly connected to national security concerns during the Cold War era.[32] While Baldwin's long essay, *The Fire Next Time* (1963), which was widely considered to be one the most important manifestos of the Civil Rights Movement – described by *Atlantic Monthly* as "so eloquent in its passion and so scorching in its candor that it is bound to unsettle any reader" – does get a mention in his FBI files, the report is surprisingly brief, comprising five lines.

In the case of Baldwin, the FBI seemed more concerned with questions of morality and decency in his work than the inflammatory political content of his essays. There are numerous pages of FBI files on Baldwin's best-selling 1962 novel, *Another Country*, focusing on the novel's descriptions of bisexuality and interracial sex, which outraged conservative readers, including the FBI's director. Hoover noted that it was banned in New Orleans (FBI, 75) and responded to several letters from outraged citizens who sought to have the novel removed from libraries and book clubs. A representative letter from one angry citizen complained that *Another Country* contained "every filthy word, compound word and phrasing that could be used to portray: Drug addiction, Sex perversion at its vilest" (FBI, 1628). Hoover's responses to such appeals to "decency" were always guarded – in the sense that his professionalism kept his own apparent revulsion in check – but it isn't hard to get a sense of what he thought. The above letter, Hoover noted, "is very much appreciated," but since no federal law had been violated, there was nothing he could do. He could, however, make his own moral stance very clear by enclosing pamphlets "which express[ed]…[his] views on the widespread accessibility of obscene and pornographic literature." These leaflets included: *Combating Merchants of Filth: The Role of the FBI*, *Let's Wipe out the Schoolyard Sex Racket!*, and *The Fight Against Filth* (FBI, 1629). The inflammatory rhetoric of the titles alone suggests that Hoover was affronted by Baldwin's literature.

Another FBI report compares *Another Country* to Henry Miller's *Tropic of Cancer* (France 1934, United States 1961), presumably because of the descriptions of "sex perversion" (FBI, 1620) found in both. The FBI's (largely self-appointed) role as the guardian of morality and decency raises important concerns about civil liberties and censorship, as well as illustrating how Hoover's power and influence extended well beyond his role as the enforcer of federal law.

Officially, the FBI took note only of materials that violated federal law. Yet it is well known that, as early as 1925, the director started an "Obscene File" listing works deemed to be pornographic and/or a federal offense.[33] Baldwin's file includes several references to the "Bureau Library," which stored certain books presumably because they were deemed "subversive," "dangerous," or "immoral" (FBI, 1592). The titles of books held in the Bureau library offer an intriguing insight into the FBI's definition of "dangerous" literature. In order for books to be held in the FBI library, they presumably needed to be read. But read by whom? Some deductions are possible; for instance, in 1972, Baldwin's *No Name in the Street* and Gayraud S. Wilmore's *Black Religion and Black Radicalism* were requested by Inspector G. C. Moore of the "Extremist Intelligence Section, Domestic Intelligence Division" (FBI, 1600). In other cases there appear headings marked "Book Review," such as in the files concerning *A Rap on Race* (1971), a collaborative work between Baldwin and Margaret Mead – who, as was noted in one file, "had been affiliated with several communist front organizations" (FBI, 1592). Despite the suggestion that *A Rap* will be reviewed, the author of the file neither analyzes nor offers a précis of the book's literary merits. Rather, the agent analyzes the book based on the premise that both authors may have communist leanings, which the author of the review struggles to locate beyond noting that both writers "agreed they had to be clearheaded as possible about all human beings," as well as highlighting one instance when the FBI is mentioned (FBI, 1593). Here, as elsewhere, the FBI agents attempt to decode and reveal instances of subversion, but they frequently fail to provide more than superficial readings of the works at hand. While the Bureau were clearly not attempting to produce literary analysis, the report on *A Rap* underscores the ways in which they struggled to decode subversive elements that Hoover and his colleagues insisted must be present.

Furthermore, the FBI's interest in Baldwin as a writer specifically connects the author's FBI file to key questions in analysis and textual practice. Baldwin's files reveal much about how the FBI analyzed and critiqued Baldwin and his work, but the files themselves, which are encoded, blanked-out, and catalogued in a complex organizational system, resemble difficult modernist texts that frequently resist close reading. In other words, reading Baldwin's FBI files and the FBI's reading of Baldwin links legal and textual interpretation, as well as connecting the roles of the FBI detective to that of the literary critic (or critic as detective). Both seek to decode or uncover meanings from the body, or the body of the text. The connections between spycraft and literary criticism were made explicit during the Cold War by James Angleton, a long-standing chief of the CIA's counterintelligence staff who developed a formal practice that he called "the practical criticism of ambiguity."[34] While the FBI's approach may not have been so sophisticated, they nonetheless undertook investigations of Baldwin's work in order to quantify and measure subversive content. Certain reports on *Another Country*, for instance, bear headings such as "Laboratory Work Sheet" and "Specimens Submitted for Examination." Under the heading "Result of Examination," the report notes that "The book described above as specimen Q1 was not identified with material of a similar nature which has been forwarded previously to the Laboratory. Specimen Q1 is being added to the Bureau's files" (FBI, 1622). The language here is reminiscent of the Cold War rhetoric of "germophobia," yet it also reads as a clinical attempt at some sort of literary analysis.

The clinical nature of this attempt is illustrated by a report that comments directly on Baldwin's literary skill[35]: *Another Country*, the assistant attorney general of the criminal division concluded in a report to the director, "has been reviewed in the General Crimes Section of this Division and it has been concluded that the book contains literary merit and may be of value to students of psychology and social behavior" (FBI, 1627). By drawing attention to the social value of *Another Country*, the report echoes the conclusions of Judge Clayton W. Horn in the notorious *Howl* obscenity trial in 1958. Clayton adjudged Allen Ginsberg's poem to "have some redeeming social importance," concluding that "the book is not obscene."[36] However, unlike the *Howl* trial, where expert witnesses such as professor David Kirk testified to the literary merit of the poem, the FBI's report highlights the Bureau's roles as judge and cross-examiner.[37] This in turn raises further questions about Hoover's attempts to monitor obscenity, and also the FBI's attempts to shape public opinion and policy related to obscenity.

The Bureau's report on *Another Country*'s literary merit, then, highlights the problematic ways that the FBI relied on its in-house literary analyses to judge the social value of books under scrutiny. Furthermore, the FBI was convinced that certain books, such as John Steinbeck's *Grapes of Wrath* (1939), contained codes that spoke to communists and "fellow travelers." An FBI memorandum of 1942 concluded that some of William Carlos Williams's poems might be written in code, arguing that "they appear to have been written by a person who is very queer or possibly a mental case." The FBI eventually conceded that Williams used "an 'expressionistic' style which might be interpreted as being 'code.'"[38] Other FBI reports read like weak undergraduate essays: one, for example, concludes that Red Stout's 1941 novel, *Sisters in Trouble*, could be "a deliberate attempt to convey a meaning other than the solution of a mystery story...note the almost exclusive German cast of characters."[39]

The Bureau's attempts at literary analysis illustrate the ways in which agents struggled to read and interpret literature that was not plotted in line with conventional American ideals. Works such as Baldwin's that deviated from acceptable parameters and tackled themes of homosexuality, race, or violence were deemed alien or subversive. In other words, the FBI readers struggled to make sense of "un-American" themes. Concomitantly, as I have suggested, the files themselves also present difficulties in terms of analysis and interpretation for the literary critic without FBI training. Nonetheless, despite these obstacles, the files are productive, for they yield both information about Baldwin and about the FBI's specific attempts to classify a subject who was notoriously difficult to pin down, not only in terms of genre, but also physically, given in his transatlantic shuffles between the United States, Europe, and Turkey.

Baldwin's FBI files – even after being declassified again in 1998, which rendered more information visible – are also full of blanked-out sections and omissions, which are classified under the Freedom of Information Act. In addition, the "final" version of the file often differs significantly from the original report. As Clarence M. Kelley, the director of the FBI during the 1970s, has noted, "[m]ost reports were written, rewritten, edited, scrubbed, and cleaned and pressed a dozen times before they were put in the mail. Reportorial accuracy was seldom a consideration."[40] In terms of textual practice, the files represent a particular challenge to the literary or cultural critic. They are, to borrow from the French critic Gérard Genette, a kind of palimpsest: they can be read as "hypertexts," in which the original, or "hypotext," cannot be traced, leading to a confusing layering of erasure and marginalia.[41] Not only are the director's barely legible scrawls visible on the margins of the files; there are also printed footers offering financial tips to employees working on the documents – such as, "Buy U.S. Savings Bonds Regularly on the Payroll Savings Plans," illustrating the ways in which these forms performed simultaneous functions. In Baldwin's files, there are reports on his activity, handwritten marginalia, and advertisements directed at agents reading the files.

If the files were "cleaned" – that is, expunged of sensitive material – then it is arguably the paratextual comments that reveal the most about the FBI's opinions. Hoover, never anticipating that the Freedom of Information Act would be introduced, thought that the numerous marginal notes he scrawled on federal files, including Baldwin's, would always be private – that such marginalia would remain in the Bureau's domain. A notable example is Hoover's 1964 jotting, "Isn't Baldwin a well known pervert?" (FBI, 1256). Yet this comment, written on the margins of a typed memorandum, was not just a personal note or a rhetorical musing: the barely legible question in fact precipitated a measured response by an unnamed agent, which illustrates the way in which Hoover's marginalia acted as a central component of the files. The official report responding to Hoover's question asserts, "It is not a matter of official record that he [Baldwin] is a pervert," adding that "the theme of homosexuality has figured in two of his three published novels" (FBI, 1258). The report concludes that "it is not possible to state that he is a pervert," but notes that "he has expressed a sympathetic viewpoint about homosexuality" (FBI, 1259). The interest in Baldwin's sexual activity – and accompanying assumption that perversion is a synonym for homosexuality – illustrates another way in which the Bureau investigated beyond the subject's political life, scrutinizing people for what they saw as moral or immoral behavior. Although this particular report on Baldwin at least has the merit of not conflating an interpretation of the author's fictional writing with a straightforward biographical reading, it raises the question of how far Baldwin's sexuality fueled further surveillance. In other words, did Baldwin's sexuality prompt intensified federal investigation?

Baldwin's description of his first encounter with the FBI is couched in notably violent and sexual rhetoric, where the author recalls feeling "humiliated" and compares the incident to being "gang-raped."

Baldwin's use of violent and sexual rhetoric to describe his first encounter with the FBI – using words such as "humiliated" and "gang-raped" – seems to support this argument.

Hoover, as emblem of the FBI, is transformed from prurient voyeur to sinister perpetrator, underscoring, as Maurice Wallace has noted, "the spectacular conditions of historical black masculine identity and the chronic effort to 'frame' the black male body, criminally and visually, for the visual pleasures of whites."[42] And yet, Baldwin's openness about this sexuality, his readiness to address the topic in his fiction, seemed to disarm the FBI, who had no leverage to blackmail a writer who was already openly homosexual.[43] While information such as Baldwin's "homosexual parties" in Istanbul underscores the Bureau's international monitoring of its targets, there is scant information to reveal about such activities (FBI, 651). For the most part, descriptions of Baldwin within his file reveal more about the FBI's assumptions about how a homosexual was supposed to behave than about Baldwin himself, exposing insights about the FBI's modus operandi and turning the gaze back to the voyeuristic reach of the Bureau's surveillance.

More damaging, however, are the FBI's records of Baldwin's sexuality in relation to his civil rights work, as public knowledge of his homosexuality almost certainly hampered his role as a spokesman for the movement, a fate also suffered by Bayard Rustin, a leading civil rights activist whose sexuality complicated his position as a spokesman in the Southern Christian

Leadership Conference.[44] In the transcript of a wiretap, Levison is recorded as having claimed that Baldwin and Bayard Rustin were "better qualified to lead a homo-sexual movement than a civil rights movement." Similarly, King's aide Clarence Jones is reported to have fallen out with Baldwin in 1963, stating that "Baldwin's sexual propensities had been known," with the implication that this would damage the Civil Rights Movement (FBI, 124).

Viewed in their entirety, the extensive FBI files on Baldwin's political and literary outputs comprises part of a larger picture that emerges in the history of the Bureau's monitoring of African-American writers.[45] As William Maxwell has documented, the FBI were "inconspicuous consumers of African American texts" who remained convinced of their subversive political potential.[46] In Baldwin's case, the files further our understanding of the complexity of Baldwin's political commitments, underscoring his relentless refutation of the sinister distinction between "American" and "un-American" that dominated the postwar U.S. political landscape, as well as highlighting how his sexuality impeded his role as public spokesman. As James Campbell observes, "In the most ruthless reading of the facts, it is possible to conclude that Hoover succeeded in his campaign against Baldwin"; he notes that the writer left the United States "at the height of his influence and at a crucial turning in the struggle for civil rights."[47] Baldwin's awareness that he was under surveillance certainly impacted the writer, who struggled to find refuge for his "private life," as he termed it, in an unmonitored space away from the sinister "hidden laws" he exposed in his writing. As is well documented, Baldwin gave up on his desire "to find a resting place, reconciliation in the land where I was born" and lived instead in Turkey and France for the rest of his life.[48] Crucially, this writer who had been watched so intensely nonetheless continued to keep his bulging, ever-watchful eyes transfixed on the country of his birth. As he stated in Sedat Pakay's 1970 film *From Another Place*, "One sees [one's country] better from a distance...from another place, another country."[49] Baldwin's courage in the face of relentless surveillance sheds light on his unyielding commitment to freedom of speech and justice. "You've got to get rid of J. Edgar Hoover and the power that he wields," Baldwin declared in 1969. "If you could get rid of [him]...there would be a great deal more hope."[50]

NOTES

1 James Baldwin, "The Discovery of What It Means to be an American," in Toni Morrison (ed.), *James Baldwin: Collected Essays* (New York: Library of America, 1998), p. 142.

2 D. Quentin Miller, *A Criminal Power: James Baldwin and the Law* (Columbus: Ohio State University Press, 2012), p. 8.

3 Baldwin, "The Fire Next Time," in Morrison (ed.), *Collected Essays*, p. 300.
4 Baldwin, "The American Dream and the American Negro," in Morrison (ed.), *Collected Essays*, p. 716.
5 See Lovalerie King, *Race, Theft, and Ethics: Property in African American Literature* (Baton Rouge: Louisiana State University Press, 2007); Deak Nabers, "Past Using: James Baldwin and the Civil Rights Law in the 1960s," *The Yale Journal of Criticism* 18.2 (2005), 221–5; and Lawrie Balfour, *The Evidence of Things Not Said: James Baldwin and the Promise of Democracy* (Ithaca and London: Cornell University Press, 2001).
6 Baldwin's FBI File, 1595. Under the U.S. Freedom of Information Act, Baldwin's FBI files can be requested by writing to the Bureau. Unlike for many authors, including Richard Wright, Baldwin's files are not available online. The FBI files are paginated but are not chronological. Baldwin's files are divided into three sections: part 1: 1–559; part 2: 560–943; part 3: 944–1884. The FBI pagination of Baldwin's files will be referenced parenthetically in the essay. For information about how to request Baldwin's FBI files, see: https://www.muckrock.com/foi/ united-states-of-america-10/fbi-files-on-james-baldwin-9724/.
7 William J. Maxwell, "African-American Modernism and State Surveillance," in Gene Jarrett (ed.), *A Companion to African American Literature* (Oxford: Blackwell, 2010), p. 255.
8 Eve Auchinloss and Nancy Lynch, "Disturber of the Peace: James Baldwin – An Interview," in Fred L. Standley and Louis H. Pratt (eds.), *Conversations with James Baldwin* (Jackson: University Press of Mississippi, 1989), p. 171. Hoover was staunchly anticommunist, and the FBI frequently linked communism to subversive, anti-American behavior. See J. Edgar Hoover, *On Communism* (New York: Random House, 1969).
9 James Campbell, *Talking at the Gates: A Life of James Baldwin* (London and Boston: Faber and Faber, 1991); David Leeming, *James Baldwin: A Biography* (New York: Alfred A. Knopf, 1994). See also Campbell, "'I Heard it Through the Grapevine:' James Baldwin and the FBI," in *Syncopations: Beats, New Yorkers, and Writers in the Dark* (Berkeley, Los Angeles, London: University of California Press, 2008), pp. 78–81, in which he details how Baldwin's FBI files were fully declassified in 1998.
10 Gary Edward Holcomb, *Code Name Sasha: Queer Black Marxism and the Harlem Renaissance* (Gainesville: University Press of Florida, 2007), p. 30.
11 Cited by J. Campbell, "'I Heard it Through the Grapevine:' See Campbell's articles for a brief discussion of Lesar. *Syncopations*, p. 100.
12 Baldwin originally took the surname of his mother, Emma Berdis Jones, as his father's identity was unknown. He changed his surname after his mother married David Baldwin in 1927.
13 The titles of Baldwin's books were of course *Go Tell It on the Mountain* (1953) and *Another Country* (1962).
14 Campbell, Talking at the Gates, p.173.
15 Campbell, "'I Heard it Through the Grapevine," *Syncopations*, p. 88.
16 Braden was sentenced to twelve months in jail for refusing to testify before the House un-American Activities Committee in 1959. Braden's wife, Anne, started a clemency appeal to get her husband released from jail. Martin Luther King, Jr. also signed the petition. See Catherine Fosl, *Subversive Southerner: Anne Braden*

and the Struggle for Racial Justice in the Cold War South (New York: Palgrave Macmillan, 2002).

17 For a discussion of Baldwin's Trotskyite past, see my article, "James Baldwin's Life on the Left: A Portrait of the Artist as a Young New York Intellectual," English Literary History 78 (2011), 833–62.

18 Baldwin, "The Devil Finds Work," in Morrison (ed.), Collected Essays, p. 547.

19 Ibid., p. 544.

20 Campbell, Talking at the Gates, p. 167.

21 Allen Ginsberg's FBI file was 919 pages; Norman Mailer's was 466. Paul Robeson's was particularly large at 2,680. See http://vault.fbi.gov/.

22 Unlike Baldwin's file, Richard Wright's is available on the FBI's Web site at www.fbi/gov/. The mention of Baldwin is in Wright's file, section 1b. There is no pagination in the online version, but it is on p. 49 of the hard copy.

23 For a useful account of this meeting, see Philip A. Goduti, Jr., Robert F. Kennedy and the Shaping of Civil Rights, 1960–1964 (Jefferson, North Carolina and London: McFarland and Company, Inc., 2013), pp. 191–3.

24 Campbell, Talking at the Gates, 169.

25 See, for example, "Conversation: Ida Lewis and James Baldwin," in Standley and Pratt (eds.), Conversations with James Baldwin, p. 92.

26 Baldwin, "The Fire Next Time," Collected Essays, p. 294; Campbell, "'I Heard it Through the Grapevine," Syncopations, p. 77.

27 Campbell, Talking at the Gates, p. 172

28 In a further twist, in 1964 the FBI sent letters to prominent individuals and radical publications to smear George Weissman, a SWP leader and managing editor of the Militant. Falsely accusing Weissman of stealing funds from the Committee, the FBI sent letters to Baldwin, Harold Cruse, and LeRoi Jones. See Nelson Blackstock, COINTELPRO: The FBI's Secret War on Political Freedom (New York et al.: Pathfinder, 1975; 1988), p. 105.

29 For a brief but useful overview of the Committee to Aid the Monroe Defendants (CAMD), see Ward Churchill and Jim Vander Wall, The COINTELPRO Papers: Documents from the FBI's Secret Wars against Dissent in the United States (Cambridge, MA: South End Press, 1990; 2002), pp. 51–2. The authors note that "One of the first 'tasks' undertaken through COINTELPRO-SWP was to attempt to abort the judicial process in the case of the so-called Monroe defendants."

30 Campbell, "'I Heard it Through the Grapevine," Syncopations, pp. 86–7.

31 Natalie Robins, Alien Ink: The FBI's War on Freedom of Expression (New York: Rutgers University Press, 1993), p. 347.

32 See David K. Johnson, The Lavender Scare: The Cold War Persecution of Gays and Lesbians in the Federal Government (Chicago: University of Chicago Press, 2004). Johnson points out that during the "Lavender Scare" many homosexual men and women were targeted as security risks on account of their sexuality.

33 Robins, Alien Ink, p. 67. See Douglas M. Charles, The FBI's Obscene File: J. Edgar Hoover and the Bureau's Crusade against Smut (Lawrence: University Press of Kansas, 2012).

34 William H. Epstein, "Counter-Intelligence: Cold War Criticism and Eighteenth-Century Studies," English Literary History 57.1 (1990), 260.

35 Andrew Ross, *No Respect: Intellectuals and Popular Culture* (New York and London: Routledge, 1989), p. 45.

36 THE PEOPLE OF THE STATE OF CALIFORNIA Plaintiff VS. LAWRENCE FERLINGHETTI (1958) Available: http://mason.gmu.edu/~kthomps4/363-s02/horn-howl.htm. Last accessed April 15, 2014

37 See Bill Morgan and Nancy J. Peters (eds.), *Howl on Trial: The Battle for Free Expression* (San Francisco: City Lights Books, 2006).

38 Robins, *Alien Ink*, pp. 293–4, 294.

39 Ibid., p. 78.

40 Robins, *Alien Ink*, p. 18.

41 See Gérard Genette, *Palimpsests: Literature in the Second Degree*, trans. Channa Newman and Claude Doubinsky; foreword by Gerald Prince (Lincoln: University of Nebraska Press, 1997).

42 Maurice Wallace, "'I'm not Entirely What I Look Like:' Richard Wright, James Baldwin, and the Hegemony of Vision; or, Jimmy's FBEye Blues" in Dwight A. McBride (ed.), *James Baldwin Now* (New York and London: New York University Press, 1999), p. 300.

43 See, for example, Joseph J. Firebaugh, "The Vocabulary of 'Time' Magazine," *American Speech* 15.3 (October 1940), 232–42.

44 John D'Emilio, *Lost Prophet: The Life and Times of Bayard Rustin* (New York: Simon and Schuster, 2003), p. 372.

45 See Bill Maxwell's forthcoming book, *FBEyes: How J. Edgar Hoover's Ghostreaders Framed African American Literature* (Princeton University Press).

46 Maxwell, "African-American Modernism and State Surveillance," in Jarrett (ed.), *A Companion to African American Literature*, p. 256.

47 Campbell, "'I Heard it Through the Grapevine," *Syncopations*, p. 101.

48 Baldwin, "Princes and Powers," in Morrison (ed.), *Collected Essays*, 161.

49 Magdalena Zaborowska, *James Baldwin's Turkish Decade: Erotics of Exile* (Durham and London: Duke University Press, 2009), p. 18.

50 Auchinloss and Lynch, "Disturber of the Peace: James Baldwin – An Interview," in Standley and Pratt (eds.), *Conversations with James Baldwin*, p. 101.

13

MAGDALENA J. ZABOROWSKA

Domesticating Baldwin's Global Imagination

In memory of Brenda Rein
A house is not a home: we have all heard the proverb. Yet, if the house
is not a home (home!) it can become only...a space to be manipulated –
manipulation demanding rather more skill than grace.
                                    – James Baldwin, *Architectural Digest* (1987)

This quotation on the paradox of house and home as discourse, structure,
and process comes from James Baldwin's short autobiographic essay published in *Architectural Digest* in August of 1987, about three months before
his death. One of the last glimpses into the writer's private life, "*Architectural
Digest* Visits: James Baldwin," describes his last abode, known as Chez
Baldwin or the "spread," as Baldwin called it, in the village of St. Paul-de-
Vence in the south of France. It offers a little-examined, complex narrative
important to assessing this writer's legacy, as well as a coda of sorts to his
quest for stability, family, and writing havens that began with his first departure from the United States in 1948.[1] "I have lived in many places, have been
precipitated here and there," Baldwin sums up his international wander-
ings, which became trips away from home once he bought the place in St.
Paul-de-Vence in the 1970s.[2]

Baldwin's succinct narrative, a house tour unfolding modestly beneath
Daniel H. Minassian's lush photographs of his abode, offers a poignant
catalogue of previous locations that failed to sustain him: "a house in
London in the sixties, a couple of apartments and a summer house on the
Bosporus in Istanbul...a house...in Corsica." These were places where he
"never expected to 'stay' " as a "transatlantic commuter, carrying my type-
writer everywhere, from Alabama to Sierra Leone to Finland."[3] Baldwin
also explains his decision not to return to the United States later in his
life: although he had bought a house in New York, he "did not live in this
building for very long," as the assassination of Martin Luther King, Jr.,
"devastated my universe" and caused him to "wander around" until, ill

and collapsing from physical exhaustion and "grief I had been avoiding," he realized that the house in St. Paul-de-Vence "found me just in time." Claiming that "[i]t is far from certain that I will live another sixteen years," Baldwin saw his last house as a subject capable of seeking and "finding," of literally "saving" its dweller from emotional devastation brought about by racist violence in his home country.[4] The unlikely location of the sleepy French village where he settled in 1971 made finding home in his later years finally, and paradoxically, possible.

This essay glimpses Baldwin's domestic space in St. Paul-de-Vence as a restorative and healing location, as well as, in his own words, a "space to be manipulated," a creative and generative abode that framed the writer's last decade and enabled his late works.[5] Bringing into a broad conversation approaches of literary, cultural, and visual studies, this chapter rests on Henri Lefebvre and Walter Benjamin's theories of social space and the private interior, and employs Gaston Bachelard's formulation of "the house image…as topography of…intimate being," one where we can read James Baldwin's "partiality of…imagination."[6]

In what follows I examine several images of Chez Baldwin and read closely the *Architectural Digest* piece as a photo-text that allows us to glimpse Baldwin's self-presentation in his domestic environment.[7] My approach to this eclectic material benefits from Diana Fuss's (2004) emphasis on the role of writers' homes as "theater[s] of composition…place[s] animated by the artifacts, mementos, machines, books, and furniture that frame any intellectual labor."[8] My framing of Baldwin's house, as a material space that he manipulated and as a convergence of imagined and metaphorical spaces – a domestic theatre – that organically enabled his creativity and staged the production of his works, suggests an artistic collaboration. That collaboration unfolds between the writer and the diverse aspects, textures, artifacts, and grounds of his last abode. This brief house tour deliberately echoes Baldwin's own in *Architectural Digest* and approaches Chez Baldwin as a character, much as the writer who occupied it. And while this approach might be read as an instance of what Anne Trubek (2011) terms "literary worship," which confirms the obvious fact of the "writer and readers…[being] already severed from the act of writing," my goal is not to elaborate on the acts of Baldwin's writing.[9] Rather, I explore possible processes of his writerly domestication in St. Paul-de-Vence, the processes to which he gives voice in his works, and whose traces we can imagine by sifting through the elusive archive of whatever remains of his life in St. Paul-de-Vence.[10]

Although the physical topography of Baldwin's house has been lost forever – there are few preserved images from the time the writer lived there, and the site remains unmarked, lost to developers – many readers and scholars have visited St. Paul-de-Vence in hopes of experiencing the structure that housed Baldwin's "intimate being." These trips come about because those who read and study this complex writer crave material reminders of his life, especially given that so few of them are present in the United States. We, the privileged few who have managed to travel to Chez Baldwin, have been trying to envisage what in its surroundings might have fed the imagination of the author's late years. As Quentin Miller explains, "I had read all of his books until the bindings fell apart, but I wanted something else, some intangible feeling for where he had been."[11] The house of James Baldwin, whether still standing or not, remains an important access point – literal and literary – to Baldwin's legacy.[12]

Witnessing Home: "The Collaboration or Corroboration of That Eye"

I first heard of James Baldwin's house in the south of France, what he called the "spread," during a summer research trip in 2000.[13] I found my way to the large, untamed property located along the sunbaked route de la Colle, right outside of the medieval city's ramparts. I stood in front of its tall, locked iron gate. A two-story garage-gatehouse with a steep external stair to its left was overrun with pink flowering vines.[14] The house was a typical, crumbling Provençal structure, perhaps with eighteenth-century origins, and a garden tightening its grip on the stone and tile of the main building at the end of a crumbling cobblestone pathway.

Although uninhabited for several years – since David Baldwin, James's beloved younger brother left in 1996 – the house was still full of both brothers' belongings.[15] The walls were generously decorated with David's collages, and atop mantelpieces, desks, and tables were stacks of James's and David's photographs, files, books, and clippings. I lingered in the study at the back, where Georges Braque had once painted, and where Baldwin had his studio, or "torture chamber," as he called it.[16] The garden, which embraced the house on all sides, was filled with places to sit and take a break; it also held Baldwin's famed welcome table under an arbor. A path dense with greenery was traced with colorful lightbulbs. On a wall by an arched passageway a small mirror blinked; Jimmy would peer into it to check his appearance before joining his visitors in the garden. There were once plans to transform the property into a retreat for writers, and it was Baldwin's wish that his legacy be honored in that way.[17] Today, there is nothing, not even a marker.

I stood for a while in the room on the main floor, the former living room, where Baldwin had been moved once he became too frail to walk down to his study, and where he died. The room contained the artist's bed and a table with a mess of books and papers. I wandered through the rest of the

Figure 13.1. Magdalena J. Zaborowska, Front door of Chez Baldwin, St. Paul-de-Vence, June 2000. Photo by author. Reprinted with permission of author.

house, peered through windows, took more photographs and felt rather distraught as a scholar: How would having seen this space affect my future reading of Baldwin's works? Almost a decade and a half since that visit, I cannot give a conclusive answer to this question, although the lessons of my overawed tour of Chez Baldwin later led me to Turkey and Baldwin's home sites there. One of these lessons is always to look for the material as the context for the metaphorical, for the literal as the context for the literary, no matter how scarce the archive. The attention we readers and scholars pay to places where important works have been created, and to structures, cities, and landscapes that inspired memorable lines of text, stems from the need to anchor in the material and tangible what is elusive and impermanent about

214

literature, and from our hope to share imagination and inspiration.[18] The need to see the places where writing happened emerges from the desire for closeness to one's subject; what better place to feel inspired than within the walls that once housed the admired writer?

I begin this chapter with these auto-ethnographic recollections of Chez Baldwin because I hope that we can save some of the material aspects of this writer's legacy, that his traces in the world will be preserved not only in his books but also in the places where he wrote them. As Diana Fuss emphasizes in *The Sense of an Interior* (2004), writers' houses invite us to enter "into conversation[s] with the dead," and the "recurrent interplay of subject and object in the space of writing reminds us that if the writer's interior is a memorial chamber, it is also a living archive."[19] Although I came to St. Paul-de-Vence looking for such an archive, I was keenly aware that I had no way of knowing whether Baldwin's last room looked exactly like the photograph I took of it in 2000, thirteen years after his death and four after David Baldwin had left it.

What I could be sure of was that the house had changed and that spatial accuracy and verisimilitude were not as important as the fact that I was able to enter it and spend some time there. In contrast to visiting a well-advertised writer's museum, where one might see a desk artfully displayed behind velvet ropes just "as she or he left it," I encountered only what remained of the messy everydayness of Chez Baldwin. As Daniel Miller remarks, studying houses involves "a willingness to step inside the private domain of other people."[20] At the moment of my visit, the ever-changing "memorial chamber" of Baldwin's domain was a collection of objects enclosed within walls to which my visitor's eye would add meaning.

As a literary scholar, I am partial to what Bachelard terms the "activity of metaphor," as well as the ways in which all kinds of "images [must] be lived directly…taken as sudden events in life." Bachelard's house poetics relies on the assumption that meanings and their material inspirations cannot be divorced from the realm of the metaphor and image that belong to the writer. It is thus possible for the actual "house [to] acquire…the physical and moral energy of the human body," to be an agent, however ephemeral, in the texts it has inspired. This approach is particularly applicable to Baldwin, who acknowledged his dwelling's subjectivity when stating that it "found me just in time." For a writer, Bachelard claims, "[f]rom having been a refuge, [the house] has become a redoubt…. a fortified castle for the recluse who must learn to conquer fear within its walls."[21]

Having seen Chez Baldwin enables me to imagine the writer's late-life transformation into the steward and homemaker of sorts that he appears to be in his *Architectural Digest* narrative and in the interviews he gave

Figure 13.2. Magdalena J. Zaborowska, Living Room of Chez Baldwin, St. Paul-de-Vence, June 2000. Photo by author. Reprinted with permission of author.

in 1985–7. Bachelard's phenomenology of the imagination allows for an organic connection between material structures, the human body, and the images and dreams of those who live in, visit, think, or write about houses. Thus, once inhabited, a house enables a "geometrical object" to undergo a "transposition to the human plane," in which the experience of material space becomes an extension of our humanity, and endows meaning-making with transformative power: "Come what may the house helps us to say: I will be an inhabitant of the world, in spite of the world.... A house that has been experienced is not an inert box. Inhabited space transcends geometrical space."[22] As a framing for and extension of the writer, Baldwin's house has evolved its own complex poetics, which inflected much of his writings, and especially his last finished yet unpublished play, *The Welcome Table* (1987), which must be read in the context of his house tour in the *Architectural Digest*.

Representing House: "The Key to One's Life Is Always in a Lot of Unexpected Places"

Baldwin's 1987 "Last Interview," with the journalist, poet, and editor Quincy Troupe, was recorded at his house only days before he died.[23] It confirms the importance of his last abode to the person he became at the end of his life and celebrates "unexpected places" in his experience and oeuvre as key to understanding his journey.[24] As Troupe emphasizes in the foreword to *James Baldwin: The Legacy* (1989), the volume in which the interview was later collected, Baldwin's last work, the play *The Welcome Table,* owed its setting and plot to "an actual event...a late-night August dinner in the gardens." The play also had "Baldwin's intense, restive and febrile persona hover...over the pages."[25] In a somewhat similar vein, "*Architectural Digest* Visits: James Baldwin" uses the writer's name in a common metonymic fashion where it stands for his immediate milieu, thus making the man and house a single entity. However, unlike the play, this popular publication seems intended for the coffee tables of homemakers rather than the desks of literary critics.

The text of "*Architectural Digest* Visits: James Baldwin" is overshadowed by Minassian's photographs of the tranquil, sunlit Provençal garden and the simply furnished interiors of the old stone farmhouse. Of the seven photographs, only two depict the writer, who seems posed to complement rather than command the scene; it is as if the piece is self-conscious about Baldwin's eclipsed celebrity in the United States. It is a "digest" piece, after all, meant to show rather than tell, or to showcase not so much the writer as the real estate he owns. At closer examination, however, it is a densely meaningful narrative, a photo-text that encapsulates Baldwin's late vision of himself, the vision seemingly intended for a popular audience but suffused with what he saw as his larger literary legacy.

After Turkey, whose impact on his works I have discussed extensively in *James Baldwin's Turkish Decade* (2009), St. Paul-de-Vence was the other exilic location where Baldwin was not only prolific, but also tried new things in his writing. These experiments included the interweaving of black musical forms into his last novel, *Just Above My Head* (1979); the new kind of playwriting inspired by the work of Russian playwright Anton Chekhov in *The Welcome Table* (1987); cross-breeding essay and reportage for his account of the Atlanta children murders in *The Evidence of Things Not*

Seen (1985); collecting poems that he dismissed as "finger exercises" for the volume *Jimmy's Blues* (1983); and collaborating with jazz musicians and providing vocalization of poems from that volume for the album "A Lover's Question," issued by Label Bleu in France.

"The spread" allowed Baldwin to slow down. Having arrived, as he writes in *Architectural Digest*, at the "age at which silence becomes a tremendous gift," he praises domestic work with the easy metaphor of "the vineyard in which one toils [with] a rigorous joy."[26] This last house of his is "very *old*…which means that there is always something in need of repair or renewal or burial," yet the "exasperating rigor" of domestic maintenance "is good for the soul," and "one can never suppose that one's work is done."[27] This sentiment contradicts young Baldwin's belief, as expressed in a 1957 letter from Corsica to his childhood friend and editor Sol Stein, that his work is "my only means of understanding the world…my only means of feeling at home in the world."[28] He beseeches Stein: "Please get over the notion…that there's some place I'll fit when I've made some 'real peace' with myself: the place in which I'll fit will not exist until I make it."[29] Thirty-three years old at the time, Baldwin casts himself as an eternal nomad "covering the earth," who believes that the best way to "escape one's environment is to surrender to it."[30] The moment for "making the place in which he fit" came after an exhausting decade and a half of writing and activism, as well as moments of despondency in the wake of backlash against the Civil Rights Movement, the murders of some of its leaders, and his waning popularity as a writer in the United States. At forty-six, he decided to surrender to the house in St. Paul-de-Vence.

Baldwin's surrender signified an important turn from being an exile and nomad to a homeowner, a turn that has not been documented extensively. Besides film footage of the place that Karen Thorsen used in her documentary, "The Price of the Ticket" (1989), precious few sources document his residence. A closer look at the photos and captions from *Architectural Digest* helps us contextualize the images that were presumably taken and arranged in collaboration with the writer.[31] The captions include snippets of Baldwin's speech, likely taken from a recorded interview, and provide detailed descriptions of key spatial elements of Chez Baldwin.

The first caption appears under the second photo in the series that depicts the writer seated at an outdoor table with a view of the village behind him. The extensive text encapsulates his life story and identifies the first photo in the series, of the house from the back garden, which appears above the article's title: "'I first arrived in France in 1948, a little battered by New York because of my anger, my youth, and my pride,' recalls James Baldwin, whose debut novel *Go Tell It on the Mountain* began his exploration of social inequality and civil liberties." It continues, "[h]e is currently working on a new novel, *Any Bootlegger*," and adds, "a bamboo-shaded table, where Baldwin and his guests eat lunch, is surrounded by the vegetation that he has let grow untamed." Two more images show the writer reading while seated on a stone patio under an umbrella, highlighting picturesque elements of landscaping and architecture around him: "'An island of silence and peace' is how Baldwin describes the terrace directly in front of his office where he can take breaks from writing"; "[r]oses surround and climb over one of the oldest parts of the house, the back entrance with a shuttered door that leads into the kitchen."[32]

Three images on the final page highlight the functionality of the interiors: "The corkboard in his office, where Baldwin often works till dawn...[p]hotographs of friends and family include one in the center of Baldwin with his brother David...two book jackets...of his most recently published works...plaster mask of Pascal"; [t]he living room...furnished with rustic Provençal pieces, in keeping with his preference for an unadorned environment"; "[p]hotographs...arranged along the living room mantel, and paintings...by his friends." The portrait of the artist in an idyllic southern French abode is complete. His sexuality is never mentioned – not one bedroom photo appears. Unequivocally single, even solitary, an intellectual cultivating his talent in a remote location in his twilight years, he is comfortably desexualized.

This portrayal stands in stark contrast to those that hail parties and entourages of friends, lovers, and family in Baldwin's biographies and memoirs about him. It also omits his connection to the local population, especially women who welcomed him into their tightly knit village community and some of whom served as inspirations for characters in *The Welcome Table*. Their role for Baldwin was crucial, as he suffered conflicting desires for home – on the one hand, he longed for domestic intimacy and privacy in a monogamous relationship; on the other, he understood that his lifestyle of nighttime work, exhausting parties, often excessive drinking and smoking, not to mention strenuous travel and a stormy love life, made stable domesticity virtually unattainable.[33] Among the inhabitants of St. Paul-de-Vence, who cared little for his fame and notoriety, the activist-writer-traveler became a homemaker-author.

This transformation is visible in the *Architectural Digest*, which juxtaposes his actions, achievements, and travels – "I had bought a building in New York...directed a play in Istanbul...visited Italy" – with the bodily and affective fallout of his whirlwind life – "I collapsed physically...[f]riends then shipped me.... It was grief I had been avoiding, which was why I had collapsed.... Why not stay here?"[34] Mary Painter, an old-time friend whom

Baldwin at one point "wishe[d] he could marry," persuaded him to settle in her favorite location in the south of France.[35] Once there, Baldwin spoke of the French women who became his friends as his guides and teachers, at the same time as he continued to enjoy the company of African-American "sisters" he had admired and loved since his youth. Both became important inspirations for his last work, *The Welcome Table*.

Staging the House of Women: "She Was My Guide to Something Else"

Baldwin came to St. Paul-de-Vence after deciding to leave Turkey for good in 1971.[36] He had been ill and struggling with the final drafts of his fourth essay volume, *No Name in the Street* (1972); he was also thin and weak, in need of convalescence after an acute bout of jaundice.[37] Brenda (Keith) Rein, his assistant and typist in Istanbul, kept him company, discussing American politics and the Black Panthers in the context of her native Oakland, California. She was one of the African-American or Turkish women – along with the singer Bertice Reading,[38] the actor Gülriz Sururi, the journalist Zeynep Oral, the actor Eartha Kitt, and the scholar Florence Ladd – who became Baldwin's close friends, confidantes, and enablers of his work, either directly collaborating or inspiring ideas about femininity and gender roles, in which he became increasingly interested as his Turkish decade came to a close.

By the time he settled in France, Baldwin was increasingly enamored of several black women like Brenda Rein, including the writer-performer Maya Angelou, the artist-writer Vertamae Grosvenor, the novelist Paule Marshall, the activist Louise Meriwether, and the scholar Eleanor Traylor. He also admired feminist poets Audre Lorde and Nikki Giovanni and the novelist Toni Morrison. Suzan-Lori Parks and Shay Youngblood studied with him when he taught at Five Colleges in the 1980s. Most importantly, from his earliest years, Baldwin adored singers like Bessie Smith, and especially the international superstar Josephine Baker and singer-activist Nina Simone, both of whom were guests at his house. Noting Baldwin's marked turn toward femininity in his self-presentation as an older man, Leeming claims that beyond sheer admiration of these women, "there was a part of him that envied their style, their clothes[, their gestures."[39]

By the publication of his fifth collection of essays, *The Devil Finds Work* (1976), on representation, cinema, and autobiography, Baldwin was confident in addressing the intersectionalities of race, gender, and sexuality, that "Identity would seem to be the garment with which one covers the nakedness of the self.... This trust in one's nakedness is all that gives one the power to change one's robes."[40] By the 1980s, "the female within the male ha[d] long fascinated" Baldwin, and he "not only enjoyed female company," but also embraced camp and gendered performativity, having "given in to a love of silk, of the recklessly thrown scarf…the large and exotic ring, bracelet, or neckpiece.…His movements assumed a more feminine character." As Baldwin succumbed to a "wish fulfillment or psychological nostalgia for a lost woman within his manhood," inspired by his female friends and visitors, he dreamt of a "character" in whom "James Baldwin would be transformed into a Josephine Baker."[41] While he perhaps wanted to be like the black women he admired, Baldwin learned how to be at home away from his homeland from the women of the town where his house stood.[42]

In particular, he became close friends with the "pied noir" Jeanne Faure, a local historian exiled from French Algeria from whom he rented and later bought the house. Though their relationship was at first "stormy," as she did not like blacks, Mlle. Faure in time came to love Baldwin, and he cherished their friendship until her death, barely a year before his own.[43] The spacious house provided a vibrant setting for meetings with friends and family visits, for creative collaborations, long discussions on politics and art, and parties famed in the region.[44] Baldwin recalls his first impressions of the place in *Architectural Digest*: "I looked around me and realized that I had rented virtually every room in the house.… It's a fine stone house, about twelve rooms, overlooking the valley and at the foot of the village. My studio is on the first floor, next to a terrace.… Visitors need not find themselves on top of each other, and there are several acres of land."[45]

Along with Jeanne Faure, "a very strange lady, solitary…a kind of legend,"[46] Baldwin became close friends with Tintine Roux, an older woman who ran the famous restaurant, La Colombe D'Or, and who "had picked herself to be my protector."[47] As he explained to Troupe, "both these women were watching something else besides my color. And they…loved me.… I miss them both terribly." He became legible to them, for they "recognized where I came from."[48] When Faure's brother died, she asked Baldwin to lead her at the funeral procession, to "stand…with her at the head of the family." The meaning of this act was "shocking" to the town, and yet symbolized the writer's full acceptance as not only a St. Paul-de-Vence inhabitant but also as Faure's kin, and thus a descendant of the town's elders: "what it meant…is that I was the next in line, when she died."[49] When Baldwin traveled to Paris to receive the French Legion of Honor medal from President François Mitterrand on June 19, 1986, he took Mlle. Faure with him, along with his cook, Valerie Sordello, to whom he had promised a trip to the big city. Hired to clean and cook for Baldwin, Valerie became a "member of the family and was with Baldwin to the end."[50] Appearing briefly in the documentary "The Price of the Ticket," Sordello has remained a fleeting presence on the pages of Baldwin's writing, having inspired the sympathetic character of Angelina, the maid, in *The Welcome Table*. In general throughout the play, the "literal point of view was very much Baldwin's Saint-Paul-de Vence scene," and "all of the main characters are female."[51]

In letters dated July 1982 and March 1983, Baldwin wrote to his friend, the actor David Moses, about his hope to finish the play. He compared the creative process to giving birth, in somewhat ambivalent gendered terms, as there was something "unspeakably feminine" about being a writer – "labor pains," the book "kicking," and then the author having to "shit it out."[52] The play proved difficult to write because he was determined to try something new in it, having been inspired by the works of the Russian playwright Anton Chekhov.[53] *The Welcome Table* takes place during one day, from early morning until "round around midnight." His detailed stage directions describe "an ancient, rambling stone house" in Provençe, a room that is a combination of "dining room and office," "an arch," "le salon," and "spiral stair-case," all of which mirror the actual interiors and architectural features of Chez Baldwin.[54]

The protagonist is the homeowner Edith Hemings, an intriguing, turban-wearing performer who can be read as a transgender figuration of James Baldwin/Josephine Baker. She was once "a skinny bow-legged child" like Baldwin, but now has become an "actress-singer/star." She is a veritable black Atlantic character, "Creole, from New Orleans."[55] Her cousin Laverne (possibly inspired by the choreographer Bernard Hassel, who managed Baldwin's house) runs the household, and employs Angelina, the maid, and Mohammed, the Algerian gardener (who was to be the hero of Baldwin's unrealized novel *No Papers for Mohammed*). Another character, Regina, is Edith's old friend who has recently been widowed and drinks heavily (possibly modeled on Mary Painter). There are also Rob, Edith's "protégé and lover," and Mark, a Jewish man who is also Rob's lover. Elderly Mlle. Lafarge is a "pied noir" (inspired by Jeanne Faure). There are also: Daniel, a former Black Panther and "clumsy arsonist" who is trying to become a playwright (modeled on the writer Cecil Brown); Terry, a photographer; and Peter Davis, a black American journalist (modeled on the scholar Henry Louis Gates, Jr.).[56] The dramatis personae section ends with a note that specifies that Regina, Mark, and Rob are "in appearance" and "legally" white, as is, with "something of a difference," Mlle. LaFarge. Terry's character is completely open to interpretation: male or female, black or white.

The play toys with drawing-room drama conventions and, echoing an actual event in 1985, revolves around Peter Davis's interview with Edith on the day the household is celebrating Mlle. Lafarge's ninety-third birthday. As we progress toward the party and the late-night interview following it, we glimpse the complex erotic entanglements between the characters, with the main emphasis on the females' life stories and their views on the social and political roles of men and women. While Peter and Edith talk, the focus shifts from one group of interlocutors to another, allowing a mixing of main and marginal characters and inviting the reader to glimpse complex forces of love, desire, fear, and need for acceptance that underlie their dialogues.[57] The way Baldwin's house engenders and embraces both the play and its characters' lives may be compared to the ways his women friends helped him to settle into late-life writing of domesticity.[58]

In an interesting historical twist on that domesticity, in "The Last Interview" with Quincy Troupe, Baldwin makes a startling claim that the house and its environs enabled his reconnection with his ancestral American southern roots. He became a "peasant" in St. Paul-de-Vence "because of where I really came from...my father, my mother, the line. Something of the peasant must be in all of my family."[59] Baldwin's musings on his "peasant" origins – a remark that should be taken seriously given that it was made on the eve of his death – came about because he suddenly felt that he fit in, albeit in a place and among people who were far from his birthplace.[60] Ensconced in his garden, Baldwin felt safe to look back at his roots in Harlem: "The beginning of my life rather recalls a shipwreck," he writes with no trace of nostalgia in *Architectural Digest*, echoing the 1955 essay on his childhood and conflict with his father, first titled "Me and My House" and later published as "Notes of a Native Son."[61] He admits to being in flight for a long time, for "the shipwrecked can find it difficult to trust daylight or dry land."[62]

By the time Baldwin wrote *No Name in the Street* (1972) – which opens with an homage to his mother and grandmother and bridges his exile in Turkey and newly found domesticity in St. Paul-de-Vence – he began to move away from his "father's house," or the masculine-oriented themes and characters that dominated his early works, toward embracing feminine-oriented ones in the works that followed. Bachelard's house poetics offers the relevant term "maternal features of the house," which implies the ways in which the structure becomes anthropomorphized in writing and bestows on its dweller a sense of safety and love.[63] Through the magic of writerly "manipulation," Baldwin makes his beloved house an important character in his last play and a generative space that gives birth to important writing during his last decade.[64] While this complex writer continues to inspire readers and scholars to work hard to feel at home in his writings, the study of Baldwin's house – with all its challenge and ambivalence – might also help us more fully to integrate black American writers' domestic lives into the nation's literary home.

NOTES

1 David A. Leeming, *James Baldwin: A Biography* (New York: Knopf, 1994), p. 313.

2 James Baldwin, "*Architectural Digest* Visits: James Baldwin," *Architectural Digest*, August 1987, 122.

3 Baldwin, "*Architectural Digest* Visits," 123.

4 Ibid.

5 Henry Louis Gates, Jr., published many versions of his encounter with Baldwin and Josephine Baker at the St. Paul-de-Vence house, for example: "The Welcome Table: James Baldwin in Exile" in Susan Rubin Suleiman (ed.), *Exile and Creativity: Signposts, Travelers, Outsiders, Backward Glances* (Durham: Duke University Press, 1998).

6 Gaston Bachelard, *The Poetics of Space* (originally published 1958), trans. Orion Press (Boston: Beacon Press, 1994), p. xxxvi. See also Walter Benjamin, *The Arcades Project* trans. Rolf Tiedemann (Cambridge: Harvard University Press, 1999); and Henri Lefebvre, *The Production of Space*, trans. Donald Nicholson-Smith (Oxford, UK; Cambridge, MA: Wiley Blackwell, 1991). My triad of influences includes Bachelard as phenomenologist, Lefebvre as sociologist and Marxist scholar of cities and social space, and Benjamin as literary critic.

7 The genre of photo-text is best represented by Baldwin's collaboration with Richard Avedon, *Nothing Personal* (New York: Atheneum, 1964). See also Sarah Blair, *Harlem Crossroads: Black Writers and the Photograph in the Twentieth Century* (Princeton: Princeton University Press, 2007); and Josh Miller, "The Discovery of What It Means to Be a Witness: James Baldwin's Dialectics of Distance" in Dwight A. McBride (ed.), *James Baldwin Now* (New York: New York University Press, 1999), pp. 331–59. Brian Norman discussed this work at the American Studies Association meeting in Washington D.C., November 2013.

8 Diana Fuss, *The Sense of an Interior: Four Writers and the Rooms That Shaped Them* (New York: Routledge, 2004), p. 1.

9 Anne Trubek, *A Skeptic's Guide to Writer's Houses* (Philadelphia and Oxford: University of Pennsylvania Press, 2011), p. 5.

10 Trubek in *A Skeptic's Guide*, "Writer's houses preserve domesticity," p. 45.

11 Quentin Miller's unpublished paper, "'It Rains Down Here, Too': Going to Meet James Baldwin in Provence," is an account of such a personal/scholarly trip to Chez Baldwin and confirms the importance of preserving it.

12 A local real estate agency confirmed that the house was lost to a developer several years after David Baldwin's departure.

13 The section heading quote refers to Baldwin, "Here Be Dragons," in *The Price of the Ticket: Collected Nonfiction, 1948–1985* (New York: St. Martins, 1985): "It is virtually impossible to trust one's human value without the collaboration or corroboration of that eye – which is to say that no one can live without it," p. 680. "Spread" appears in Leeming, *James Baldwin*, p. 313. Coleman A. Jordan assisted me during that trip and helped document it.

14 See the Web site of the Musée & Office de Tourisme: http://www.saint-pauldevence .com/en/history/personalities/james-baldwin

See also the French interview on that site, "James Baldwin à propos de son enfance à Harlem." See also: http://savejimmyshouse.blogspot.com/; http://www .youtube.com/watch?v=8pE_Kp8aLW4 links a French television documentary.

15 I saw the house thanks to Jill Hutchinson, late David Baldwin's partner, who took care of the place after he left.

16 Georges Braque was an important twentieth-century French modernist painter who helped develop the Foundation Maeght for the arts in St. Paul-de-Vence in the 1960s.

17 David Leeming, discussion with author, November 2012.

18 Daniel Miller's *Stuff* poses a "challenge to our common-sense opposition between the person and the thing, the animate and inanimate, the subject and the object." (Cambridge: Polity Press, 2010), p. 5.

19 Fuss, *Interior*, pp. 213–14.

20 Miller, *Stuff*, p. 109.

21 Bachelard, *Poetics*, pp. 47, 46.

22 Ibid., pp. 46–7.

23 This note refers to the section Representing House: "The Key to One's Life Is Always in a Lot of Unexpected Places". "The Last Interview" (1987), in Quincy Troupe (ed.), *James Baldwin: The Legacy* (New York: Touchstone-Simon and Schuster, 1989), p. 207.

24 Troupe, who was also a performer, playwright, and nonfiction writer, was part of the Black Arts Movement.

25 Troupe, *James Baldwin: The Legacy*, p. 11.

26 I develop extensive descriptions of Chez Baldwin as a queer space in my book, from which this essay comes.

27 Baldwin, "*Architectural Digest* Visits," 124. See also David O'Reilly, "A Play This Time: The Fire Has Not Dimmed for James Baldwin, Whose 1950s Work 'The Amen Corner' Opens at the Annenberg Center Tomorrow Night," *The Philadelphia Inquirer* (December 2, 1986), E1.

28 James Baldwin and Sol Stein, *Native Sons* (New York: One World, Ballantine Books, 2004), p. 96.

29 Ibid., pp. 96–7.

30 Ibid., p. 97.

31 The captions' authorship is unattributed but may be Baldwin's.

32 Baldwin, "*Architectural Digest* Visits," 124.

33 David Leeming, discussion with author, New York, March 2004.

34 Baldwin, "*Architectural Digest* Visits" 123.

35 Leeming, *James Baldwin*, p. 377.

36 This note refers to the section Staging the House of Women: "She Was My Guide to Something Else". Troupe, "Last Interview," p. 199.

37 Brenda Rein, discussion with author, May 2007.

38 Mea culpa: I misspelled Reading's name in *James Baldwin's Turkish Decade* (Durham: Duke University Press, 2009). So did Leeming.

39 Leeming, *James Baldwin*, p. 377.

40 James Baldwin, *The Devil Finds Work* (New York: Dial, 1976), p. 93.

41 Leeming, *James Baldwin*, p. 377.
42 Baldwin's late-life turn toward feminine self-presentation and gender politics must be read in the context of his rich oeuvre and life story; this brief chapter glimpses it as part of his aforementioned domestic "manipulation."
43 Troupe, "Last Interview," pp. 197–201.
44 See also Cecil Brown's recollections in: http://nabcommunities.com/2012/02/23/culture-a-real-life-midnight-in-paris-with-james-baldwin-part-iii/
45 Baldwin, "*Architectural Digest* Visits," 123–4.
46 Troupe, "Last Interview," p. 197.
47 Ibid., p.198. Baldwin's frequent drinking companions were the actors Simone Signoret and Yves Montand.
48 Ibid.
49 Ibid., p. 200.
50 Leeming, *James Baldwin*, p. 313.
51 Leeming, *James Baldwin*, pp. 374, 376.
52 James Baldwin to David Moses, July 6, 1982 and March 10, 1983. Manuscript, Archives, and Rare Book Library. Emory University, Atlanta.
53 Anton Chekhov was one of the most prominent authors of plays and stories in nineteenth-century Russia.
54 The Baldwin Estate does not allow direct quotations from the play; hence I offer limited references to this text. Baldwin, *The Welcome Table*, manuscript, n.p. Schomburg Center for Research on African American Culture.
55 Baldwin, *The Welcome Table*, manuscript, unpaginated, pp. 5, 9.
56 Henry Louis Gates, Jr., "The Welcome Table: James Baldwin in Exile," p. 318.
57 I offer a detailed introduction to the play, its summary, and links to Baldwin's other works in Zaborowska (2009 and 2011). The play, originally conceived in Turkey in the late 1960s, was an organic product uniting Baldwin's domestic and authorial labors. He elaborated on his need to write it in letters to his brother David after his first decade in St. Paul. Originally entitled *Inventory or Investments* (Leeming, p. 356), it later took shape in collaboration with Walter Dallas, an African-American director who taught at the University of the Arts and headed the Freedom Theater in Philadelphia.
58 Baldwin's interest in gender politics suffuses *The Welcome Table*, as well as the late essays that provide its context and appeared in *Playboy*: "Freaks and the American Ideal of Manhood" (1985) and "To Crush the Serpent" (1987). This is also apparent in his transitional works, such as his last two novels that feature important female characters and narrators, *If Beale Street Could Talk* (1974) and *Just Above My Head* (1979).
59 Troupe, "Last Interview," p. 198.
60 Leeming, *James Baldwin*, p. 314.
61 The piece appeared in *Harper's Magazine* (November 1955).
62 Baldwin, "*Architectural Digest* Visits," p. 122.
63 Bachelard, *Poetics*, pp. 7, 45–6.
64 Recent publications on home as feminine: "The Writer's Room," *The NYT Style Magazine* (February 16, 2014), M2226; and J. D. McClatchy, *American Writers at Home* (New York: Library of America, 2004), which lists only Frederick Douglass's house among the twenty-one that "remind us of…our passions and sorrows turned into the books that have told us…how we are Americans," p. 9.

D. QUENTIN MILLER

Coda: The Heart of Baldwin

Having read the essays in this *Companion*, I turn to the chaotic bookshelf behind me and stare at the rows of books by and about James Baldwin. Fittingly, given the author's life and oeuvre, it's a messy and motley collection, including everything from cheap pocket paperbacks to first editions. I see three separate copies of *Another Country*, two copies each of many other titles. In my own critical journey through Baldwin's work, I have been more prone to accumulating than selecting. I have described Baldwin as a jigsaw puzzle, and over time, I feel as though critics have found more and more missing pieces and are considering new ways to make them fit together. It's a difficult job, for Baldwin can be puzzling indeed. Moreover, the puzzle seems to grow with every new piece. Baldwin was not one to be contained.

For some reason, I pull down my copy of *Notes of a Native Son*. Maybe I feel sorry for it – it's held together with layers of Scotch tape. I open it gently. It contains an archaeology of sorts. Thumbing through, I see that my margin notes appear in five different pen colors, plus one yellow highlighter: a rainbow of critical responses, collected over more than two decades of my life. I wonder why I chose this book as I begin to write this reflection in this important *Companion*. Some explanations come to mind: I sit right around the corner from Beacon Press in Boston, where it was published; I believe it was the first book by Baldwin I read. Its taped spine and worn cover testify to its endurance.

But there is something else. Pondering the patterns I see in this *Companion*, I had been thinking about archetypes and tropes. These essays highlight a number of Baldwin's important archetypes: the fiery, sermon-delivering, commanding patriarch. The vulnerable child, or childlike adult. The artist straining against convention. The public figure yearning for privacy. The anonymous figure desiring fame or love. The wise leader. The wandering sufferer. It could easily be said that these are all aspects of Baldwin himself, but they are also the fodder for the subjects of the essays contained herein. The tropes are also evident in this volume: the enduring power of music, the furious quest for love, the importance of witnessing, the conversion of suffering into art. We see them in a concentrated way in the title of his first collection, *Notes of a Native Son*. Put a "g" on the end of that title and the collection becomes music, its notes as plaintive as the blues that are so often Baldwin's subject. The "native" of the title highlights Baldwin's peregrinations: native to where? He wrote these essays from another country. The young author conceives of himself as a son: the overt allusion to his complex relationship with Richard Wright yields to his equally complex relationship with his own father and indicates further his fraught relationship with Christianity from the point of view of the son who is sacrificed to atone for the flawed world his father created.

I have looked at this book a hundred times, but, as Nicholas Boggs says in his essay in this volume, there is always the imperative to "look again," with new eyes, through new critical lenses. I was drawn back to "Notes of a Native Son" (the title essay) because it is an origin story, the genesis of Baldwin's journey as a writer, out of the Eden of innocence and into the world of experience. It is, if I may make an evaluative judgment, the finest essay Baldwin ever wrote, and one of the finest in the English language. It begins with the extraordinary confluence of four events: Baldwin's father dies on July 29. Baldwin's youngest sibling is born that same day. The funeral takes place a few days later, on Baldwin's nineteenth birthday – signifying his adulthood. A few hours after the funeral, a major race riot breaks out in Harlem.

Birth, maturity, violence, death. The intensely personal demons Baldwin confronts in the essay, such as his father's bitterness ("he was certainly the most bitter man I have ever met"[1]), connect to public, collective demons. The Harlem race riots and his father's "disease" (a word as common as "bitterness" in the essay) are connected in the author's mind. As the second half of the essay begins, Baldwin describes how he and his family were waiting for the arrival of his baby sister and for the death of their father, but also, "All of Harlem, indeed, seemed to be infected by waiting" (98). The word "infected" stands out when this sentence is lifted out of context: Why wasn't Harlem just "waiting"? But in the context of the essay, "infection" develops an important theme. His father's bitterness may have originated in society, but it is *inside* him: in his "spirit," his "mind," and his "body" (88, 89, 90). It is an infection that is hereditary: "this bitterness now was mine.... The bitterness which had helped to kill my father could also kill me" (88, 89). Baldwin, sojourning into a segregated New Jersey where he is denied service at various restaurants because of the color of his skin, begins to feel the effects of his father's illness within himself: "having an unsuspected predilection for it, I first contracted some dread, chronic disease, the unfailing symptom of which is a kind of blind fever, a pounding in the skull and fire in the bowels" (94). In the famous scene when he throws a water mug at a waitress who refuses to serve him, his "frozen blood abruptly thawed" (97). His disease, like his father's, is experienced deep within, and it is then that he realizes that "my *real* life, was in danger, and not from anything other people might do but from the hatred I carried in my own heart" (98).

Hatred, heart: nearly anagrammatic words that have a mutually destructive relationship. Baldwin's deep look into his own body, infected as it is, causes the reader to look at the fever in the blood that infects our country. In the first paragraph, Baldwin refers to the race riots that precede his father's funeral as "one of the bloodiest...of the century" (85). When blood is spilled, it leaves a mark on history. The race riots Baldwin describes are part of a pattern of racial violence in the country: from Tulsa in 1921, to Harlem in 1935 and 1943, to Watts in 1965, Detroit and Newark in the Long Hot Summer of 1967, and Los Angeles in 1992 – to name only the most egregious – blood was spilled everywhere. And yet, Baldwin describes himself as equally worried about the blood that had not been spilled. The infected blood in his veins connects him to his father. He also worries that his baby sister will inherit the bad blood that connects families.

What to do, then? Riots, Baldwin suggests, are not the answer: even though "Harlem had needed something to smash," just as Baldwin had needed to smash a mirror and water glass when the New Jersey waitress wouldn't serve him. He says of the riots, "None of this was doing anybody any good" (111). Nor had it done him any good to lash out at the waitress, and it could have gotten him killed. The hatred he feels, though valid, is "an exhausting and self-destructive pose. But this does not mean, on the other hand, that love comes easily: the white world is too powerful, too complacent, too ready with gratuitous humiliation, and, above all, too ignorant and too innocent for that" (112).

To keep one's hatred inside is to exacerbate the disease, though:

> One is always in the position of having to decide between amputation and gangrene. Amputation is swift but time may prove that the amputation was not necessary – or one may delay the amputation too long. Gangrene is slow, but it is impossible to be sure that one is reading one's symptoms right. The idea of going through life as a cripple is more than one can bear, and equally unbearable is the risk of swelling up slowly, in agony, with poison. (112)

This is what happened to Baldwin's father. This is what Baldwin fears will happen to himself. Spilled blood and poisoned blood both lead to death. Writing his essay during the immediate aftermath of the famous *Brown vs. Board of Education* desegregation decision, Baldwin was skeptical that the cure to America's race problem was going to be simple. Love isn't easy. A deeply entrenched disease resists panaceas.

What do we continue to find and admire in Baldwin, then? Certainly not someone who was so eaten up by a disease of the heart that he was paralyzed. What Baldwin offers, and what each of the essays in this *Companion* highlights, is a man dedicated to searching for the cure to this American disease. The cure is not the point: the *dedication* and the *search* are. Rarely have we seen an author more dedicated, more earnest in his quest than James Baldwin. He was not without his shortcomings and flaws, but his passion and his awareness, no less than his gifts and his hard work, cause readers to look again, to look deeper, and to repay his creative efforts with our own critical ones.

Baldwin knew, in 1955, that the recent legislation outlawing segregation would not end racial hatred – at least, not overnight. The disease is systemic: to concentrate only on the visible symptoms is to overlook the fact that the infection runs deep. And racial hatred is only one manifestation: the disease is hatred more generally. The conversion of difference into enmity breeds the virus. He concludes, "Hatred, which could destroy so much, never failed to destroy the man who hated" (113). Baldwin realizes that he can't change the world: "it goes without saying that injustice is a commonplace" (113). At the same time, he commits himself to struggling against injustice: "one must never, in one's own life, accept these injustices as commonplace but must fight them with all one's strength. This fight begins, however, in the heart and it now had been laid to my charge to keep my own heart free of hatred and despair" (113–14).

Here and elsewhere, James Baldwin lays bare his heart for us. He offers his blood, sometimes frozen in fear, sometimes boiling with fever, so that we may learn to diagnose that disease in our own time. Like love – the heart's greatest achievement – there is nothing easy about this process. The price, the cost, the suffering, the failures as well as the triumphs, the fight that begins in one's own heart: these are what bring us to Baldwin in the first place and what keep us coming back.

Amen. *En avant.*

NOTE

1 James Baldwin, "Notes of a Native Son," in *Notes of a Native Son* (originally published 1955), (Boston: Beacon Press, 1984, 87). All subsequent notes cited parenthetically.

GUIDE TO FURTHER READING

Biography

Boyd, Herb. *Baldwin's Harlem: A Biography of James Baldwin*. New York: Atria Books, 2008.

Campbell, James. *Talking at the Gates: A Life of James Baldwin*. New York: Viking, 1991.

Eckman, Fern Marja. *The Furious Passage of James Baldwin*. New York: Lippincott, 1966.

Field, Douglas. *James Baldwin*. Tavistock, Devon, UK: Northcote House/British Council, 2011.

Leeming, David Adams. *James Baldwin: A Biography*. New York: H. Holt and Co., 1995.

Weatherby, William J. *James Baldwin: Artist on Fire: A Portrait*. New York: D. I. Fine, 1989.

Selected Critical Studies

Balfour, Katharine Lawrence. *The Evidence of Things Not Said: James Baldwin and the Promise of American Democracy*. Ithaca, NY: Cornell University Press, 2001.

Bloom, Harold. *James Baldwin*. New York: Chelsea House, 2007.

Brim, Matt. *James Baldwin and the Queer Imagination*. Ann Arbor: University of Michigan Press, 2014.

Dickstein, Morris. *James Baldwin*. Pasadena, CA: Salem Press, 2011.

Field, Douglas. *A Historical Guide to James Baldwin*. Oxford and New York: Oxford University Press, 2009.

Hardy, Clarence E. *James Baldwin's God: Sex, Hope, and Crisis in Black Holiness Culture*. Knoxville: University of Tennessee Press, 2003.

Harris, Trudier. *Black Women in the Fiction of James Baldwin*. Knoxville: University of Tennessee Press, 1985.

Kaplan, Cora, and Bill Schwarz. *James Baldwin: America and Beyond*. Ann Arbor: University of Michigan Press, 2011.

King, Lovalerie, and Lynn Orilla Scott. *James Baldwin and Toni Morrison: Comparative Critical and Theoretical Essays*. New York: Palgrave Macmillan, 2006.

Macebuh, Stanley. *James Baldwin; A Critical Study*. Vol. 1. New York: Third Press, 1973.

231

McBride, Dwight A. *James Baldwin Now*. New York: New York University Press, 1999.

Miller, D. Quentin. *A Criminal Power: James Baldwin and the Law*. Columbus: Ohio State University Press, 2012.

Re-Viewing James Baldwin: Things Not Seen. Philadelphia: Temple University Press, 2000.

Porter, Horace A. *Stealing the Fire: The Art and Protest of James Baldwin*. Middletown, CT: Wesleyan University Press, 1989.

Scott, Lynn Orilla. *Witness to the Journey: James Baldwin's Later Fiction*. East Lansing: Michigan State University Press, 2002.

Troupe, Quincy. *James Baldwin: The Legacy*. New York: Simon & Schuster, 1989.

Wedin, Carolyn. *James Baldwin*. New York: Ungar, 1980.

Zaborowska, Magdalena J. *James Baldwin's Turkish Decade: Erotics of Exile*. Durham: Duke University Press, 2009.

Interviews

Baldwin, James, and Audre Lorde. "Revolutionary Hope: A Conversation between James Baldwin and Audre Lorde," *Essence*, 1984.

Baldwin, James, and Studs Terkel. "James Baldwin Talks with Studs Terkel." September 29, 1962. https://archive.org/details/popuparchive-1854433. Accessed July 2014.

Elgrably, James. "James Baldwin. The Art of Fiction No. 78," *Paris Review* 91 (Spring 1984). http://www.theparisreview.org/interviews/2994/the-art-of-fiction-no-78-james-baldwin. Accessed July 2014.

Mead, Margaret, and James Baldwin. *A Rap on Race*. Philadelphia: Lippincott, 1971.

Standley, Fred L., and Louis H. Pratt (eds.). *Conversations with James Baldwin*. Jackson: University Press of Mississippi, 1989.

International Reception

Bobia, Rosa. *The Critical Reception of James Baldwin in France*. Vol. 68. New York: Peter Lang, 1997.

Köllhofer, Jakob J., and Deutsch-Amerikanisches Institut. *James Baldwin: His Place in American Literary History and His Reception in Europe*. Frankfurt am Main and New York: P. Lang, 1991.

Selected Video Recordings

Burch, Claire, and Christopher Sorrenti. *The James Baldwin Anthology*. Regent Press. 2008. https://www.youtube.com/watch?v=N7OfoAbi1oA. Accessed July 2014.

"Debate: James Baldwin and William F. Buckley." Sponsored by the Cambridge Union Society, Cambridge University. 1965. http://vimeo.com/18413741. Accessed July 2014.

Fontaine, Dick, and Pat Hartley. *I Heard It through the Grapevine*. New York: Living Archives, Inc. 1982. http://www.dickfontaine.com/1980page.html. Accessed July 2014.

"Take This Hammer." San Francisco: PBS Channel Thirteen, American Masters Archive. 1989. http://www.pbs.org/wnet/americanmasters/episodes/james-baldwin/am-archive-take-this-hammer/2332/. Accessed July 2014.

Thorsen, Karen, et al. *James Baldwin: The Price of the Ticket.* San Francisco: California Newsreel. 1989. http://www.thirteen.org/programs/american-masters/james-baldwin-the-price-of-the-ticket/. Accessed July 2014.

WORKS BY JAMES BALDWIN

These titles include novels, plays, essays, short stories, articles, and reviews published by James Baldwin during his lifetime, listed in chronological order of publication.

"Maxim Gorki as Artist," *Nation* April 12, 1947

"When the War Hit Brownsville," *New Leader* May 17, 1947

"Smaller than Life," *Nation* July 19, 1947

"Without Grisly Gaiety," *New Leader* September 20, 1947

"History as Nightmare," *New Leader* October 25, 1947

"Battle Hymn," *New Leader* November 29, 1947

"Dead Hand of Caldwell," *New Leader* December 6, 1947

"Bright World Darkened," *New Leader* January 24, 1948

"The Harlem Ghetto: Winter 1948," *Commentary* February 1948 (reprinted as "The Harlem Ghetto")

"Present and Future," *New Leader* March 13, 1948

"The Image of the Negro," *Commentary* April 1948

"Literary Grab Bag," *New Leader* April 10, 1948

"Lockridge: The American Myth," *New Leader* April 10, 1948

"Change Within a Channel," *New Leader* April 24, 1948

"Modern River Boys," *New Leader* August 14, 1948

"Previous Condition," *Commentary* October 1948

"Journey to Atlanta," *New Leader* October 9, 1948

"Too Late, Too Late," *Commentary* January 1949

"Everybody's Protest Novel," *Zero* Spring 1949

"Preservation of Innocence," *Zero* Summer 1949

"Death of the Prophet," *Commentary* March 1950

"The Negro in Paris," *Reporter* June 6, 1950 (reprinted as "Encounter on the Seine: Black Meets Brown")

"The Outing," *New Story* April 1951

"Le Problème noir en Amérique," *Rapports France-Etats Unis* September 17, 1951

"The Negro at Home and Abroad," *Reporter* November 27, 1951

"Many Thousands Gone," *Partisan Review* November–December 1951

"Roy's Wound," *New World Writing*, Vol. 2. New York: New American Library, 1952

"Exodus," *American Mercury* August 1952

Go Tell It on the Mountain, New York: Knopf, 1953

"Stranger in the Village," *Harper's* October 1953

"The Amen Corner," Act One, *Zero* July 1954

"Paris Letter: A Question of Identity," *Partisan Review* July–August 1954 (reprinted as "A Question of Identity")

"Gide as Husband and Homosexual," *New Leader* December 13, 1954 (reprinted as "The Male Prison")

Notes of a Native Son, Boston: Beacon Press, 1955

"Life Straight in De Eye," *Commentary* January 1955 (reprinted as "Carmen Jones: The Dark Is Light Enough")

"Equal in Paris," *Commentary* March 1955

"Me and My Home…," *Harper's* November 1955 (reprinted as "Notes of a Native Son")

Giovanni's Room, New York: Dial Press, 1956

"The Crusade of Indignation," *Nation* July 7, 1956

"Faulkner and Desegregation," *Partisan Review* Winter 1956

"Princes and Powers," *Encounter* January 1957

"Sonny's Blues," *Partisan Review* Summer 1957

"Come Out the Wilderness," *Mademoiselle* March 1958

"The Hard Kind of Courage," *Harper's* October 1958 (reprinted as "A Fly in the Buttermilk")

"The Discovery of What It Means to Be an American," *New York Times Book Review* January 25, 1959

"Sermons and Blues," *New York Times Book Review* March 29, 1959

"On Catfish Row: *Porgy and Bess* in the Movies," *Commentary* September 1959

"Letter from the South: Nobody Knows My Name," *Partisan Review*, Winter 1959

"The Precarious Vogue of Ingmar Bergman," *Esquire* April 1960 (reprinted as "The Northern Protestant")

"Fifth Avenue, Uptown," *Esquire* July 1960

"They Can't Turn Back," *Mademoiselle* August 1960

"This Morning, This Evening, So Soon," *Atlantic Monthly* September 1960

Nobody Knows My Name: More Notes of a Native Son, New York: Dial Press, 1961

"The Dangerous Road before Martin Luther King," *Harper's* February 1961

"The Exile," *Le Preuve* February 1961

"A Negro Assays the Negro Mood," *New York Times Magazine* March 12, 1961 (reprinted as "East River, Downtown: Postscript to a Letter from Harlem")

"The Survival of Richard Wright," *Reporter* March 16, 1961 (reprinted as "Eight Men")

"On the Negro Actor," *The Urbanite* April 1961

"The Black Boy Looks at the White Boy Norman Mailer," *Esquire* May 1961 (reprinted as "The Black Boy Looks at the White Boy")

"Theatre," *The Urbanite* May 1961

"The New Lost Generation," *Esquire* July 1961

Another Country, New York: Dial Press, 1962

"The Creative Process," in *Creative America*, New York: Ridge Press, 1962

"As Much Truth as One Can Bear," *New York Times Book Review* January 14, 1962

"Letter from a Region in My Mind," *New Yorker* November 17, 1962 (reprinted as "Down at the Cross")

"A Letter to My Nephew," *Progressive* December 1962 (reprinted as "My Dungeon Shook")

"Color," *Esquire* December 1962

The Fire Next Time, New York: Dial Press, 1963

"The Fight: Patterson vs. Liston," *Nugget* February 1963

"The Artist's Struggle for Integrity," *Liberation* March 1963

"Letters from a Journey," *Harper's* May 1963

"We Can Change the Country," *Liberation* October 1963

"A Talk to Teachers," *Saturday Review* December 21, 1963

Blues for Mister Charlie, New York: Dial Press, 1964

Introduction to an exhibition of paintings by Beauford Delaney, Galerie Lambert, Paris, 1964

Nothing Personal (with photographs by Richard Avedon), New York: Atheneum, 1964

"The Uses of the Blues," *Playboy* January 1964

"What Price Freedom?" *Freedomways* Spring 1964

"Why I Stopped Hating Shakespeare," *Observer* April 19, 1964

"The Harlem Riots," *New York Post* August 2, 1964

"Words of a Native Son," *Playboy* December 1964

Going to Meet the Man, New York: Dial Press, 1965

"The American Dream and the American Negro," *New York Times Magazine* February 1965

"The White Man's Guilt," *Ebony* August 1965 (expanded and reprinted as "Unnameable Objects, Unspeakable Crimes," in *The White Problem in America*, Chicago: Johnson, 1966)

"To Whom It May Concern: A Report from Occupied Territory," *Nation* July 11, 1966

"God's Country," *New York Review of Books* March 23, 1967

"Negroes Are Anti-Semitic Because They're Anti-White," *New York Magazine* April 9, 1967

"The War Crimes Tribunal," *Freedomways* Summer 1967

Tell Me How Long the Train's Been Gone, New York: Dial Press, 1968

The Amen Corner, New York: Dial Press, 1968

"Why a Stokely?" *St. Petersburg Times* March 3, 1968

"The Nigger We Invent," *Integrated Education* March–April 1968

"Sidney Poitier," *Look* July 23, 1968

"White Racism or World Community?" *Ecumenical Review* October 1968

"Sweet Lorraine," *Esquire* November 1969

"Dear Sister...," *Manchester Guardian* December 12, 1970

A Rap on Race (with Margaret Mead), Philadelphia: Lippincott, 1971

No Name in the Street, New York: Dial Press, 1972

One Day When I Was Lost: A Scenario Based on Alex Haley's "The Autobiography of Malcolm X," London: Michael Joseph, 1972

A Dialogue (with Nikki Giovanni), Philadelphia: Lippincott, 1973

If Beale Street Could Talk, New York, Dial Press, 1974

Little Man Little Man: A Story of Childhood, New York: Dial Press, 1976

The Devil Finds Work, New York: Dial Press, 1976

"How Once a Black Man Came to Be an American," *New York Times* September 26, 1976

"An Open Letter to Mr. Carter," *New York Times* January 23, 1977

"Every Goodbye Ain't Gone," *New York Magazine* December 19, 1977

"The News from All the Northern Cities," *New York Times* April 5, 1978

Just Above My Head, New York: Dial Press, 1979

"If Black English Isn't a Language, Then Tell Me, What Is?" *New York Times* July 29, 1979

"An Open Letter to the Born Again," *Nation* September 29, 1979

"Of the Sorrow Songs: The Cross of Redemption," *New Edinburgh Review* Autumn 1979

"Dark Days," *Esquire* October 1980

"Notes on the House of Bondage," *Nation* November 1, 1980

"The Evidence of Things Not Seen," *Playboy* December 1981

"Roger Wilkins: A Black Man's Odyssey in White America," *Washington Post Book World* June 6, 1982

Jimmy's Blues: Selected Poems, London: Michael Joseph, 1983

"On Being 'White' and Other Lies," *Essence* April 1984

The Evidence of Things Not Seen, New York: Holt, Rinehart and Winston, 1985

The Price of the Ticket: Collected Nonfiction, 1948–1985, New York: St. Martin's/Marek, 1985

"Freaks and the American Ideal of Manhood," *Playboy* January 1985 (reprinted as "Here Be Dragons")

"Letter to the Bishop," *New Statesman* August 23, 1985

Selected Posthumous Publications

A Lover's Question (with David Linx and Pierre Van Dormael), Brussels: Les Disques Du Crépuscule, 1990

Native Sons (with Sol Stein), New York: Ballatine Books, 2005

The Cross of Redemption: Uncollected Writings (Randall Kenan, ed.). New York: Vintage International, 2011

Jimmy's Blues and Other Poems, Boston: Beacon Press, 2014

INDEX

Cambridge Companions to . . .

Milton edited by Dennis Danielson (second edition)
Molière edited by David Bradby and Andrew Calder
Toni Morrison edited by Justine Tally
Nabokov edited by Julian W. Connolly
Eugene O'Neill edited by Michael Manheim
George Orwell edited by John Rodden
Ovid edited by Philip Hardie
Harold Pinter edited by Peter Raby (second edition)
Sylvia Plath edited by Jo Gill
Edgar Allan Poe edited by Kevin J. Hayes
Alexander Pope edited by Pat Rogers
Ezra Pound edited by Ira B. Nadel
Proust edited by Richard Bales
Pushkin edited by Andrew Kahn
Rabelais edited by John O'Brien
Rilke edited by Karen Leeder and Robert Vilain
Philip Roth edited by Timothy Parrish
Salman Rushdie edited by Abdulrazak Gurnah
Shakespeare edited by Margareta de Grazia and Stanley Wells (second edition)
Shakespeare and Contemporary Dramatists edited by Ton Hoenselaars
Shakespeare and Popular Culture edited by Robert Shaughnessy
Shakespeare on Film edited by Russell Jackson (second edition)
Shakespeare on Stage edited by Stanley Wells and Sarah Stanton
Shakespearean Comedy edited by Alexander Leggatt
Shakespearean Tragedy edited by Claire McEachern (second edition)
Shakespeare's History Plays edited by Michael Hattaway
Shakespeare's Last Plays edited by Catherine M. S. Alexander
Shakespeare's Poetry edited by Patrick Cheney

George Bernard Shaw edited by Christopher Innes
Shelley edited by Timothy Morton
Mary Shelley edited by Esther Schor
Sam Shepard edited by Matthew C. Roudané
Spenser edited by Andrew Hadfield
Laurence Sterne edited by Thomas Keymer
Wallace Stevens edited by John N. Serio
Tom Stoppard edited by Katherine E. Kelly
Harriet Beecher Stowe edited by Cindy Weinstein
August Strindberg edited by Michael Robinson
Jonathan Swift edited by Christopher Fox
J. M. Synge edited by P. J. Mathews
Tacitus edited by A. J. Woodman
Henry David Thoreau edited by Joel Myerson
Tolstoy edited by Donna Tussing Orwin
Anthony Trollope edited by Carolyn Dever and Lisa Niles
Mark Twain edited by Forrest G. Robinson
John Updike edited by Stacey Olster
Mario Vargas Llosa edited by Efrain Kristal and John King
Virgil edited by Charles Martindale
Voltaire edited by Nicholas Cronk
Edith Wharton edited by Millicent Bell
Walt Whitman edited by Ezra Greenspan
Oscar Wilde edited by Peter Raby
Tennessee Williams edited by Matthew C. Roudané
August Wilson edited by Christopher Bigsby
Mary Wollstonecraft edited by Claudia L. Johnson
Virginia Woolf edited by Susan Sellers (second edition)
Wordsworth edited by Stephen Gill
W. B. Yeats edited by Marjorie Howes and John Kelly
Zola edited by Brian Nelson

TOPICS

The Actress edited by Maggie B. Gale and John Stokes
The African American Novel edited by Maryemma Graham
The African American Slave Narrative edited by Audrey A. Fisch
African American Theatre by Harvey Young
Allegory edited by Rita Copeland and Peter Struck
American Crime Fiction edited by Catherine Ross Nickerson
American Modernism edited by Walter Kalaidjian

American Poetry Since 1945 edited by Jennifer Ashton
American Realism and Naturalism edited by Donald Pizer
American Travel Writing edited by Alfred Bendixen and Judith Hamera
American Women Playwrights edited by Brenda Murphy
Ancient Rhetoric edited by Erik Gunderson
Arthurian Legend edited by Elizabeth Archibald and Ad Putter
Australian Literature edited by Elizabeth Webby

Printed in the United States
By Bookmasters